Harriet Cooper Corbus

April 1931.

Background with Figures

MRS. HENRY S. DRINKER AND SON
(Les Derniers Jours d'Enfance)

BACKGROUND
WITH FIGURES

Autobiography of
CECILIA BEAUX

WITH ILLUSTRATIONS

Boston and New York
HOUGHTON MIFFLIN COMPANY
1930

The Riverside Press
CAMBRIDGE · MASSACHUSETTS
PRINTED IN THE U.S.A.

To
MY SISTER

PREFACE

THIS book owes its existence to a dual motive. On one hand it is a purely selfish desire to retrace a series of adventures touching upon characters of world interest. The second motive rises nearer home, indeed so near as to be chiefly of family interest, and primarily for family record. As an introduction it precedes the adventure, and is responsible for it. It will be found to be an illustration of a certain type of education, now obsolete, but which is hoped to be worthy, albeit still in the making, of wearing the patine of a veritable antique.

C. B.

GLOUCESTER, MASSACHUSETTS
October 5, 1930

CONTENTS

I.	Parentage	3
II.	Childhood and First Impressions	13
III.	Education	29
IV.	Class and Studio	64
V.	Europe	100
VI.	Incidents and Episodes	135
VII.	An English Visit	179
VIII.	Return to America	193
IX.	War Portraits	235
X.	Cardinal Mercier	239
XI.	Clemenceau	278
XII.	Quinze Rue de Cherche Midi	307
XIII.	Baron Beatty of the North Sea	317
XIV.	Green Alley	338
Appendix		347
Index		351

ILLUSTRATIONS

Mrs. Henry S. Drinker and Son (Les Derniers Jours d'Enfance)   *Frontispiece*

Cecilia Kent Leavitt, Grandmother of the Author   4
    From an early miniature

John W. Leavitt, Grandfather of the Author   4
    From an early miniature

Miss Eliza Leavitt   8

The Book of Wolves (*aquatone*)   22
    Drawing by C. Beaux

Cecilia Kent Leavitt (*aquatone*)   40
    Drawing by C. Beaux

Child with Nurse: 'Ernesta'   56

Ernesta   72
    Reproduced by permission of the Metropolitan Museum, New York

Sita and Sarita   88

On the Terrace   104

Mrs. J. H. Richards   120
    Reproduced by permission of the Pennsylvania Academy of Fine Arts

Cecilia Beaux   136
    From a photograph

Mrs. Robert Chapin and Child   152
    Oil drawing by C. Beaux

Flora Whitney   168

Mrs. James B. Drinker and Son   184

Richard Watson Gilder   210

ILLUSTRATIONS

DOROTHEA AND FRANCESCA   218
Reproduced by permission of the Chicago Art Museum

AT HOME   222

MRS. THEODORE ROOSEVELT AND DAUGHTER   228

S. E. CARDINAL MERCIER   242

MRS. ALEXANDER SEDGWICK AND CHRISTINA   258

CECILIA BEAUX   274
Self-portrait

GEORGES CLEMENCEAU   292

ADMIRAL LORD BEATTY   324

MORNING AT GREEN ALLEY   338
From a photograph

IN THE LOGGIA   342
From a photograph

NATALE   342
From a photograph

Except as otherwise indicated the illustrations are from paintings by Cecilia Beaux

BACKGROUND WITH FIGURES

BACKGROUND WITH FIGURES

I

PARENTAGE

MY mother, Cecilia Kent Leavitt, was the eldest of the eight children of my American grandparents, the first born of their strong youth and rapture. I can quite clearly imagine the young pair, in their modest house in Dey Street, New York.

Two fine miniatures remain, painted in those first years, for my grandfather, even when a very young man, was keenly alive to fresh ideas of life and to a general survey of the moment. Though not well off, he thought it fitting that portraits of his young wife and himself should exist for their children, the little family just appearing. As the miniatures themselves attest, the best artist of the day in such work was commissioned. Unfortunately, no sign of signature can be found upon the pictures, set in oval frames, with red morocco cases.

The portrait of my grandfather represents the handsome Puritan head of a young man about thirty, with strong dark eyes, firm mouth and jaw, enveloped in the white stock and wearing the high-collared coat of the period. The likeness of my grandmother was less successful. Her mobile face, a long oval, with dark eyes slightly pointing upward at the corners, and flexible lips, could not be seized so easily by the firm hand that modelled my grandfather's muscular, clean-shaven face.

My grandmother's small head on a very slender throat rises from a broad, delicate, lace-and-muslin collar. Her bodice is very short — a little jacket, in fact, of black velvet and silk, and high sleeves, plain, but very stylish, and fortunately still preserved. Her dark hair is dressed high, in puffs and a comb. I remember her telling me that her sister used to say, 'Cecilia, your hair is like a pound of black sewing silk.' Wonderful hair, fine and straight. In the last year of her life, when she was ninety-three, there was still a remarkable quantity of it, and I had the privilege of being chosen to brush and arrange it.

My grandparents were both of New England Puritan stock, English entirely. Their ancestors had been early settlers in the northern and western part of Connecticut. My grandfather, John Wheeler Leavitt, came from the township of Washington; my grandmother, whose name was Cecilia Kent, from Suffield. Her older sister, Sarah Evelina Kent, had married and was living in Brooklyn, and thither she brought her pretty young sister, twelve years her junior.

It was there that Cecilia Kent met young John Leavitt, lately started in business with a cousin of an older generation in New York. Both were young, earnest, handsome, and vital. The same principles of life and religion were theirs; the same ideals of living and character. Her humor offset his sterner qualities; their mutual trust was perfect, and was never broken. Both had strong constitutions and perfect health of body and mind. In romance their married life began and continued, without record of obstacle or disaster, through the birth and upgrowing of their large family. My grandfather was more and more prosperous, and became a rich man for those days.

The two elder children of my grandparents were girls, only a year apart, Cecilia and Eliza.

As the family increased, it is probable that the earnest ideals of the young parents suffered some relaxation. They could hardly have maintained the personal watchfulness with which the two oldest were guarded and trained. But

CECILIA KENT LEAVITT

JOHN W. LEAVITT

no time was wasted in applying to these two the 'early lessons' which in those days many parents believed to be indispensable for the proper equipment of their children for life.

The little sisters were full of energy, and apparently found no hardship in the accomplishment of their daily 'tasks.' Bible reading was replete with interest; sewing brought into being actual and finished objects, the sweetest and only real reward, of labor. Many walks and excursions were made. Dey Street, where they lived, was only a short distance from Broadway, and one could walk there in the wide and elegant street, and to the Battery, a lovely park on the water, or at the foot of Wall Street take the ferry to Brooklyn to visit cousins on Brooklyn Heights.

The happiness of these busy little lives is charmingly reflected in records which have fortunately been preserved.

Cecilia, my mother, was not yet five years old, and her sister Eliza less than four, when their young father brought them each a diary. These were neatly bound blank-books, evidently carefully selected and with their names stamped in gold, on red morocco. Although both the little girls could read, and probably write also, it was thought best by their mother that the daily story should be dictated, and the carefully written volume before me bears evidence of being a direct and unedited setting down of little Eliza's account of her day.

* * *

As the family grew, the house in Dey Street became too limited, and my grandfather built a house on the south side of Barclay Street facing what is now the Woolworth Building. This house disappeared some years ago to make room for, or to be converted into, warehouses.

There was also a country estate, across the river upon the Palisades, at Hoboken. This place was called Oakland and was greatly beloved by all the family.

For the Barclay Street house my grandfather had the whole attic constructed as a gymnasium for the children; also the first bathroom with accessories known to New York was put in, and the water piped to the second floor — an innovation greatly relished by my grandfather, who welcomed all new conveniences.

As the older children matured, it was a very lively household. There were tutors, German and French, music lessons and indefatigable practising: Professor Gloubenskly (and a tall, bony, and rather fearsome Scott for mathematics), and Otto Dresel, a young German musician, who later became very well known. He was a pupil of Mendelssohn, and my grandfather, hearing of him soon after his arrival here, and eager to give his daughters all possible advantages, engaged him at once to instruct them. This opened the new and fascinating world of German music to the two older girls, who never forgot the charm and happiness, as well as the immense advantage, of this connection. My Aunt Eliza, who became herself a brilliant musician, and who outlived her sister many, many years, looked upon Otto Dresel as the mainspring of her musical life. When I was a child, to whom, of course, these masters only existed as names, I never wearied of hearing my aunts chatting together over their work about former days in which strange foreign persons took an often amusing part. Rippling laughter, which was frequent in our house, nearly always accompanied these recollections.

When they were considered to be of the proper age, the three older girls, Cecilia, Eliza, and Sarah (the beauty of the family), began attending Miss Green's school at No. One Fifth Avenue. The large square house until a short time ago was still the same as in those days, and in passing it, I have often pictured to myself the gay little party walking up from Barclay Street on cold winter mornings, the three girls, their brother, and his friends, who later were to take a more serious part in their lives.

When my mother was about twenty-three, the clouds began to appear. My grandfather, in some large connection in the South, in which his relation to the cotton industry was involved, failed in business, and his anxiety broke down his health. Everything went to his creditors. Both houses were sold. There were still young children. The family, from comfort and plenty, went into a small house in Twenty-Third Street, then a rough suburb. My grandmother cheerfully took up her new cares and economies; her chief anxiety being the state of her husband's health. The two elder sons, just through college, were entirely impractical. One of them, Samuel, was a rivetted reformer, and went through life in poverty trying to establish impossible Utopias. The older son, whose tempestuous babyhood is much dwelt on in little Eliza's diary, lay, I remember hearing, all day on three chairs, eating nothing but dry bread, and reading Swedenborg.

It was better than if the boys had been dissipated or spendthrift. Dreamers and reformers are seldom of much assistance in family crises. At least, their mother might have said that she 'always knew where they were.' But they took no part in retrieving the family fortunes. The two older sisters immediately took up the whole burden. Teaching was the only way open to them, and they were well educated, in music and languages especially. The part taken by my mother in this was truly heroic. For women, teaching in those days was not the honorable and diploma'd profession it is now. Cecilia and Eliza could only hope for positions little above menial.

Oakland had been bought by a gentleman of means. He sought a governess for his daughters, and my mother, not willing to postpone for a day her valiant effort for her family, applied at once, and was accepted. A few weeks after the disaster in her father's business took place, she returned to the home and the scene of all her young happiness and power, for she was always the leading spirit in the house, returned to serve, and to see others enjoy what had been hers, and the scenes that were full of the faces and the hours she had loved best.

* * *

The family had friends and distant relatives in Philadelphia, and after a year or two opportunities began to appear from this quarter for the young instructors. Cecilia went first, and soon her warmth and vivacity made her many friends. She saw much of the worldly side of the Quaker City. Although a poor girl earning her living, her brilliant spirits never failed. She was not handsome, but her beautiful carriage and figure and her flashing smile were perhaps more effective than more regular charms. There were, of course, lovers, and some of those who sighed for the interesting stranger would have been very eligible 'partis.'

But an admirer appeared upon the scene, unexpected, alien, foreign: M. Jean Adolphe Beaux, of Avignon and Nîmes in Provence. Perhaps my mother's knowledge of the French language was a little more fluent than that of the Philadelphia belles. At all events, the Frenchman of thirty-eight, recently arrived in America, fell desperately in love with Cecilia, who wrote home that she had met a French gentleman; then that he had 'beautiful blue eyes.' She was in no haste, however, to succumb to their charm, and it was some time before M. Beaux was permitted to go to New York and call on her parents, which he did with both formality and determination. He, of course, had to undergo a grilling examination. He had come to this country to found a business, a silk factory. It was a recent enterprise, but promised well. He had many well-known friends to vouch for him, but letters from France and exhaustive research were necessary before her father would approve of Cecilia's choice. They were married in New York, and in the shadows overhanging the family destiny, it was a bright moment, especially in the eyes of the bride's young sisters, who

MISS ELIZA LEAVITT

accepted their new brother with eager approval, and often repeated, many years after, the words of the bridegroom (my father never achieved perfect knowledge of English) when he saw his bride in her wedding dress: 'She is fit to give the hand to a King.' Long afterwards, when I was a growing girl, watching me with saddened eyes, he said, 'You will never have shoulders like your mother.'

* * *

My grandfather's death occurred only a few years after the marriage, and it must have greatly lightened the gloom of his last days to know that his French son-in-law, besides being a devoted husband, was making his wife's family his own. This my father did generously and delicately, as long as it was in his power to do so. He was an idealist, not a successful business man. He never neglected his affairs, but it was not in his nature to — as the saying is — turn over money. He was a Huguenot, a devout Protestant, with the blood, if not of actual martyrdom, still with religious persecution, in his veins. Never has the battle between the two great opposing forces of the Christian Church been more bitter than in the South of France: one to reform, the other to maintain. Also, my father's character and personality glowed with the passionate idealism which is the birthright of the inheritors of the sunny land, where Greek, Roman, and Gothic power strove for possession, bringing together currents that were to civilize Europe and be the crucible in which the spear of Gallic intellect was to be forged. One of the well-known descents of the Nordic race was by the Rhone Valley, and there was a more profound origin than she was aware of in the great blue eyes that so captivated the young American girl. Of course, the sympathy between Puritan and Huguenot was a powerful bond between my father and his wife's family. Neither had inherited the harsh dogmas that had grown out of a too determined zeal, and done such harm to the first principles of Protestantism.

Their ideal hope and belief was in the purest form of spirituality, an ideal, alas, impossible to apply to poor humanity, or to be maintained by them in the mass. They were lovers, as well, of Art and beauty, and willing to make constant sacrifices to enjoy them.

My father was intensely interested in the French Collegiate Church in America, and religion, as a part of daily life, took a deeper and deeper hold on him. M. Fargue, the French pastor, was a frequent visitor at our house when I was a child. My father often selected the hymns for the services at the church from a volume of *Psaumes et Cantiques*, with music. All the music was in the plainest choral form, measured, and entirely in harmony with the solemn emotion of the verses. One was my favorite, and never forgotten:

> Du Rocher du Jacob,
> Toute l'œuvre est parfaite.
> Ce que sa bouche a dit,
> Sa main l'accomplira.
> Alleluia, Alleluia,
> Alleluia, Alleluia,
> Car il est notre Dieu,
> Car il est notre Dieu,
> Notre haute retraite.

Nothing could be plainer nor simpler than were these services, but there was something alive in the hearts of the small congregation that filled the bare ritual with a passionate ardor. A child could not be mentally aware of this, but could feel it with wonder, and almost with tears.

These worshippers were all exiles, voluntary, perhaps, but the French never forget France, and, like my father, in their blood was the idealism that could make of religious belief, or had made of it in the past of their race, something worth dying for. Most of the congregation were poor and obscure people. Nothing in the service had cost or could cost money. The sermon was important, and the pastors of the Col-

legiate Church were few and were chosen for their spiritual
ity and eloquence. I believe that real refreshment was received by these humble and often homesick souls. The great
theme was nearness to God and communion with Him; perhaps more possible with the exile than with the comfortable
American citizen, thoroughly at home by this time and
prosperous.

**

Strange is the existence in which there is no memory of a
mother; no vestige of even a momentary, vague, child-im-
pression. This was my fate, and, although it was so, there
has been no stronger reality in my life than the reality of my
mother's person and influence. She was an adored being,
and all through my childhood and youth, the friends who
had worshipped her used to gaze long at me, in pity, and de-
siring to find traces in me of the beloved. I was accustomed
to, and took great pride in, this pity and interest. I knew
her to have been one whose memory caused the eyes turned
on me to have that strange absorbed gaze, in which com-
passion and wonder were blended.

Sometimes chests were opened, and cloaks, dresses she had
chosen and worn were taken out and refolded. There was
an exquisite fan or two; a bit of frilled ribbon, and, above
all, the square white box edged prettily with gold, in which
lay her wedding veil and the wreath, the narrow satin slippers, and a pair of short white kid gloves, with lace at the
wrists.

The glamour and awe which lay about these relics was
one of the great emotions of my childhood. Their elegance
was to me a positive possession, a sort of patent of nobility, I
would not have parted with for the most longed-for and
special personal adornment of my own.

I was proud, too, of not being thought worthy to be called
in any ordinary way by her name; that name which was
pronounced by the last breath upon her dying lips, as the

name to be given to me, the newly born she hardly knew herself.

What of those twelve first days of my life which were passed near, or upon her breast, before the chill, and the devastating fever, and the end? No one ever did, or could, speak of them to me. Those who knew what they were turned away speechless when they were alluded to. I never knew aught of them except that whisper of my name, her sister's and her own, 'Eliza — Cecilia.' After two years these names were formally given to me in baptism, and I walked up a long aisle between my grandmother and my father, to receive them; but my father could not endure to hear her child called by his wife's name for years, after her death, and I was always called 'Leilie.'

II

CHILDHOOD AND FIRST IMPRESSIONS

A MOTHER, in her thirty-third year, has died. We would say now, unnecessarily, perhaps, but there again are the stars, the never interrupted current of destiny. She has left an infant daughter, and her mother, who has borne eight children, has taken the child. She is a widow and will always remember. She has little to live upon and is of independent spirit. She has taken also Aimée Ernesta, the older sister of the child, and the father, in his distraction, and as far as the children are concerned, leans completely upon his dead wife's mother. There, too, are the sisters — Eliza, whose name the child bears, and a girl of sixteen, Emily, both ready to serve and able. She, the grandmother, is the child's first visual memory. It is morning; there is a pleasant light room, with two windows. The small girl is standing up in her crib, having just found herself awake, and alone. The door opens, and her destined friend and protector enters; a small stout figure in black, gliding swiftly, with white cap a little flowing, perhaps. The child does not remember the embrace, nor greeting; only that her hands are joined, and upon the dear shoulder she whispers the morning salutation: 'I laid me down, I slept, and the Lord sustained me.'

The second vivid memory of Leilie's earliest years is of the afternoon of her third birthday. It is the first of May. She is sitting on her nurse's lap, before an open window, looking out on Locust Street. The gliding step and silken rustle are heard in the hall. The same figure enters. The grandmother has been out, shopping. She wears a black silk mantilla, and her bonnet is tied under her soft chin with a bow of black ribbon. A gauzy black veil floats out, and she carries a small parcel. The box is opened. The child has never known such joy. It is a very small, bright, silver thimble.

She has been promised to learn to sew, and very soon may wear it. Before the thimble was outgrown, it was worn out. Firm usage had pierced it with several holes; firm usage, but without tears.

There is one more memory of this time. The child is seated upon a low stool before a chair (a chair-seat was frequently used as a work-table); she is drawing upon a slate framed in wood. She, herself, has no memory of the drawing, or of the effort of producing it, but only of heads bent over her; the slate exhibited among delighted young aunts; exclamations, calls to look; 'Leilie has drawn the organ-grinder!'

* * *

Although my grandmother never gave me 'lessons' (that service falling to the aunts until my fifth year), I was very close to her during morning hours, and in those very early years certain habits became fixed. I sat on a little chair beside her and learned, chiefly, that anything undertaken — whether it was threading a needle, finishing off a hem, or conquering a line of three-letter-word-reading — everything undertaken must be completed, conquered. Oh, the joy after the struggle with the obstinate thread, the knot, to fold up the finished dish-cloth, close the defeated spelling-book, and spring into well-earned release!

In my opinion, no child's life should be without the zest of such contrasts. They are like the strong summer breeze shaking out the dew from young branches, and teaching them to bend, resist, and regain their poise.

Such very early memories are, of course, significant only in the revelation they give of an important truth; that before the seventh year a child has not been *consciously* mixed with the life around it, or rather with the scenes. Impressions are made in the very young years, which later are remembered as being the first realization of something ever after familiar or beloved, but never again so separate or so clear. In childhood, attrition has not begun; the page is spotless, and in some natures, at least, is open to receive what will be remembered during a lifetime, as the moment or two, and the first, of ecstasy.

In the case which I am trying to record, these impressions are almost entirely visual; that is, they are not dependent on incident or other forms of sensation.

There is a carriage full of people; who must have been the grandmother, the aunts, and the older sister. They are going on a journey; it is morning, in early summer. The carriage hurries along through unknown, narrow streets. It has rained; the pavements are wet. Every one knows where we are going, except the youngest one, who is absorbed by her mysterious joy. Only one moment, however, does she really remember: the arrival at what must have been a dock. Out of a delicate mist, shot through with morning sunlight, stand the masts of ships, and some drooping sails. It is the child's first realization of the light of morning on such — or, indeed, on any — scene. Where we went, the journey, the details of travel, all are a blank, but nothing in the years between has dimmed the peerless vision; the child's first meeting with the sun-god, or rather the first flash of his spear in rising mist. Little did she know that it was the hour, always destined for her to be the best, the productive, the creative hour; the hour of fearless hope, for in memory it is sheer beauty, at its opening, and nothing else, that remains.

* * *

There are two more of these supreme child-moments: one was in the morning, the other at noon, and neither could have been complete at other times of day. The first is Mallory Brook. It is a warm morning in the hills of western Connecticut. Broad hats and sunbonnets are the equipment, and with other delicious odors, such as that of cows, hay, and the general sweetness of the place and time, is mingled the good homely one of fresh-starched muslin, spreading its shade over a freckled nose, and the best of all perfumes, where the grassy road passes through the woods. It rained yesterday, and now the sun is drawing out the pine and the earth's essence, where arbutus was and has left its breath behind.

This memory, it is plain, will be complex, not entirely of the visual sense, nor nearly all of it. Scarcely less sweet is the fresh touch of the breeze on hot cheeks and forehead, when we stop in the shade on a big rock and hats and sunbonnets come off. There is the short steep descent of the Connecticut hillside, so steep that it is pleasant not quite to know what is coming below. Then a silken rustling sound, a cool odor, pungent, new, mint; Mallory Brook.

The first sight of crystal water purling over warm-hued pebbles, and foaming around dark-hued stones, struck through and through the city child's heart, and made channels there through which all after beauty, seen, would find room to pass. The pain of the inexpressible was there, too; the child's first sense of the inarticulate.

Paddling in it would not do; it was soon evident that this stirred up murk and the loose débris under shelving stones. The confluence of the ripples was broken, too, around ankles and over toes that the cold water soon troubled, for the stream was not far from its rocky source.

Crouched on a warm stone, one could touch the ripples with a fern or twig, or bit of mint. Her vast ignorance of what it was that formed the diapason of her bliss had no power then to puzzle the child, nor hinder visual emotion, which was as supreme perhaps at that moment as it ever would be. Long afterwards, she knew more about it; knew why it was that a child who wanted all there was of sensuous joy, and all at once, should have apprehended with unconscious directness a brook's high place in created things; a portion of one of the indispensable elements close to its virgin spring and just emerged toward the sun; the best of earth's distilled offerings, under the rays of the source of life.

Children easily accept a miracle, even when it is *only* beauty, and have no sense of being 'marked for life' by it. That knowledge comes later, when memory records and feels again the charming details. It is a miracle that something as invisible and pure as atmosphere should have conduct, action, so much more actual and present than air, to our faculties. Unseeable clarity, that we have known as water, have drunk in hot thirst, and bathed in in ignoble tubs, now is ours without benefit of clergy. It ripples around her fingers, as, crouching, the child presses them inches down upon the very color of the pebbles, that are strangely cold, firm, and resistant to the tender intruding substance of her palm; cool runnings are about an arm turned so much whiter below the surface. These cannot be *seen*, only revealed, by a film of sky reflection on a ripple's tilt sunward. But that dove's iris moves, for an imperceptible instant only, over the yellow, bronze, and white of the brook's floor that lies between grey rocks and the fern's dipping. Thus heaven and its blue summer mood touches and joins in the miracle.

Clumsily, indeed, one sums up a drama where all Nature at her dearest is present, and there is soon even the pine perfume of high noon.

* * *

There are one or two adventures in this early period of the child's life which have the importance of being all but the final one; such as her narrow escape, at the age of four, from drowning in the dark waters of the cistern, beneath the kitchen floor in the old house at Washington, Connecticut. Heedless, as usual, she walked into the square of darkness, left uncovered by some careless person. She was carrying a clam-shell full of peas from the garden, gathered for the enrichment of earnestly constructed mud pies. Some one entering saw fluttering petticoats in the black abyss, and, directed by the stars, put down the long, hooked stick used for drawing up the rainwater by bucketfuls. Rising from her plunge, perhaps for the third time, as only her sister had seen her disappear and had rushed for help, the small adventurer clutched the bent pole and was drawn up and out, safe and sound. Her own memory has no record of fear; in fact, contains nothing but the square of light she saw overhead, and the black-and-gold motion of the smooth element she had disturbed. For some reason a vision of the group she had left just before her adventure still remains, also. Ladies, her aunts and cousins, are seated together under tall trees on the grass, reading aloud, as usual, and working at crochet or embroidery. There is a wide leghorn hat or two; flowing skirts of white, or pale colors, and one very smooth, dark head. The alarm, the rush for help, not needed, shall not be dwelt on. The only concern of the 'casualty' being the loss of her clam-shell.

Scenes reappear, but only the clearest should be recorded. It was at about this time, and while the white clematis bloomed, that I saw death for the first time. A playmate, just my age, died suddenly. I was taken to see him, and to leave a flower beside him as he lay upon his little bed; his pale beauty noble, beyond all words, in memory. Richard's curls, fallen back from his forehead, lay upon the pillow, and wreaths of clematis, fresh, white and green, and perfumed, seemed the covering of his bed. There was sorrow, a new pain I had not known before, in my heart; but no shock, no horror, not even surprise. Absorption in the unimagined loveliness that I *saw* transcended every other emotion, and that is what remains. The odor of clematis never reaches me without this memory, and it is one of the ones I should most regret to have missed. Doubtless the appreciation of this beauty, in the mind of the one whose hand led me into that not darkened room (I remember the afternoon sun came in), was the motive in leading me to receive the accolade of death, and beauty, at the same moment. The guardian was right, as seen from the result upon my consciousness, even in that unformed hour of my life.

* * *

My sixth summer was memorable from a complete change in the family environment. We turned from our native Connecticut hills from necessity, not choice, and united with a whole series, uncle, aunt, and cousins, in settling for the summer in a farmhouse in middle Pennsylvania.

I was not very happy; there was a roughness in existence I had not known before. On the way I encountered a great, hot feather bed, and a tiny basin to wash in, and there was a husk mattress at the end, and gingerbread for breakfast. The latter I approached with joy, but found not to be quite up to the level of the routine I knew. There was a screaming baby in the group, and two boys older and younger than myself. Of one of these I stood in terrible fear; the other was a spoiled darling with long golden hair. I suspect that a proud little girl was rather envious of the charms of this pretty child who was the pet of the household. But all this is dim, fortunately, in recollection. It has become only general noise and turmoil. What clearly remains is full of pleasure.

The farmhouse stood on a side hill, its rear and barns looking down on a pretty valley, where a small river, called a creek, passed through wood and meadow. A long footbridge crossed it where it was broad and shallow, and lower down it narrowed into a dark deep pool among evergreens, where the grown-ups, or a big companionless boy, might bathe. This was a dismal spot to me. The bottom could not be seen, and contained all sorts of probable horrors, such as slime, old roots and creepers, and what not — even eels, perhaps.

The house, which was of unfinished stone and partly whitewashed, had the pleasantest verandah facing the slope upward of the orchard. The porch, which ran the length of the house, was really a grape-arbor, over which spread an old vine, where, later, purple clusters hung. It had a brick floor, often dappled with leafy shadow and light. Here the elders sat with their work, although one or two of them, who had hearts for child adventure, were generally with us at our favorite playground, the creek. Above the bridge we could bathe, and the strong and fearful boy was too busy to be alarming.

But in all this there is only one very vivid recollection. Perhaps, for a wonder, I was alone with the aunt who always had her sketch-book and pencil with her. Strangely enough, though the scene before me was to bewitch memory for a lifetime, I had no wish to draw it.

Looking up the stream, the little river was quiet, almost noiseless, and, unusual in an American landscape, its banks and stretches, as far as one could see, were lawns of vivid green; a grassy pasture, kept close by grazing creatures of the farm. Great trees, without undergrowth, threw broad delicious shadows, between which long shafts of summer sunshine lay upon the grass, and down the greensward walked solemnly a long line of snowy geese, bending necks here and there, spreading wings, or lowering yellow bills to taste the grass. From shadow, through streams of light, they came. It was my first conscious perception of the beauty of white plumage moving in a setting which had the undisturbed perfection of a classic pastoral. I knew nothing, probably thought nothing; I am sure said nothing; I was nought but an unsullied page that was constituted to hold unfaded the scene impressed upon it by the same hand that made the image. Later there accompanied this memory, and became part of it, the incomparable language of the Twenty-Third Psalm:

'Thou makest me to lie down in green pastures;
Thou leadest me beside the still waters.'

And since I have known whence I came by birth, it does not seem strange that my infant soul should have suddenly been at home in a scene where Nature has made use of a few creatures as her craftsmen, in forming a place fit for the *gods* to rest or wander in, or pursue their careless joy.

Perhaps the stability of memory is always due to the influence of atavism, upon the subconscious mind. What we have come from — which is what we fundamentally are — revives suddenly, under the stimulus of a remote, germinal, ancestral urge, recognized and desired as it appears unsummoned, in the unlike present; and so it passes into the crucible of performing energy, as the closest, strongest ally of creative impulse; in fact, the guardian and inspirer of our *Taste*. Taste that in its indomitable demands has nothing in common with the ready-made whimsicality dictated by weariness and satiety.

* * *

The aunt, doubtless thinking of her unfinished sketch and her vagarious niece, trudged up the dusty hill to the farmhouse, the noisy family, and dinner, neither of them aware that anything had happened during their quiet morning. The child, perhaps, lagged behind to pick and peel a mullen pod, and had to be called and hurried on. She hated the dusty road that burned her feet, hated the roadside dust on leaf and fern. At all events, the fecund morning passed unnoticed. Well is it that most really important matters are unobserved at their advent, that no ticker-tape is thrown upon the breeze, nor are reporters present, when a seed falls into a furrow that will bear the richest corn in the crop, or the small hard vessel drops to earth with the grandest of oaks in its vitals.

* * *

For the next few years very few indelible impressions of beauty, or indeed of anything, are to be recorded. The child

— 21 —

could read now, for her own pleasure; did not like fairy stories, nor the abridged edition of the 'Arabian Nights,' which was bestowed upon her and was expected to entrance her. 'Mother Goose,' with a few crude illustrations, was her secret favorite; perhaps from its rich assimilation of intimacy, with unsoundable mystery. She loved to sit upon the stairs in the city house, on the first flight from the lower hall, at the hour just before the gas was lighted. She exactly fitted the stair-lifts at this time, her feet on one and her back against another. The front door and the hall table could be seen and a glimpse of the parlor — all quiet, no one about. But it was not lonely, for voices on the second floor were audible, grandmother and aunts finishing their evening toilet. Mysterious it was on the stairs without being fearsome, and here the child said over to herself Tommy Tucker, and enjoyed the leap from the problem of cutting white bread and butter, so comfortable and pleasing, to the strange and sudden problem of something called a wife. She knew all the ageless lines by heart, and tasted and savored each in turn.

Another keenly relished moment was that when she could stand by her grandmother's toilet-table and watch the process of dressing. This procedure had really something in it akin to the quiet order, and Nature's exquisite way of 'finishing,' that had appeared in the valley at Eschelman's. She, of course, was only present at the closing scenes of the drama. But she knew the then important garment, that, in the instance before her, depended alone for its charm on the finest of linen and needlework; it had not other decoration. Grandma's stockings were the whitest — in summer called 'open-work'; her slippers the blackest. Dresses were various in form, and never colored, and are unremembered; but the hair, fine and abundant, was brushed and patted to satin smoothness. The last touch, a small lace cap, being carefully adjusted, was secured by two gold pins whose points never came through nor appeared. The child's idea was

THE BOOK OF WOLVES
Drawing by C. Beaux

that the pins entered the dear head itself, and that only the calm and courage of her gentle divinity could have sustained such torture with a smile. She would have died rather than question this, and the goddess never knew of this tribute to a more than mortal fortitude.

* * *

It was at or near this time that the family moved to West Philadelphia. The house was not a 'country' house, but it had a garden, or what could become one, and there were at that time outlying fields, a spring-house, a tiny stream, and a few large trees. There was a hillside, with a small farmhouse at the top, and on the slope a fallen apple tree, not too derelict to prevent its producing in the spring a full harvest of blossoms, which could be climbed in, sat in, and gathered, with perfect freedom and happiness. A bed of violets spread beneath it, which gave the ultimate touch of ecstasy to a city-bred child. But the constant and devouring interest that life developed in these and the next few years was in the existence and persons of dolls. Privately there were two families, her sister's and her own. Husbands were absent on business, but often and solicitously mentioned in family letters that passed between the sisters on rainy days. The ladies, earnest mothers of three children apiece, were Mrs. Henry Franklin and Mrs. Charles Wood. Every available moment of the day was given to maternal duties.

Mrs. Wood's family was younger than their cousins, which was natural, and she was the mother of the only infant in long clothes. Providing for the needs of these children; concocting doses in bottles for their frequent illnesses; making their dresses, and full line of underclothes; hemming and marking dozens of miniature towels, napkins, and bed linen — certainly developed real skill with the needle which was already well advanced. Mrs. Franklin possessed a bureau and bed. There was a cradle for the baby, but sleeping accommodation was limited, and 'tucking in' almost impossible. A constant source of anxiety during the winter months was the sense, the certainty, that the children were not warm in their beds. The third story of a not very well-heated house was the scene of these domestic crises. The dolls' beds and the cradle were in our room, and many a bitter night have I risen from my sweet warm nest and my sister's dear proximity, to gather up two of the least protected, as any mother would, and go to sleep clasping their icy china heads to my breast.

I see 'Mrs. Wood,' even in her earlier years, as both a realist and perfectionist, pursued by an uncompromising passion for 'carrying through.' Perhaps it was the perception of what might be the value of this characteristic in the child's future that made her elders and guardians so indulgent of this intense preoccupation. Her sister's conviction was less strong, perhaps on account of her superior age. She had zest, but there was a lurking sense that it was only a game after all, which damped the energy of her attention to details; or did some fairy whisper that she was to brood, some day, over living children?

* * *

As there has thus far seemed to be one aspect only, and that a happy one, in this story of infantile years, I feel called on as a truthful historian to record the only really ugly episode in the child's life. A tardy justice calls for it, also, but the narrative shall be short.

An uncle, the reformer mentioned some way back as having made no effort to assist his parents in trouble, made a visit to his family, and when he inquired for his nieces, who had long since retired, and wished to have a look at them sleeping, he was permitted to do so, and was escorted upstairs by a young and mischievously inclined brother.

When the uncles entered and turned on the light, the scene before them produced an effect quite the opposite of what a civilized soul should feel. A redresser of wrongs done to humanity, that is, to the 'working' classes, and a careless youth, thought it was humorous to drag all the dolls from their beds and hang them by legs, arms, and hands to gas fixture, door handles, and any exposed point. The night was bitter cold, and when the girls awoke in the early morning, the shadowy forms hanging about the room proclaimed the outrage. Here a veil must be drawn. Suffice it to say that there were neither tears nor cries. The effect was far-reaching. The nieces went down to the breakfast-table silent, and refusing to salute or to notice their visiting relatives, who were quite ready to be forgiven. They never forgot to shrink from the reformer when he appeared as a guest. His mother had had a severe reproof for both her sons who wished to conciliate, and it is not going too far to say that one of the mothers has since then never really trusted the ethical principles of professional philanthropists.

* * *

In spite of the early and intense development of the maternal instinct, the education of the child went on. Although the aunt (with the sketch-book) was devoting all her energy to giving music lessons, and returned from long courses to inconvenient places with dripping skirts and wet gaiters, she had time, not only to correct French exercises and hear French read aloud, and to instruct in history, but she also put in thousands of fine stitches in delicate cambric, that her youngest niece might be suitably arrayed. When the loveliest of these garments was outgrown and letting-out of tucks would no longer suffice, it was a great grief to the child, who can remember and cherish the memory of the dress's beauty, and the sweetness of the act that produced it, in combination.

The grandmother's part, as the years passed, was to read aloud while work went on. She was the house's head and director, and took no part in actual lessons, nor in needlework, except to examine and criticize.

Until my fourteenth year I had no schooling outside the home circle. I was slow to learn, or to remember what was dealt to me through channels unmixed with some sort of 'æsthetic' (for lack of a better word) appeal. I learned, by heart, long portions of both the Old and the New Testament, revelling in such passages as Jacob's address to his sons: many of the Psalms, the 'As the hart panteth' being my favorite; also the Twenty-Third before alluded to; the impassioned appeal of Isaiah; the Song of Solomon; and in the New Testament, the visit to Emmaus, and the last chapters of Revelation. There was less eloquence in the Shorter Catechism, which I was expected to learn by heart, and in which I was pretty nearly letter perfect, but the English language at the time it was produced has been the model for the centuries since, and moved me profoundly even when I did not exactly apprehend the doctrines set forth. Some of the rhythmic phrases sound now in my ears, and their 'tempo' is slow and measured, like the theme in a choral.

Lighter excursions in poetry were Scott's poems, the poetry of Thomas Hood, and of course Longfellow. The 'Pilgrim's Progress' was read aloud, and the opening lines charmed me so that I used to steal away to con them over to myself. I had a common, abridged copy of 'Robinson Crusoe,' and knew later, when the real one fell into my hands, why I had not relished the book more.

Our house had a third story, which had all the virtue of an attic, as no one passed through or beyond it. It was automatically private. Dim sounds came up from below. The piano, flights down, was like smooth waves under a light pinnace. There was no harsh voice in the house, so that the mingled tones and often laughter that rose from downstairs were only agreeable.

I often ask myself, when I glance up at the mountainous

perforated cubes of Park Avenue, how children are raised without a third story. How can an apartment, however spacious, be anything but promiscuous? Children, as individuals, need privacy far more than grown people, and it should be automatic. It should not be obviously provided, still less should they be sent to it. Clumsy methods, where delicate tentacles shrink and are folded away to atrophy.

The third story of a semi-country house is a place free from jar or intrusion. The upper hall was the very home of silence, and, as for the guest-room at its far end, a heart stung by supposed injustice, or wounded by misunderstanding, might find place for alleviating recollections in its deep armchair, and the mere sight of the white bed, the Marseilles quilt, and the full dimity valance were comforting. The fact that the room was not lived in and belonged to no one, not even myself, made it as distant as a cave in the hills, yet withal sweet with protection and homeliness.

But beside the soothing elements of the place, there were shelves, where books, outgrown by progressive minds or 'read to pieces,' rubbed shoulders with a little light Victorian fiction for the sleepless guest, and a few standards. Here I discovered a volume bound in brown cloth — 'The Cabinet Edition of Classic Tales.' Its contents were ample, being printed in two columns in the smallest type. In it I found 'Gulliver's Travels,' 'The Sorrows of Werther,' and the 'Castle of Otranto.' These were my favorites. The 'Sentimental Journey' and 'Theodosius and Constantia,' I looked into, but they were too mature for the taste of a girl of my age. Children's minds are, I believe, rarely 'poisoned' by browsing undirected among grown-up books. What they do not understand they glide over, and seldom ask questions about books they have discovered themselves. If their private researches have been in real literature by chance, which they may be incapable of grasping, they will still, if they are sensitive, get the flavor, the aroma, of certain sentences that will throw an armature around their tender taste, which will guard it from the attraction of poorer stuff and make arid for them books of shallow import and clumsy workmanship.

III

EDUCATION

IN an attempt to gather and observe the formative influences in the life of any child, exact sequence is not worth attention. All that this record holds occurred before the age of fourteen, when, although she was to remain more or less a child to the end of her days, the one in question mourned deeply on her fourteenth birthday that her childhood was over.

One of the aunts, the youngest, the one with the sleek brown head and long, shy, dark eyes, had married a Philadelphian who was of the old school; an engineer by profession, who had served on McClellan's staff during the Civil War. My aunt had assisted in my education, and my uncle was to be, after my grandmother, the strongest and most beneficent influence in my life. I know that my Aunt Emily's contribution to my bringing up had several channels. My lessons, with her, took place in the dining-room, rather a gloomy spot by day, on winter mornings, and we sat at either end of the green-felt-covered table. I am sure she labored over the sums and geography we bent over, but what remains consciously of these hours are the periods devoted to dictation. The use of the pen did not trouble me. Spelling was not one of my difficulties, and the appearance of new words, and of phrases far from anything I could have dreamed of, were a delight. Above all, and the real source of the living word enduring in this episode, was the choice of the material used.

How had her Puritan ancestors managed to bequeath to my instructress the really elfin slant of her humor, the soft droop of her head, and her almost whispered sallies, that were followed by the shouts of the family? It must have been something of this strain that caused her to choose from our library, for the hour of dictation she was to offer to her young niece, Heine's 'Pictures of Travel.' A translation, of course, it was a green cloth volume much used, and, as the sentences clearly and softly issued from her curving lips, the child before her passed far away from the chill dining-room and irksome tasks.

Around her was warm sunshine and above her heaven's loveliest blue, in a glamorous land that her imagination seemed to actually move in, as the words, slowly pronounced, gave her time to conceive the reality. But infinitely more relished were the intimate presentments of sensation and emotion, always exquisitely balanced, and graced, by the only witty German. She knew nothing of style, or penetration, and form without emphasis, but the paragraphs glided in upon her welcoming consciousness and remained.

Chapter IV of 'Italy,' beginning, 'While the sun gleamed ever lordlier and lovelier from heaven,' and the next, 'As I drew aside the green silk curtain, which covered the entrance to the Cathedral,' etc., had even a more subtle flavor. There were other portions, one about 'The little Veronica,' which charmed me most of all. I am sure that I took dictation from many other sources, but certainly these had less penetrating power, for I remember none of them.

The same sleek head and wily humor took part in my instruction as a beginner in music.

**

Music, in our house, was of capital importance. Of three grown-up members of our family, one was a finished artist; another, the uncle mentioned above, was not a brilliant performer. He was a learned musician and explorer in new fields, with full veneration and constant study of the old masters. His wife, my youngest aunt, was able and ready to take her place in a duet when needed, and when, at odd moments, when no one else was at the piano, her hands stole over the keys, I always stopped to listen, for always some of her fluent charm swept into the chords.

Being, of course, introduced to music very early, and given my opportunity, I was her pupil. I practised dutifully and learned to play 'The Happy Farmer,' and its like, when alone; but I was bitterly afraid of the standards of those who might not help hearing me, upstairs, and if either of them was present, all connection between hand and spirit ceased.

They tried to encourage me, but I did not like my playing, not being accustomed to mediocrity, or worse, and had an instinctive feeling that I should never admire it. I hated blundering, and did not see that it would ever be a satisfaction to try to convey my feelings crudely.

Of course, I did not know what the trouble was, but when at the age of eleven it was decided that there was not enough of the essential gift to make it best to devote me to it, I was not sorry. There was no trifling on our piano; there were too many sensitive ears about; and also it would never have occurred to me to drum on the piano. It was sacred. It was a privilege, and often mine, to dust it carefully, with its especial silk handkerchief. I crawled about under it, knowing every line of the pedals, and the rest of the fine light wood of its under side.

In fact, I was often crouched beneath it when some one was playing, and loved the muffled, thunderous sound that flowed about me like a cataract. The piano was a Chickering grand of a *souche* now unfashionable, but immensely esteemed in its day. Years afterward my uncle changed it for what became a succession of later makers' models that he esteemed for one reason or another, and the really aged instrument had to retire. I fear that there are no pastures where fine old pianos can be turned out to finish a beautiful life in comfort, like old horses who have been family pets. It was rosewood with lines, but no carving. When later I saw a black glistening instrument, with elaborate and bunchy carved legs, I was shocked, and never knew a rack that compared in elegance with the fine straight lines of ours.

* * *

So much for the sanctuary. Its oracular demonstration established my taste. In our house there was music every evening, generally duets, when my uncle was at home. If not, the chief artist put down her embroidery early in the evening and sat down to the piano for as long as she wished.

But there were unwritten, and really unspoken, rules. The musician must never be asked to play, nor might any given piece be asked for, and in the long narrow 'parlor,' where the piano occupied the whole end of the room, there must be silence. In the adjoining room, the family in general sat with open doors. But a child might lie all the evening, face downward, on the parlor sofa, or on the rug, or under the piano; a beating heart makes no noise; and I dare say the musicians had some idea when they rose that something equivalent to instruction had been going on in the tousled head on the sofa pillow.

My uncle brought home all the new music, and as they, the chief artists, were consummate sight-readers, there was no jar from stumbling, and no repetition, except of the whole piece. There was little of what could be called practising, though they once worked over the Jupiter symphony for a whole winter, and my uncle was sometimes, for months, at grips with certain compositions he could not master, technically. He played with superb tone, conception, and feeling, but could never reach my aunt's virtuosity in the left hand. One of my choicest memories is of warm mornings in spring, when, with open glass doors upon the side verandah and little garden, we women-folk noiselessly busy with the breakfast silver and glass, passing in and out, could do so to the rhythmic passion of the Chopin Polonaise, Op. 53, which my uncle was drawing from the very vitals of the piano. Over and over the bass octaves rolled, under never-satisfied fingers, until, between the morning moment, always pregnant for me, the tides of spring in my veins, and the vast billows of romantic rhythm and sonority, my small heart seemed actually to experience an ecstatic growth, and bounded in my breast. Years afterwards, when I was at the accepted age for romance, and was having my share, some one played the same music in my hearing with what seemed a prophetic significance and deep note of warning.

* * *

Was it because it was too good, too far out of my reach, that I never could throw myself into actual participation in an art which was such a necessary part of my life? I was to participate, but as a communicant only. I was never to serve at the altar. In 'Indian Summer,' Emily Dickinson has spoken for me. How often she has done so....

> Oh, sacrament of summer days,
> Oh, last communion in the haze,
> Permit a child to join.
>
> Thy sacred emblems to partake,
> Thy consecrated bread to break,
> Taste thine immortal wine.

* * *

But, although I was to do nothing in instrumental music, other doors were open. I had as much voice as the average child, and could be counted on for surety of ear and for time and rhythm. My sister and I always did close harmony (we did not know its name), and wove about between soprano and alto, while we were at work, at anything but lessons. Somewhat before this, however, when I was nine, something quite ambitious was undertaken. At this time the uncle and aunt mentioned above were living near an 'iron works,' called Freedom, in central Pennsylvania, of which he had charge. My sister and I spent the winter there with them, in a long, interesting old house, in a big abandoned garden. A rough shaly mountain rose at one side, and at its feet ran a gruff sort of river, unapproachably guarded by thick alders, and, as an unwelcoming meadow came first, the stream had little part in our lives. The house was charming, though shabby. It was spacious, and just enough mysterious, and it seemed the sun had full entry everywhere and made up for rather scanty furniture.

We had lessons every morning. There were no neighbors, and no visitors, except an occasional official caller on my uncle.

There was only a square piano, which was much in use, and during several long absences of my uncle, when my aunt, my sister, and myself were entirely alone, she organized and directed a surprise for him. We learned, in fact, to do such parts of Mendelssohn's 'Elijah,' as could be performed for home consumption only, by three voices, soprano, contralto, and tenor, which part was taken by my aunt, who led, and played the piano accompaniment. Of course, my little voice was soprano, and my sister took the contralto parts. Needless to say, we did not perform the solos, though we were familiar with them. I suppose I never knew again a rapture more moving than that which I felt in the tenor solo, 'If with all your hearts.' I knew all the soprano parts, except the solos. We did the *Terzetto*, of course; and 'O rest in the Lord' in unison, the quartette, 'Cast thy burden,' without the bass, and could sing them correctly with some shading and without strain.

Later, at home, and with the assistance of tenor and bass, we did choruses, arranged for eight voices, from other oratorios; the entrances and weavings of the parts in 'He watches over Israel,' from the 'Elijah,' again, and, apart from its solemn beauty, no country dance or cotillion could have been more relished. When I was seventeen or eighteen, we were singing English madrigals and German quartettes with our boy friends, and duets, and even had singing lessons, though we were never expected to become soloists.

Sunday evening hymns had always been part of the home ritual. My uncle was deeply interested in church music, and gave his services as organist to our suburban church. He compiled a hymn-book, rearranging much of the music. A whole shelf in our musical library was devoted to hymn literature, as my uncle drew much of the material for his book from the English school of cathedral music.

* * *

Long before it was discovered that I had more proficiency with a pencil than I had on the piano, I accompanied my aunts on visits to what picture galleries and special exhibitions there were.

The Pennsylvania Academy of Fine Arts was at that time quite far downtown, in a dark old building. Memory retains only one impression of our visit there. While my aunts were wandering and examining, I fell behind, 'intrigued,' as they say now, by an enormous oil painting which hung over a descending stairway. A railing, or balustrade, prevented visitors from plunging downstairs from the gallery floor, but also prevented guests of my size from adequately viewing the picture. No one was near to see, and I lay down with my head on the floor and 'got' the picture very well from between the posts of the railing. The huge canvas depicted three life-size horses in full career, ridden by enigmatical personages; cloud and flame surrounded; prostrate and suppliant figures filled the foreground. The foremost steed was white, with flowing mane and tail, and was rearing in the pride of conquest. The title of the picture was 'Death on the Pale Horse,' by Benjamin West. I knew my Book of Revelation, so it was only an illustration, to me, and in spite of foaming bit and stretched nostrils of Arabian flexibility, not a very impressive one. Still I remained curiously gazing until I was found and put upon my feet.

Children register their impressions with astounding exactness, but they seldom manifest, or remember, surprise or
astonishment. To them one novelty is no more wonderful
than another, and lighting the gas quite as much of a miracle as Aladdin's carpet, so there is no registered sensation,
though a perfect recollection, of the first painting I consciously observed.

*_**

It must have been several years after this that a private
collection was opened in Philadelphia to privileged persons
on certain days. Mr. William C. Gibson was the fortunate
and generous owner, and my uncle had a card for the gallery, which was in the Gibson house.

Mr. Gibson had progressed beyond, and no doubt believed that he had improved on, the old red brick and
marble that, where it remains from the eighteenth century,
is the only architectural glory of Philadelphia, now. His
new house was on Walnut Street, and people knew no more
what to think of it than they do now of 'l'art moderne' in
furniture.

The façade of the four-story 'residence' was of grey granite, in large blocks. The steps and entrance were massive,
and were of the same stone, brilliantly polished. Over the
front door was a portico of elephantine lines and Egyptian
suggestion. As the house faced north, all this stood in
shadow, and was of a gloom that would have befitted a
mausoleum or a prison. As a witty French critic has said,
'Art changes; it does not progress'; and this house, built
by a collector of works of art, is a forcible supporter of the
theory.

I was first taken to the gallery on a cold winter day. After
our long bleak journey in the horse-car, the entrance, and
the door opened by a solemn servant, were not very hopeful;
but once inside, at the end of a dark hall shone Paradise
itself. Light filtered through immense pale green fronds of

lofty ferns. Here were perfumes of hidden flowers and moist earth; the voice of a bird; delicious warmth; summer.

I had never dreamed of a conservatory before, and my delight was unmixed with knowledge of a furnace and steam pipes. But, far more than even this, there were a number of small galleries opening from it where the pictures hung. The lighting, all daylight from above, was soft and equal, and showed every touch of color and value at its best.

Very few of the pictures were large, and all could be easily seen. Of course, I knew nothing of these virtues of presentation; I knew nothing but my own happiness. I must have been taken several times to the gallery, for I had my favorites and was unembarrassed by the difference of schools. The pictures were all as 'modern,' or nearly so, as the front entrance of the house, only Art, in her wilful way, had not answered when evoked for *it*, and had turned in many differing directions indoors.

My favorites were, first of all, a head of a young man, by Couture. It hung rather high, but this suited the design of the head, which had been seen from below. The rich modelling — 'found' as the French say with learned accuracy — had been mixed with the eye's brooding imagination; the beauty of the head itself, in which no choice line had been missed by the artist; the ripe, fruity quality of the very substance of the material that had conveyed all this were felt with awful joy and ignorance, the former of which has never changed or diminished.

The 'Angelus' itself was there, with less of the sensuous in its purple-grey and black, and, to my ignorance, this reduced its power, for, as to the subject, no one explained to me that there was a kind of prayer that could be uttered publicly, in a wide field, by two people facing each other. Of course, the picture had a central position, where its romantic dignity made the paintings near it look common. This I dumbly felt. The idea of the French peasant and his life, I met first here. Utterly unknown before, I saw it with a sort of wondering recognition, as of something appearing dimly, out of great distance. The pink and polished sweetness of the peasants of Bouguereau and Merle had the appeal of dimpled flesh, limpid eyes, and dewy lips, and the much more realized costume touched my curious eye with something of the same atavistic mystery of when and how and 'Where hast thou stayed so long?'

I little knew why I liked the great tree by Courbet, standing alone in a smallish canvas, and the only object there, but it is one of the pictures most vividly remembered.

On one wall bloomed in foamy splendor Cabanel's 'Birth of Venus.' I am not sure that it was not opposite the 'Angelus.' I can remember only a sense of unfamiliarity. It was not one of my friends among the pictures. It was some one else's friend, but what child's eye is not pleased by turquoise and cream?

If I did aught but gaze, if I pondered at all, it was before the Boldini and the Fortuny that I stood longest and puzzled most. The Boldini was a small picture. A young lady walked on a summer day, in France, when the air was fresh and pure. French clouds I did not know, but they seemed somehow good, marshalled overhead. There were a few strange-looking small trees, of a bluish-green color, unfamiliar to me. But the mystery of the *painting* was quite another thing. It is sometimes difficult to separate memory from later knowledge, but I am still thrilled by the recollection of those fresh, pure strokes, mixed with morning light, the pearly light of France, strokes so enigmatical when examined, so wrought with whim and fantasy, yet so sure, with the firmness of reality when one walked away. 'I cannot understand, I love,' I would have thought, if I had known my Tennyson. The small Boldini and I were more than friends, but it must be confessed here that it is the only Boldini I ever really loved.

Then there was the Fortuny, a little canvas in a wide black frame, which was much more puzzling, and even more magical, though it had no beauty except in the making of a chicken-fight, in a small green *patio*, a solved problem in art.

* * *

There were handsome compositions in the collection by Gerôme, Vibert, Madrazzo. By the latter, a pretty Spanish girl at a window. In all such pictures as these I plunged at once into the story, of course, and above all into the aspect of life that they explained, without compromise. I found much more in the gallery than painting. I had my first taste of foreign ways, places, light, palaces, churches, gardens, and ceremonies and people of the past, or moving in the scene and atmosphere of old Europe. My embryonic sense took hold, once for all, of something that was mine, and that nothing should cheat me of some day; but I had no conscious reservations in past or present, and 'time to go' was the only interference of which I was aware.

How could I dream of being an artist? I never did. I was too much occupied, and I did not see 'myself' as having any possible relation or participation in what I saw around me.

This gallery was my outstanding opportunity, but there was also the sporadic exhibition of 'important' single works, which, placed alone in a darkened room under a strong light, might be seriously viewed by art-lovers for whom were arranged chairs in shadow. Under such circumstances I saw Bierstadt's 'Rocky Mountains,' a monumental example of German, or Swiss, faith and energy. Indeed, I highly honor the artist's pursuit of place and proper distance, across the wide valley, where rivers, forests, fields, and 'laboring wains' maintained their dignified existence, until the eye reached (though it did this first, by the way) the snowy peaks and perilous crevasses of the backbone of our country.

I was quite cool about the picture, but my eye enjoyed travelling from one natural object to another, over cascade and precipice. Where is the picture now? Its green was fresh then and its shadows no darker than the unrelated truth. Now, what color it had must have sickened and perished in a brown-grey limbo, although its excellent drawing and well-arranged masses may have embalmed it in a dignity, and even fearsomeness, and almost poetry, it never had before.

Damascus is said to be no hotter than Philadelphia in summer, and as our house stood rather low, with a hill in front of it, this was probably true for it. Generally the family scattered to any possible refuge during July and August, but I remember rather pleasantly one year, when my grandmother, my sister, and myself went into summer quarters and remained. The garden and side porch were shaded in the afternoon, and in our thinnest of summer garb did very well, for us. The morning hours were intolerable out-of-doors. In the house there was cool semi-darkness of shuttered windows, India matting on the floors and linen-covered furniture; and my grandmother in her 'linen-cambric' dress would have freshened any environment. She was well aware that an occupation must be devised that could be combined with entertainment. She brought down from the storeroom a pile of immense, slightly worn linen sheets. My task was to restore them. I was to cut out weak places and put in enormous patches. The most worn of the sheets were to be cut up for this, choosing the strongest parts. The sheet in hand was spread upon the floor, and I crawled about on it, cutting out and laying on the patch, with perfect precision, and the neatest stitches. There were no crooked corners — all was done by the thread. The preparation needed for this, the skill to be expended, the delicious cool fabric which the needle seemed to rejoice to enter — all these things had a quality for me that gave them a place with other pleasures in memory, but whether the hours would have flown as they did, without my grandmother's

CECILIA KENT LEAVITT
Drawing by her granddaughter, C. Beaux

contribution as a stimulant, I cannot say. She gave all her mornings to this. In our house much had to be done in the family that, in easier circumstances, would have been put out or done by servants. These tasks were always accompanied by loud reading, which for us eliminated all of the monotony and much of the fatigue. On this occasion my grandmother chose an American novel, 'The Gayworthys.' She probably chose it first because the scene was laid in a village that might have been our beloved Washington, Connecticut. The characters resembled, remotely, people we knew. If we could not go to our dear Connecticut hills, we might (never seeing the book, which was put away between-whiles) have them with us fresh and lovely during hot mornings in Spruce Street. This was my first novel (to be more than peeped into). I was eleven at this time. The interest and expansion I found in it were devouring, and occupied my thoughts much of the time when the precious volume was closed and put away. My grandmother had never heard the dictum of Anatole France, '*Pas d'emphase,*' but she illustrated the maxim in her reading.

In her earliest girlhood she had assisted one of her older brothers, Aratus Kent, in his theological studies. The young man was to become a pioneer missionary in remote Illinois, and had a serious handicap in very inferior eyesight. His young sister, Cecilia, was wont to read aloud to him many hours a day, I know not from what sources of Philosophy and 'Divinity.' Clarity, and just the right amount of deliberation, were needed for this, and the sister never forgot her training. Her reading was so little personal that one's own interpretation or conception of the drama or scene described always found room for harmonious development and realization, unencumbered by any claim from the reader, who had no personal tricks of accent or pronunciation; no mannerisms.

A description by negatives, however, can give no idea of the voice or of the phrasing so unconsciously practised. She would have said, 'I know no other way,' and for her hearers, engaged in patching and perhaps furniture polishing (my sister could not use her eyes for sewing), she knew just when the moment had come for a break, and one would be sent flying on some errand downstairs or up.

Furniture polishing — a great deal of it was done in our house, and not by servants, and of course never without the accompanying mental stimulant. There was quite a little of the old waxed furniture in the house, and once a year these pieces, generally table-tops or the fronts of large, deep bureau drawers, had to be treated. This was done by the use of a hard lump of beeswax about the size of one's fist. The lump was irregular in shape, and one could only rub it on in streaks and patches. Having, so to speak, 'written' the wax pretty generally over the table-top or bureau, one took a strong, short-bristled brush, somewhat like a scrubbing-brush and proceeded to exercise it strengthily upon the surface. This was done until the wax, warmed by friction, was perfectly distributed over the whole — no streaks visible. Then came rubbing with a soft old linen cloth, until, final test, a finger-mark would not show upon the wood. The result was not a shining sparkle, which would have been thought vulgar, but a soft, delicious patina the hand loved to linger upon, and a profound reënforcement, rich and sombre, of the color of the wood.

How could a child with a natural *penchant* for textures help developing into an individual to whom liquid dressings, artificial silk, and impure linen were anathema, and who found that touch was a close second to eye in the appreciation of plastic art?

I was now a nondescript girl of thirteen, well-grown, amenable, and with energies too deep for evidence as yet. I was, in fact, languid, but my guardians saw to it that I did not waste my time. I felt unoccupied. Secretly I wrote verses, and kept a journal, long since disposed of. I had perfectly straight and very thick light brown hair, my father's fair complexion, and, people were foolish enough to tell me, his eyes.

My instructress in drawing, though I have no recollection of further work with the Harding studies, used to brush my hair for more than an hour a day. The brush used freely and vigorous patting were an effort toward the much-desired shiny smoothness that in default of curls was considered the only alternative, and it was then braided in two tight substantial plaits upon my shoulders.

There is one more short halt to be made before closing the door on childhood.

My aunt, the chief musician, was also a painter of flowers in water-colors. She also designed the patterns for her embroidery and had been present with her sketch-book at Eschelman's and our other summer sojournings.

She returned from town one day with a small package of lithographs, drawings by the English artist, Harding. They were in outline only and were the simplest form of presentment of a small house and tree, careful studies of leafy boughs, stones with a neighbor weed, or plantain drawn with fond attention to every curve and curl of large leaves.

I was entirely ready to undertake what was suggested, that I should try to copy one of them. Harding was a true artist. Every touch had quality and charm. Selected content and simplicity were predominant. I did not think of the Couture, but the little studies had the same spirit, full of grace and truth. But my dear aunt had not thought of introducing me at a lithographing establishment. She had carefully selected the models; I had a well-sharpened, hard lead pencil, and a nice sheet of fine white drawing-paper, a rubber, and a penknife. How good it all looked. I took a deep breath, and began to find, by dots and almost invisible lines, the proportions of the little hut, the size of the tree, etc. All very well so far, but I began to see, as I continued,

that there was something about the soft black broken line of
the model that my lead pencil would not produce. I tried
to exactly imitate the breaks; no good. Nevertheless, I persevered. Frequent approval came from my instructress
leaning over me. The house was exactly the right size; the
walls upright, and the drawing was in exactly the right
place on the paper. The joyless adventure grew pale,
monotonous; hard and hairy, at the same time. I wondered
why my touches had no beginning or end. What was the
matter? With my usual reticence, I did not ask. I was told
that it was quite good, and that I might do another one to-
morrow; but I remained alive to this early disappointment
for the rest of my life.

Later I was to know more of lithography.

* * *

Home education continued for me until I was fourteen,
when it was thought best to send me to the school in town;
that is, in Philadelphia, where my sister had preceded me.
The school chosen was considered the best and was certainly the most exclusive school in Philadelphia.

It was by no means an Institution or Academy. The
principals were Miss Lyman and Miss Charlotte Lyman, of
the pure New England strain of that family. Miss Lyman
was a queen, benignant and charming, who held the school
in the hollow of her small, plump white hand. She had a
rich, deep voice, which she never had to raise. Her astonishment, when there was occasion for it, was conveyed by a
slight but fearful gesture of raised eyebrows, and, in extreme
cases, the culprit's name pronounced with resonant suggestiveness of judgment. She reigned over the whole school,
but had emphasized contact with the big girls, some of
whom might have been seventeen or eighteen years old, and
whose desks were in the vicinity of her throne. Could this
have been nothing but an ordinary chair, beside a small
table? How I venerated the group! Ellen and Rosalie

Evans, Rebecca Lewis, Julia Strong, Mary Whitney, Charlotte Humphrey, Susie Ritchie, and Lily Moore could not err, or fail in anything. At least they never did. The school was not graded, and I have always felt that this method was a much more intelligent and direct one, from being more stimulating, than the usual one of classification, where the pupil is put through a course of several years, never leaving the group into which she is placed on entering, and which is regulated largely by age. There were no examinations in our school, but there were monthly reports, which were a serious or happy occasion, as the case might be, when set before parent or guardian.

I was placed, regardless of age, where I was thought to belong. In Latin, in which I was a beginner, and arithmetic, I was with girls younger than myself. But in French, English composition, and natural history, I ranged with the peeresses and heard their clear, able statements to Mr. Chase or M. Gardel. In other classes, I was with girls of my own age, and in history (American) was even led by Miss Lyman herself, and suffered shame unspeakable by utter loss of memory through agitation.

Two-Twenty-Six South Broad Street was one of the deep, roomy red-brick and white-marble houses for which Philadelphia is famous. The big front parlor was Miss Lyman's throne-room. Her entrance at nine punctually was dramatic. She was of medium stature (a really commanding person is seldom tall) and verging on *embonpoint*. Her step was gliding and noiseless. Her habitual dress — I never saw her in any other — was a light-grey Irish poplin, with a short train. If I had ever heard of Worth, I would have believed that no one else could have fitted it. Her head was superbly set, and she wore upon her grey hair's smooth waves a bit of fine old lace and lavender ribbon. The same lace showed below her firm plump chin, and at her wrists.

In the silence that greeted her approach, the only sound was the soft rustle of her train, until she was seated, when prayers were at once read to the whole school, kneeling at their desks. This ceremony was punctilious, and, without a shade of sentimentality, it was faultless in style, the rich timbre of Miss Lyman's voice lending itself perfectly to the 'office,' which might have been as conducted by a Bishop.

After this, the whole school standing, a general spelling exercise took place, the girls in close rank around the front room. There was no preparation for this, nor for the exercise in mental arithmetic which followed. Both were conducted by Miss Lyman with great promptness. Swift currents of shame and exultation swept about the room. Miss Lyman's 'Next' instantly followed failure, and little time was given for reflection.

By this time every girl who had arrived in the mood of having overslept, was wide awake, and the irrepressible and recalcitrant were ready with fresh devices for tormenting the teacher who remained in charge when Miss Lyman had taken her august departure. There were many who were 'good' only when she was in the room, though the influential dignity of the older girls, who sat at their desks with lowered eyes and open books, had a certain effect upon the incorrigible whisperers in the back room, some of whom, in response to the rebuke of poor Miss M——, made use of the wit they had inherited from ancestors who had mingled the same with their Madeira and terrapin.

Although individually I entered very little into the sphere where Miss Charlotte Lyman moved, the dramatic contrast between the two sisters was one of the most vivid of my many impressions.

Miss Charlotte's domain was in the second story 'back-building,' the room that, if the house had been inhabited by a family, would have been the library or dining-room. Here all the younger girls in the school, some of them not more than ten years old, and wearing pinafores, spent their days, under the firm and gentle rule of Miss Charlotte. She was a good many years younger than Miss Lyman, a brune, with clustering jetty ringlets, arranged, however, with dignified reserve. She had the kindest of twinkling black eyes tilting up considerably at the corners, behind high *pommettes* of bright color. Her face was full of pleasant, homely curves, which were much set off by her dress, which was habitually of soft woolen material, of a rich red. I went up the back stairs to her room for Latin and algebra, in which I took my first steps with the 'little girls.' Although I did not continue long enough in the school to feel the zest of these studies, and have very little memory of them beyond rules learned by heart, Miss Charlotte's room had a pleasant atmosphere, and I was always glad to go there.

The absorbing novelty of my whole school experience was greatly intensified by the fact that I witnessed nearly every phase of the school's life. Each class was a pageant to my devouring observation. Teachers, small girls and big, and the intermediates to which I belonged, offered endless new objects to my gaze. Some of the girls of about fifteen were unimaginably beautiful; some of the little ones had thin pale faces and irregular teeth, which I had never seen before. Stringy hair, or hair that had known curl-papers, were equally unknown to me, and aroused endless curiosity. Some of the larger girls had the tiniest feet ever seen, and wore high buttoned kid boots, made to exaggerate this very much esteemed charm. Many of my mates, though there was nothing to indicate this at the time, belonged to wealthy families and lived within the sacred precinct that lay between Spruce and Chestnut Streets, but to the credit of their parents be it recorded, none of these showed the slightest sign, on their persons, of either money or fashion. We all wore woolen dresses; sometimes these were a homely plaid and were made at home by the seamstresses, who, in all well-

ordered households, sewed all day long in some remote upstairs chamber which the furnace could not reach, and
which was made rather cosy by a small coal stove. Very
familiar was that bowed silhouette against the window, surrounded by billows of tulle that had been torn to shreds in
last night's ball, or making over the heavy edges of skirts
that had swept the pavement of Walnut Street. I am sorry
for the young who in town can visit only in apartments, and
am thankful that I have the memory of long vistas in deep,
quiet houses, where there were high ceilings, rich damask
curtains, long wide halls, softly carpeted and curving stairs,
mounting up and up to regions where running and peeping
could be slyly enjoyed. There were views, too, of great bed-
rooms, where everything was ample and spatial; big smooth
pillows, white bedspreads, heavy furniture, for which there
was plenty of room, and spotless comfort, everywhere.

But the luxury of home was little reflected in the habits of
the young daughters of the house. Dresses were plain and
rather formless. Stockings were black or white cotton, our
shoes low-heeled and nondescript. Most of us kept an apron
in our desk, which we put on on arriving at school.

One or two of the older girls had watches, and some of
those of my age had a little jewelry, which they were asked
to show at recess, and which always gathered a group of admirers, begging to be allowed to try on the ring or bracelet.

One of my especial friends had a sister, perhaps four or
five years older than herself, who was 'out,' and nothing
could be in greater contrast than these two in dress and
manner. Christine's appearance on Walnut Street showed
all that the extreme of fashion could add to her own beauty
and elegance. How we all admired her, her proud carriage
and marvellous hats and dresses! But imitation, even if it
had been possible, no one would have dreamed of. Her
younger sister, in her comfortable dress and coat, would
have been the last to even wish for it.

I can remember only one incident among my experiences at school (in fact, I believe there was but one) that was in the least flattering to my pride or ambition. The distraction and novelty of the whole scene, and the actors therein, so absorbed my attention that I never gave to my 'lessons' the concentration they should have had. My reports were not bad, but they were not very good, and I fear rather saddened those at home who were making real sacrifices for my education.

In English composition I was entered among girls of my own age. Our master in this was Mr. Chase, a serious man, who had the appearance and manner of an Oxford Don, humanized and disciplined by life, though, even to us, he was not old. I believe the idea of our behavior never crossed his mind. It was entirely unnecessary that it should. His personality had a governing charm which never had, consciously, to deal with our conduct. Any of us would have died rather than be eligible to a rebuke from him, and our tremblings before him did not arise from any severity on his part. I still believe (what I then felt as only a sort of stammering obsession) that he was one of the most charming men I ever knew, and, alas, how little I knew of him. I suppose he taught all day long, Latin, the higher mathematics, rhetoric, in various schools. Even then I had a groping consciousness of what this meant and his resigned steadfastness in relation to it.

Mr. Chase sat at a table with our productions, which he had already gone over, before him. He picked up one of these, smiled a little, and then began to commend it, not discussing, as usual, only the spelling, punctuation, and grammar. The paper was mine. No one looked my way, or guessed this, but he seemed to know it, for after the class he 'saw' me, and raised his hand. When I stood quaking before him, he looked down on me with kindly eyes and said:

'You don't belong here. After to-day you will be in the first class.'

How long can emotion last and be forever fresh; not a memory, but a present actuality? Perhaps its life is longer when it has never been expressed. There may have been tears in my eyes, but what I said was, 'Yes, Mr. Chase'; which was proper, and I passed out with the others.

I cannot help feeling that the quiet mornings at the big green table at home, the dictation from Heine, my discovery of the 'Essays of Elia,' the hours of reading aloud from Scott's novels and his poems, as well as the Psalms and Bible chapters, learned by heart, had a good deal to do with my small superiority over my mates, in English, at this time.

As in all schools at that time, at Miss Lyman's there were 'extras' in what might have been called 'accomplishments' at a still earlier date. There was a drawing class, which was held somewhere in the upper regions of the house. It was popular, and quite a number of the girls rushed gaily off, on certain days, to partake of it. I never saw the teacher nor the models, but when the participants descended in about an hour or so they brought the results with them, upon sheets of Academy paper, held high for fear of rubbing, and indeed the drawings were 'loose' enough to have come off very easily, and resembled uniformly the eternal series of beginner's use of charcoal, which I was later to know so well in selecting the candidates for admission at the P.A.F.A. This was my first sight of student's work and it was indeed revolting. I would have had to be dragged to the class in irons if it had been my fate to go. One could discern that casts of various kinds had been the models. Blackened hands and aprons testified to the diligence of the students, who were highly delighted with the performance, and many of the less favored, whose parents could not afford this 'extra,' envied them.

How thankful I was that the opportunity was not mine!

Perhaps the only prominence my sister and I ever had at Miss Lyman's was owing to our very differing inheritance, by birth, from at least our comrades in the particular groups in which we moved; she among the older girls, I in the lower series. Our Provençal blood was probably responsible for our being called upon to do most of the verse-making that was produced, of course privately, in the school. Rhymed verse flowed from us almost as easily as speech. Some of our comrades were descended from the best Quaker settlers, or bore names of Philadelphians who had had factories on the Wissahickon for two hundred years. Mingled with these, but of equally practical mind, were the children of the ultra-fashionable; those who were rather proud of having had not too respectable ancestors. Their elders sat at the windows of the Philadelphia Club in the afternoon, and no well-brought-up girl was even to glance across the street towards those fine expanses of shining glass, behind which were mischievous old gentlemen who might have ogled them from over their newspapers.

But this race was not productive of sentimental or indeed any kind of 'poetry'; and there was a real demand for it, before the end of the term, when there were to be partings, and the adventures and sentiments of the winter were to be memorialized. Folding fans, made of slats of white Bristol board, were greatly in favor, as each slat could contain a verse glowing with either sentiment or humor as desired.

We wrote most of the lines by request, and they were then copied upon the fan by those who felt more than they could express.

We wrote also — not by request — a set of verses, inspired, I am ashamed to say, by one of the finest and most able of our teachers. Miss G. L. was a tall Quaker lady of great distinction. She wore the Friends' costume in its most exquisite form. She had the finest of mouse-colored shawls, soundless silks, and spotless, folded mull. Closely fitting sleeves on her shapely arms set off, at the wrist's perfection, very white, large, tapering hands. She had a really grand head and countenance, and never descended from her sphere of pure intellectuality. If there were glances or smothered giggles at the far end of the line of her pupils, or even notes passed, she was unaware of it. Miss G. L. brought many large charts which she unrolled and hung before us; geological and zoölogical classifications of endless complexity. These were all of vivid interest to her, and we never got so far as the microscopic creature or prehistoric monster that might have fixed our phlegmatic attention.

There must have been at proper times exchange of courtesies between Miss Lyman and Miss L. How I wish that I could have witnessed them!

* * *

If there was not much storing-up of useful knowledge on my part, during my two winters at Miss Lyman's, it was not the fault of my instructors. The classes were not large, and one always had the personal attention of the teacher, who made her appeal to each pupil as to a well-known individual whose name, character, and possibilities were familiar and interesting.

Mr. Chase and the old French teacher, M. Gardel, were more remote, and the latter, absolutely impersonal. His severity was for one's work, if it was deserved, and there was no compromise, no excuse accepted.

'You must not "think." You must *know*.'

He generally refused to correct mistakes himself, and 'Go to your Young Student,' was frequently on his lips.

Poor old man; he suffered from some malady which caused him to keep his left arm constantly pressed against his breast. How gallantly he bore this and how precise and *soigné* was the appearance of his thin, stooping person! A young girl, perhaps his granddaughter, always came with him and accompanied his departure. We were all fond of him, and I am glad to say no one would have dared or wished to irritate him.

My two winters at '226' opened up new vistas, and in some ways liberated a budding character. Humanly, I learned more at Miss Lyman's than I realized until long afterwards.

* * *

There is strong evidence at the present moment of a universal disposition toward dramatic art, toward the theatre, especially with young people. There is nothing intrinsically new in this, for no period can be named when some form of play-acting, of the dramatic scene, was not the most popular of the arts, and this, whether it was Art or only its travesty. Much of this lay in the easy distraction of the unfamiliar upon the stage, though the distraction was equally efficient if the scene was a close reproduction of what was familiar to all. The mirror was as interesting as were strange fashions, because the public had not taken the trouble to observe itself.

* * *

I often wonder why the school I attended for two seasons was to me a drama of unforgettable vividness. It was not so much the clash and magic of feeling. True the 'heart-interest' of the piece was keen, absorbing, and almost painful in its intensity, and not exactly to be called school-girl infatuation, but whether hidden, manifested, or in abeyance to the 'code' of a period, such seizures lie too near the roots of humanity to be at the command or denial of any age. They continue; hearts remain the same.

It was far more as a spectacle that the perfectly usual and unaccented association took my eye's mind captive. How far the Miss Lymans were from perceiving that their school for young ladies had, to one of them, at least, all the fascinating appeal of an original and perfectly set play! It has taken

their obscure pupil many years to realize this, and to guess
'what it was all about.'

Fundamentally it was the falling of seed upon a prepared
and virgin soil. The group of elders, some of them not very
old, in which I had been born and reared; *their* culture, occupations, and unspoken ideals, were responsible for this.
Before my fourteenth year, I had had very few young
friends, and those I had were as members of my family. I
had lived on the outer edge of a suburb, close to fields, great
trees, slopes where beds of violets grew in May, a spring and
a tiny stream. I have already made mention of the silences
and the music.

In fact, I was just ready for what life presented without circumstance or announcement, a scene peopled with characters clearly marked and original, in appearance and action.
What could be more diverse in effect, as well as in their pro-
founder motivity, than the leading performers?

Every phase of Miss Lyman's appearance and presence, in
the rich *chiaroscuro* which the high windows of the rooms
happened to provide, was a 'tableau' at which one longed to
gaze, yet dared not. M. Gardel, the delicate, strained old
man, seated in his class of blooming, careless girls, was another 'feature.' No detail of perfectly appropriate costume
was omitted from our Professor of Zoölogy, in her floating,
yet how reserved garb, of every tone of a dove's plumage, to
dear Miss Charlotte, bending over a little pinafored girl her
ebon coiffure, and the deep glowing red of her modest morning dress.

And the girls — The *jeune première* was not the prettiest
girl in school. She was a slight, boyish witch, neither noisy
nor talkative, who never lifted her long straight eyelashes, or
the corners of her proud little mouth, in any gesture of in-
gratiation or coquetry. She had a smooth dark head. Her
hair was drawn tightly back from a high forehead, and
braided as usual. Her dress was brown; she was all brown
save for the clear color of her spare little face. Her eyes,

grey, of great beauty, were, in spite of her mirth and mis-
chief, made almost tragic by dark eyebrows, mounting in
Sorrow's own upward curve. She was a teasing, honest boy.
How came she to have a nun's face? There was a certain
shaft of light from high up, entering the back school-room
windows, from a narrow cleft between roofs. When this
light happened to fall on the charmer sitting in class, all the
beauty that one might imagine in rapt saint or martyr
shone out, and she was indeed transcendent, though she
might have just pinched the arm of her neighbor, who would
be delighted with the attention. Holiness, all unconscious,
clothed her delicate mortal features. In the street she wore
a shiny sailor hat and a loose brown raglan overcoat. She
would not be bound, and none of those who waited in the
hope that she would have a whim to join or to attach a
comrade would have dared offer her their company. Yet
later she was to resign all her liberty of will and conscience.
She became, after years of approach to it, a devout convert to
the Church of Rome. Perhaps nothing less universal or majestic could have conquered her. In her youth she was irresistible, as a *jeune première* should be, and doled out happiness or misery in slight, unconscious acts, or omissions. Is
this not the chief prerogative of charmers?

I give thanks that my childhood and youth were not
stuffed, gorged, with a multifarious fodder that deadened all
appetite. I am glad that the world I saw immediately
around me had the endless variety of appearance that my
eyes were so eager to enjoy. Whether my mind 'registered'
or not, my eyes were not bored with monotony, and did me
the service of storing up in my uncluttered memory fragments of scenes, or groups in their own atmosphere, of
which nothing seems to remain except what was more than
worthy to live as long as I might. Grandmothers, aunts,
teachers, 'young ladies,' girls, and children, each wore the

'costume,' one might say, and coiffure of her age. Sounds could be heard far off on account of near-by stillness, and had a greater charm on a rainy morning. Is it hard to believe that there *was* charm in such homely sounds as the rumble of cart wheels in a distant street, a horse's hoofs on wet cobble-stones, the crowing of a cock at the little farm that lay beyond us, the click of the latch of the garden gate, when some one was expected and one was not at the window, and even the scream of a locomotive passing with its train, perhaps miles away, through the fields and hills?

Oh, educators and child analysts, see that you do not handle the delicate fibres of young consciousness and perception until the antennæ are limp and powerless to feel. Do not maul them, or, gorging them with your experimental diet, deprive them of all appetite — appetite, their supreme prerogative and birthright as developing creatures. Do not rob the maturity or age of these children. Give them a chance. They have a right (thirty or forty years later) to turn over the jewels of memory, to taste, feel, see, hear, again, what for such simple reason was so sweet and so dear, and which, but for a clear page, would have been an illegible blur. How many hearts have warmed over that line of Thomas Hood's,

'The little window where the sun came peeping in at morn.'

Recollections of childhood have all the super-grace, the quality, the *patine* of the best antiques; their mystic beauty, their value as the furniture of the soul.

The spring term at Miss Lyman's ended in June, and it was thought that I had shown enough inclination and aptitude, in my home drawing-lessons, to warrant my having regular instruction.

I had not the slightest idea of being an artist. The gulf between me and such an ambition was too great. I could not

CHILD WITH NURSE
'Ernesta'

see across it. When I thought of the Gibson Gallery, and the few other paintings I had seen, they were as remote from me, personally, as the Ark of the Covenant, and as much revered. The almost holy ecstasy I had felt at the sight of that head by Couture did not stir either ego or ambition. It was rather a winged flight outside of these and had nothing to do with any sort of performance of my own. I had never seen painting materials, canvas, colors, palette, etc. I had, I think fortunately, never seen first attempts in the use of these. In fact, my feeling for what lay about and around Nature and the life of my environment was really an unconscious perception of Art; my eyes eager for the enjoyment they were able to feel in every variety of perception made of me an absorbed spectator, rather than a performer.

Of course, I never had heard of 'self-expression.' Life to me was something to be relished. If I had dreams, they were of poetry, or of houses; not fairy palaces, but very real abodes; such, indeed, as would have been exactly right for our family if we, that is, our means, had permitted. They were not town houses, such as I had seen, but stood in gardens, with tall trees and slopes, where lay the trees' shadows on perfect lawns. They had no porches, at least in front. There were high ceilings with windows to the floor of large rooms. My mind rocked with the possibilities of furniture, carpets, curtains, gleaming silver. The beauty of the latter I knew well, and in these appropriate surroundings the ladies of my family moved or sat, in soft, rich, silk dresses and lace. There was, indeed, a gold thimble for even me. I had always seen my grandmother and aunts using these, but mine had been only silver. These fancies, however, had no tangible form and could be enjoyed as an accompaniment to nearly any occupation. I was delighted with the plan proposed for me.

My uncle, who from this time forward became the directing power at every point in my development, had a relative, Miss Katharine Drinker, who soon after this became the wife of Thomas A. Janvier, the writer. Miss Drinker was an artist who devoted herself to the painting of historical and Biblical pictures. She gave endless research to her work, which was irreproachable on its historic and archæological side. I think that, secretly, my uncle shrank from launching me away from the close circle of home, and thought that if I must go out, I could not be in a safer place. He knew his cousin well, and admired her intellectual powers, which were great. I would be near a highly cultivated mind, and a lady of his own *souche*.

Cousin Kate Drinker's studio was at the top of an old house at Fifth and Walnut Streets, on Independence Square, so that that exquisite monument, standing in its grove of trees, was always near and visible to me as I came and went.

I am glad that the studio was typical, traditional, and not to be confused with any ordinary or domestic scene, for it was the first studio I ever entered. On its threshold, everyday existence dropped completely out of sight and memory. What windows there were, were covered with hangings, nondescript, as they were under the shadow of the skylight, which was upright, like a broad high window, and without glare. There was a vast sweeping curtain which partly shut off one side of the room, and this, with other dark corners, contributed to its mystery and suggestiveness. The place had long been a studio, and bore the signs of this in big, partly obliterated figures, outlines, drawn in chalk, upon its dusky wall, opposite the light. Miss Drinker had spent her early life in China, whence her family had brought many examples of Chinese art and furniture. The faded gold of a large seated Buddha gleamed from a dark corner. There was a lay figure, which was draped for a while in the rich robes that Miss Drinker had used for her 'Daniel.' But the manifestation of what proved to be a life-long first cause and study, that of the miracles of light and what they could develop and hide, were here first revealed to me in all their full volume and simplicity. There were no cross-currents. Objects and people took the light, or were hidden by it, as they are in Rembrandt's paintings. Large spaces of obscurity swept upward from gleaming forehead, or fold of silk. This was all an everyday matter in the studio, and it was never mentioned to me, but I ignorantly revelled in its deep enchantment, in no way understood, and asked no questions. It was a place that might have been called gloomy or shabby. It was not so to me. I sat nearly all day at an easel with my back to the room and the light. Visitors, some of them keenly interesting, came and went. Sometimes I was introduced. Human interest was present. One young gentleman, as handsome as a troubadour, with a gay romantic head, came often. Miss Drinker was some twenty years older than I, and, in my ignorance of life, I thought that only youth had a right to love. I never suspected that her young friend was the fiancé of my instructress. There are powers more potent than the freshness of youth.

* * *

But about my work; I had to suffer the same 'deception' with which the Harding drawings had mocked me. I was set to copy with Conté crayon, on a yellowish paper, very glaring in the light, a series of lithographic drawings.

The subjects were beautiful, and I knew it and adored them. It was my introduction to Greek sculpture, as interpreted by 'Julien,' * and the prints were very well known as school studies, but not to me.

The lithographs were in outline. The heads were life-size, and printed on a greyish paper of a quiet tone. I have always been glad that in my novitiate the gods permitted me to touch with fresh, reverent fingers the bowed profile of the Hermes. The lines of the drawing were broad, pale and unbroken. No accent marred their suavity. Their movement was slow, pure and resolved. The soft, oily chalk must have

* Now, of course, the manager of the Paris 'Cours.'

been used as the Chinese use a brush and pale ink, once for all and from the shoulder. But the line ended always calmly, as perfection should. I knew later the grand solidity of the lithographic stone, the deep support of its gravity, its tender, receptive surface.

The broad spaces of the drawings, their evolved finality, that permitted not the slightest deviation in scale, measure, or direction, put them much farther beyond my powers than I knew. But by my sheer ignorance of the difficulty, and a vaulting desire for victory, I overcame these chimeras without remembered struggle. But the quality of the line baffled me completely. The gritty blackness of the Conté crayon, the harsh glare and impervious texture of the yellow paper, were untamable. Even the caress of a soft finger-tip to unify the line would not avail. My copy was correct and ugly, a hateful travesty to my eyes. Yet my teacher leaned over me to say that I was doing very well. She did not seem to understand my stammered, almost tearful, complaints.

* * *

The studio does not reveal later impressions, or, if there were any, they did not 'take' or last. My teacher became more and more friendly, and I was often invited to her, or rather their house, for there was a grandmother at home, many years older than mine, and a great little person, a sprite, in full Quaker dress. I loved her at once, and she as quickly adopted me, calling me 'Bo,' the first to do so. What happy evenings I spent in the tiny house on Pine Street! I always passed the night, and after supper, Mrs. Shober retired with her kinsman and friend, 'Cousin Harry Biddle,' to the parlor sofa and gossip. The old gentleman was very deaf, as was also Mrs. S., but they always seemed to understand each other. He wore a brown wig, had a long white nose, and a quavering voice. It was he who discovered the diary of Elizabeth Sandwith Drinker, kept meticulously during the War of the Revolution. It was contained in many small notebooks, and 'Deaf Harry,' as my uncle, whose cousin he also was, called him, thought best to leave out many appetizing passages in the volume he published.

The young troubadour was always present on these evenings, and when the elders were settled, the lovers (how well they concealed the fact!) bore me with them to a room, a sort of study, in the third story. Another precious retreat. Softly lighted, warm, full of books, and all the contribution of studious years. Here our little party sat till late, reading, talking, laughing. I was introduced to 'Alice' both in Wonderland and behind the Looking-Glass; to the 'Bab Ballads,' to the 'Nonsense Verses' of Edward Lear. All of this, I was ready to saturate, and relish. 'Tom' was then on the Press, and could produce verses of fun by the yard, but had not yet made manifest his great talent as a writer. Before he left, we always descended to the dining-room and had beer, which I did not much care for except the first bitter sip, but did not see the fairy grandmother again until next morning.

As I was then not much past sixteen, the uncle at home did not always approve of the rich pabulum dealt out to me by his very sophisticated kinswoman, and when one day I brought home 'Clarissa Harlowe,' which she had pressed upon me as great literature, he was thoroughly indignant. If any explanation was asked for, I never knew of it. I was not ripe for the book, nor much interested, and I think returned it pretty soon. A few years ago I picked up a contemporary set, eight volumes with engravings, and, to my astonishment, read every word of it. I shall always be grateful to Lovelace for one of his expressions, 'a riveted hatred'; but as the author, no doubt, intended, it was difficult to succeed in disliking the wicked creature as much as he deserved.

* * *

Among the interesting contacts that my new-found guide and monitress offered me, the most prized and most keenly remembered were our visits to her devoted friend, Mr. John Phillips. This fine old gentleman, who looked like Father Time in black broadcloth, lived alone in a charming old house at Tenth and Clinton Streets. 'Tom' was never with us on these occasions, not being of a temper eager to admire even magnificent proofs of steel engravings. Our visit was always in the evening and arranged beforehand.

The rooms below, which I would have loved to explore, were not much lighted, and I could catch only a dark glimpse of old portraits and furniture on our way up to Mr. Phillips's workroom, which was at the top of the house at the back, and where he was awaiting us.

Certain of the great portfolios had been chosen and were laid out on the broad work-table. The collector made all his own cases and portfolios and mounted and catalogued his treasures, unaided.

The light was concentrated, of course, on the table, but all about and in remoter corners, always in perfect order, were the signs of the dual mystery of the artisan and his tools, methods and materials. My desire for these visits was not all due to the privilege of turning over (oh, in a very special manner of handling!) rare proofs and historic plates. The tall, spare figure of our host bending his majestic head, beneath the single light; the gleam of the collector's zest in his fine dark eyes, as well as their kindness and courtesy, the lonely halls and rooms below; all the concentration and purpose toward perfection, in the house's living heart, were 'meat convenient for me,' that for which my appetite was strong and joyful. But also did the engravings reveal to me a whole field of art that I knew nothing of. I longed to hear something of the a b c of the processes; there was a language of the craft, too, of which I was ignorant, but I would not for the world have broken in on our host's soliloquy, and took what I could get, by way of feeling, without much mental satisfaction.

At ten o'clock a little maid entered softly with a silver tray.

There were Queen's cakes, a specialty of the house, and a decanter with, of course, historic Madeira. I was as ignorant of dates and vintages as of the masters of steel engraving, but was not indifferent to perfume and flavor. Our old friend's hand trembled a little as he filled the delicate glasses; not from age, but from the emotion of the preceding hour, and my constrained young heart knew and was shaken also.

The evening was over. He accompanied us downstairs; it was our last visit. He put an arm around each of us, bending to look into our faces. 'My fine friend, my fair friend,' he said.

I never saw him again.

IV
CLASS AND STUDIO

AT seventeen, life begins to open up very perceptibly. Horizons broaden, consciousness appears, and more of this than desired. Even without brusque changes of circumstance or important events, one might say that the day was altered.

One development, however, was clearly marked. I began going to Art School. It was not one that became permanent in Philadelphia, though it promised well and was the only one of its kind. A Dutch artist, Van der Whelen, being obliged, just as his career was opening, to give up painting on account of eye trouble that threatened blindness, had come to America and, under responsible patronage, opened a school. My uncle, who decided, and with great generosity gave me, everything that related to my art education, one day escorted me thither. There were many steps to climb, but we, that is I (for my uncle had already investigated it) found two large rooms, flooded with light; freshly painted walls, many casts, easels, a blackboard, and a few pupils. These were girls like myself, with one or two exceptions of somewhat older women.

There was nothing romantic or glamorous about the place. The director was a solemn, good-looking, youngish man, with the historic Dutch complexion and abundance of auburn hair and beard. After a preliminary conversation with my uncle, he turned to me and asked me if I had ever 'enlairrchet' anything. This had to be translated and turned out to be the Dutch pronunciation of 'enlarged.' I did not then know what he meant, but thought it safe to say I had not.

A small-sized lithograph of a bearded old man was then

produced, and I was told that I was to begin by making a life-size copy of it in crayon.

I felt quite lost when my guardian and protector left me and had small confidence in my ability to succeed with what was required. I dare say this was only a 'preliminary canter,' a test. I was rather tired of copying lithographs, but the difficulties to be met in the change of scale and the effort of mastering the loose hair and beard gave a zest to the task, which turned out to be not so dull after all, and I got quite a 'thrill' from the tufts of hair around the ears and the shadow of an eyelid upon the pupil. Then, too, the crayon and paper exactly suited the style of the drawing. (How could a Dutch artist think of arranging it otherwise?) In a day or two the study was finished. Mr. Van der Whelen gave me a sharp look, and said that I need do no more 'enlairrching,' and, like Alice, I passed into the next square.

* * *

Some of my fellow pupils were drawing from the casts; that is, busts and fragments from the antique. These were not very well chosen, but I longed to undertake them, especially as this was my first view of student work of this kind, and I felt I might surpass it. But other *épreuves* were to be met first. On a shelf there were rows of geometrical forms, also, in plaster, cubes circular and pyramidal, blocks and a sphere.

Plaster is sometimes beautiful when fresh, its substance milky and almost luminous. But when it has been handled and exposed for years, unlike worthier materials, it deteriorates. A leaden grey surface obscures the modelling; its shadows are monotonous and its lights spotted.

Above all, the mechanical forms were abhorrent to me, and I think that my immediate revulsion from cubism, years afterwards, was due in part at least to the recollection of the machine-made angles and ruled edges that I had shrunk from in my student days. A group of these was arranged for

me on a table by the director. At all events, there was no
cant in the presentment. The purpose was simple. Perspective and light and shade; values, in fact.

The group was placed under the light, and there was no
mistaking the absolute, in every phase of it. There was very
little explanation. Probably there would have been more of
this if my master had had a better command of English.
But when one was once in front of the group and had forgotten dimension on one's right, left, and all about, the abstract forms, entirely unrelated to life and less part of it than
the moon's bleak crevasses, began to act upon a girl's imagination, or was it only the stimulation of a new venture?
There were cast shadows; one block nearly hidden in half
tone. Across a prostrate cone's round slope fell a curved
shadow, fading as it turned. Into the central cave slanted a
beam from above. I remembered the landscape, the
mountains, dark valleys and plains, in the rumpled blanket
that covered me, in bed, a convalescent from some child's
disorder, and my group of blocks became, though very and
only 'mental' in their forms, something cosmic and almost
legendary.

Then, too, the soft Conté crayon, used with stump, and
the paper, had a far better tone and color than the plaster.
The possible depths of velvety black (oh, only an accent,
perhaps) pleased me greatly, but I did not find in my performance, when I regarded it with that critical 'other eye'
which had already developed in me, any reflection of gigantic spaces and lonely cliffs. The director seemed satisfied;
at least he never made up another group for me.

I doubt whether I really understood what I had been at,
but I had been shown and had myself executed a complete
series, illustrating the whole principle of light and shadow,
uncomplicated by color, local values, and natural forms. I
had been taught by this exercise, if I chose to apply it, every

rule of linear and aerial perspective. I did not wonder then, but often have since, whether Van der Whelen's method was accidental, and the easiest way, or part of the evolution, traditional in Flemish art for beginners, perhaps a way of finding out what an apprentice could do, besides color-grinding. It was far from being wasted time for me, but I soon found myself before a large piece of white paper and one of the plaster busts. It was not the head of the Medici Venus, which I had never seen, of course, but something like it, and even less interesting, and it was placed in a broad hard light and had no silhouette, or mystery of light-ing, no motivity. It was an object which took me no-where and brought me nothing, as I now see, because it represented a series of contradictions. I suspect that it was a Roman bust, and without original impulse. Of course, it had the highly sophisticated syntheticism of the Greek ideal for its origin, but, refined away to negative import and diluted artificialdom, it had only in the plaster pretended substance, which the marble would have made existent and absolute, even in abstraction.

The surface of plaster of Paris gives no clue to its sub-stance, though the forms it is the mould of were decisive, though abstract. So firm, in fact, that thinking back to the original that must have been, the idea of youthful body, tender cheek, lip and throat, seem to have been qualities to be rejected. Marble, bronze, and even wood, give their as-sent to this elimination, promising their own intrinsic, rich value, of which their surface gives proof, instead of contra-diction.

Any cool statement of beauty, intently, purposely, cool, must be supported by constructive, intrinsic, substance, gravity, the long evolution of a cohesive operation. Marble seems sometimes to have a more than earthly origin. Per-haps it is the gods' legacy to eternalize their glory. Gilding the marble was not the Greek sculptor's idea. Architect, politician, and priest settled that, and Nature claimed it back as her own by laying the magic of her age-long alchemy upon it.

Yet this cast that I was to copy, at once hard and fragile, to which light brought no radiance, whose weight scarcely held it upright, might have been forced, by an applied understanding, into an even inspirational presentment.

* * *

A few years ago, I was escorted through the *ateliers* of one of our most important museums by one of the trustees, a gentleman who had spent his early years in the study of art. In the 'Antique' we found his son, languidly at work. 'How long are they going to keep you at this?' the father asked.

The youth groaned, and I did not blame him. His was the mood of the whole group, among the casts. Everything was being missed. It looked as if the preceptor himself was an unbeliever. Why, then, did he not revolt, reform, or investigate?

The bust I have described occupied me for a long time, but I suppose I must have made other cast drawings, under as impoverished an opportunity, for I have no recollection of them. I doubt very much whether anything of value survives, in contacts where insufficient warmth has failed of reaching the imagination.

Our director made a very strong point of linear perspective, although its principles could have been very clearly perceived in the groups of blocks we drew from. There was, in fact, a class in perspective where the blackboard was used, and Mr. Van der Whelen appeared as a lecturer. He drew for us long, diminishing lines of lamp-posts; showed us the vanishing point where all lines converged; and to which every object is obedient. We made large drawings at home, with ruled lines to illustrate the theory, and I rather liked to create a street, or even a procession of people (very scant in detail), and see it developed so reasonably. Also, it was amusing when Mr. Van der Whelen held up a block and, turning it slowly, said, 'How more you see on *this* side, how less you see on *that?*'

* * *

What criticism we had always took place in the morning. We might stay all day if we liked. Our director never appeared again, and my pleasantest recollection of the school is that of quiet afternoons, when my special friend among the students and I sat together at the big, comfortable table, under the light, and drew from a set of models she provided. H. T. was twenty-four, seven years my senior, and far ahead of me in attainments.

I have clear memories of water-colors done by her at their summer place by the sea, in New England. The bringing-up she was born to was the same as mine, only more luxurious, and her gaiety and earnestness were combined in a truly endearing *ensemble*. During that winter she had become engaged to a young physician, and although she beamed with the happiness of an alliance as perfect as may be, her work at the school was uninterrupted. Glowing with satisfaction, she one day brought her latest gift from her fiancé. When unwrapped, a cigar box was revealed which contained, daintily done up in cotton and tissue paper, a complete set of the bones of the skull. They were exquisitely separated, not an edge or a suture imperfect. How marvellous was the sphenoid, the core and centre of human osteography! Double-winged it was, almost glittering in its translucence, and seeming to be the armor of some creature whose destiny it should be to float like the nautilus in a tropical ocean.

The external members were more opaque. They had the firmness and color of ivory, only without polish, and also without stain or discoloration, anywhere. They did not have the appearance, precisely, of natural objects. They seemed to have been formed by the hand of a master-artist. Having no polish or surface which could reflect or glisten, their quality of line was supremely in evidence. Forms supplied new lines at every turning. Effort at comparison with known masterpieces showed only Greek sculpture of 400 B.C. to be their worthy rival, and so closely resemblant were they to these in style and feeling that they seemed to be résumés of the Greek ideal.

It will be understood that these were not my then reflections, but when memory preserves an impression which is of basic significance, its clarity is indisputable, though analysis may appear much later. I learned the names of the parts from H. T. We spread a white paper on the table, and each chose a member as a model, placing it before us on the paper to please ourselves as to curves, modelling, and lighting. The despised lead pencil was found to be a perfect tool for this work, which called for the firmest type of delicacy in treatment. We did them all, becoming, led by our burning interest, more and more expert, and I dare say my experiences with the endured group of blocks and the unloved bust put me far forward in ability to render fine bony contours and vanishing curves.

More than all, the knowledge to which I had been so accidentally admitted (or was it a momentary access of generosity from the stars?) accompanied all the years (and accounted for much) of my predilection for portraiture, and the manifestations of human individuality. I always saw the structure under the surface, and its capacities and proportions.

When my second winter at the class opened, its principal had turned elsewhere. One of the maturer students, a lady with something of the pleasant physiognomy of Miss Charlotte Lyman and having the same jetty curls and high color, succumbed to the manly charms of our director. He became Mr. Van der Whelen-Brown, and her ample fortune floated them away, far from the ennui of class exercises in drawing.

The following winter, Mrs. Thomas A. Janvier took the directorship of the Van der Whelen School, as it was still called, and she was so much occupied with her duties there that she was obliged to give up some of her classes in private schools. She proposed me for Miss Sanford's, where she had for years been in charge of the drawing. 'Miss Sanford's,' from its high eminence as a thoroughgoing institution, had no rivals. It had not the social tone, if that was valuable, of Miss Lyman's, but her personality was even more marked if less picturesque. Every girl in the school was to her a moral and intellectual problem, and she was, through her consummate skill in handling, able to touch and twine budding soul-tendrils, without bruising them. She expected the young creatures in her care to mount and be at home upon the high plateau from which she looked down on the silver linings which appeared from below to be only narrow fringes around dark clouds. If the strong atavism of later years caused her charges to descend, and even lie down, in the lush valleys below, it is certain that they never forgot the clear blue light of the upper world and the keen bracing wind that sometimes took a frowsy hold of *them*, but could not disturb the smooth parting of grey locks upon Miss Sanford's high forehead. She wore her hair in side curls, looped back. The stillness of her presence, the clear, low enunciation of careful words, did not chill the warm motion of her brooding solicitude, which every girl's heart felt and loved her for.

* * *

I cannot remember my first meeting with Miss Sanford's blue-grey eye, but there is a piercing and ineffaceable composite of its impression. Her acceptance of me as Mrs. Janvier's successor must have come as near to being a compromise with her judgment as she ever permitted herself to allow. I turned my hat into a sort of bonnet, in order to look at least as old as the big girls in the class, and went to be proved, having been assured by Mrs. Janvier that I would have no trouble. She had left no footprints into which I could fit my undirected steps. I had to invent my own method. The classes were two; big girls and little girls, one morning in the week on following hours. They sat at desks, their own or others', in one of the school-rooms. Materials were the blank pages of drawing-books, pencils and rubber. I imagine that there was no grading or marking except for behavior. Miss Sanford had made out, no doubt, a theory of the service of this class as a protoplasmic exercise; perhaps it was merely an interval of release in the cause of subconscious elasticity. As the class was held in the open school-room, it never occurred to me to attempt to make it an exercise in fantasy. I turned instinctively in the direction which would lead naturally to order, as my main anxiety (remembering Miss Lyman's) was that I might not be able to maintain it. But the material I had to deal with was of another kind. The forebears of most of my pupils had not been fed on terrapin, nor had they lingered over the Madeira. Also, the Sanford-bred atmosphere of the school pervaded and remained. One or two of the older girls were of the rich type that could have outstripped the keenest of the insubordinates at Miss Lyman's, and I hope they never knew that I realized this, and feared them. At least, they never proved their metal on me, for which I now render thanks. In pursuit, then, I fear, chiefly of order, rather than the liberating paths of imagination, I turned to ideas of construction, using small objects such as a desk would accommodate, and for the older girls exercises in memory and observation, sometimes drawing for them on the blackboard.

* * *

Other demands for teaching — this time for private pupils — developed, without much idea on the part of parents, it may be supposed, except to keep the children busy and entertained. They were a very proper, well-behaved boy of

ERNESTA

twelve, and a girl somewhat older, whose golden tawny locks and dimples gave promise of abundant interests she might have in other directions, and quite soon, so that it seemed almost superfluous to provide her with other occupation or diversion. The two children came from different families and had different hours, hence requiring the entire attention of their instructor for two hours twice a week. Direction was very simple; following was another matter. Neither of the two had any perceptible degree of natural aptitude, so docility had to furnish all the ways and means. I soon found that positive inhibition followed constant surveillance, and that an occasional word of counsel and encouragement produced better results. I therefore 'sat by' and concluded that a book would be the best provisional alibi.

But it must not be a too absorbing book, not, of course, a novel. I remembered that I was ignorant of the works of Milton, not extraordinary at seventeen, and sought for a thick volume I had noticed on the shelves. It was a cheap, commonplace edition, but complete — fine print and no notes. Still the pages were full; rich lines caught the eye; one could see a whole passage at once, without interruption of commentator or editor. No encumbrances prevented the reader from being carried away through abysses of space. No scholar's voice halted the majestic periods. In these days it would be said that spring afternoons could have been better spent. This was quite likely for all it ever meant to the boy and girl, though the teacher was rather faithful, and did not forget either to drop from the empyrean, or climb out of the confines of hell, when the moment for supervision came. But she had been greatly mistaken in her choice of reading. She had expected to have to drag a rather heavy load, and instead was carried, borne away by one mighty creation after another. 'Paradise Lost,' 'Paradise Regained,' 'Il Penseroso,' 'L'Allegro,' 'Lycidas,' 'Comus,' the Sonnets, in fact, the whole volume. Many years later, I was to know more of this, explicitly and finally, from my friend Raymond Dexter Havens (now of the English Department of Johns Hopkins) in his book, 'The Influence of Milton on English Poetry.' Also our friendship was to bring me in touch with a mind deeply bred and absorbed in the very nature of poetry, which has always been to me the brightest vision of the unattainable. Did the pupils get any 'reaction,' as we say now, from the lightning and tempest and the Heavenly Host, by way of their so near, yet so transported, critic?

What if the poet's Dæmon could glance through the flame he has kindled, and make it a medium by which light could reach the slumberer one step further down? Speech is too clumsy, the story too long to tell. Will its warmth ever pierce through and into without encumbrance, and as power without word or sign? Was it guilty negligence on the part of one possessed by the poet to make no effort to pass on the magic to a young creature close at hand, who was occupied in collecting absolute pebbles on the shore of another mystery?

Confession is that nothing passed if emanation did not take place. Charity would call it incapacity on the part of the agent in charge, who could only have transmitted the golden ore in broken fragments, a sacramental act too holy for hands still more weak than unconsecrated.

So the feaster partook alone, with one hand guarding the mystic chalice, and with the other guiding a faltering pencil.

The miracle of transmission was of another kind. Fate used it as an aid to ordered destiny. The idea of language as an instrument of the imagination, of language outstripping content even as such, and in its nearer kinship with thought outstripping plastic expression, began to germinate in a mind much inclined toward it.

Fortunately I had enough common-sense and self-understanding to prevent my even wishing to attempt to write Miltonic verse, and neither did I know of the many who had attempted it. The plastic art which I was beginning to handle and deal with appeared to me to be in another world, gratifying and alluring, and containing the soul-satisfactions of a purpose to express special phases of life. I did not know, I drifted, satisfying my super-life cravings with the poets easily to be found on our shelves.

* * *

I had found Keats at fifteen, too early, of course, but not too soon to cause me to beg for a volume of my own, and which my father handed me with a smile on my birthday. Shelley, Wordsworth, and especially George Herbert, sped my little shallop as before the morning wind, and this was only the beginning of such voyages. I fed on honey-dew and drank the milk of Paradise in the quiet suburb where to a restless striver, who knew nothing of the beneficent results of repression, life did not contain half enough to satisfy her voracious appetite.

Needless to say, however, none of these perplexities troubled the mind of the young drawing-teacher. There were developments for work at home, the Van der Whelen School having dissolved, when Mrs. Janvier resigned from the directorship.

I began to make use of some of the practice I had gained there. I had been using lithographic crayon, on paper, and my uncle thought I might do something on the stone itself. He accordingly took me, one fine spring morning, far downtown to a lithographing establishment, in order that I might see the process of printing, etc. The son and manager of the firm was eager to take us about. I always felt when with my uncle that I was appearing to the greatest advantage possible. The place was thoroughly commercial and was, indeed, a factory. There were floors full of printing-presses, in action. The great stones lay in them, sliding back and forth to receive contact with the ink rollers. The process of color lithography is too well known to be described here. I was more impressed by the stones than by any part even of the color process. Many of them were five inches thick, two feet by one and a half in horizontal dimensions. In the surface I now saw the beautiful quality of line I had always wondered at, fully accounted for. I longed to touch it, and it seemed a sacrilege to use such a rare and exquisite object as an instrument for producing the hideous chromos which were being turned out. The great solidity and weight of the stone made the tender grey surface even more alluring. Mr. S. asked if I would like to draw a head on the stone, of course, in black-and-white only, and later sent one out to the house on which I drew the head of a young actress from a photograph.

It was printed and used as an advertisement. It met with the approval of the young lady, who wrote to the firm: 'I'm pleased to death with the picture and everybody thinks it's lovely.' Which amused the family and was my first commission.

I loved the feel of the crayon on the stone, and its perfume, which had a sort of woody sweetness, like burnt almonds; but the use of it for any kind of exactness was full of difficulty and anxiety. Nothing could be erased or altered. Approach was by way of a carefully prepared drawing, whose outline must be transferred to the stone by the use of tracing paper. Then, in order to have the print repeat the original drawing in facsimile, the stone drawing must be reversed, which added enormously to the strain and concentration necessary for complete success.

As I did not care to repeat my adventure with the lithographed head, the next consignment was a group of small fossils. Carefully arranged, the plate would hold nine of these. They were palæontological specimens, fragments of bone, some of them partially embedded in the rock and cut away enough to display integral parts. Photography would not have been sufficient for a good deal of the work Mr. S. gave me to do. If successful, the plates were to be included in the Report of a Geological Survey of many volumes. I was expected to define and develop the fossils, making the forms more clear and accenting special parts. Some of them had the appearance of lumps of dry mud. I sat by a window where there was a steady north light, and under this tiny cavities and prominences became what might have been craters and mountains in the moon, and with much more realism than did the blocks at the Van der Whelen School. Sometimes the subject would be a fragment of a jaw with teeth, black and shiny as ebony, and with deep grooves. These had to show, of course, their local texture in contrast to the bone. The reversed drawing had to be made first, perfect in size and proportion, an exact guide, though not modelled. After tracing, it was tentatively massed on the stone, a delicate nebula that could be developed without error. Firm black strokes, if such there were to be, went in last, and one could finally scrape out a tiny light to accent a tooth or salient elevation. Form in half tone was (as always) the greatest difficulty. But all this was what might be called 'natural process,' all the real strain coming with the necessity for extreme caution in reversing. This operation being quite new and *hors la règle* was profoundly resented by the solar plexus, and I was obliged frequently to take it for a run in the garden or other diversion.

My grandmother, though strongly approving as she did of work and discipline, understood perfectly the high degree of concentration the stone required, and with her usual gallantry took part in the struggle.

She devoted all her mornings to giving me the greatest assistance possible. In her clear, quiet voice, she read aloud untiringly, and never allowed interruption except when I got up to take breath. Mrs. Janvier had made a drawing before I knew her, which she called 'Geoffrey Rudel Dying in his Lady's Arms.' I had found on one of the lower

— 77 —

shelves of our library three grey volumes, Sismondi's 'History of the Literature of Southern Europe.' The author gave substantial prominence to Provence and Languedoc, and, as I turned the pages, I felt that it would be good to have a glimpse of my father's country through the troubadours. There was, indeed, the story of Geoffrey Rudel who loved the lady in Tripoli by report only, and died on his way to visit her, not without seeing her, however, for she went to meet him and received him and his love on their way to a destiny they had not chosen. There, too, was a translation of his poem written when his hope of seeing her was still uncertain:

Angry and sad shall be my way if I behold not her afar;
And yet I know not when that day shall rise, for still she dwells afar.
God who has formed this fair array of worlds and placed my love afar,
Strengthen my heart with hope, I pray, of seeing her I love afar.
If but one blessing should repay the thousand griefs I feel afar,
A brighter one where'er I stray, I shall not see or near or far.

In the Provençal the repetition of the final syllable was doubtless more spontaneous and musical. Alas, I never learned that language, and have often wished since then that my first instructor in drawing had taught me what she knew so well. She became later an intimate friend of both Mistral and Roumanille and a member of the Society of the 'Felibrige.' Sismondi was rather dry reading as I remember it. It was strong in the matter of research and minute historical detail, and after the chapters relating to Provence and the Midi, I am not sure that we persevered. I do not, indeed, remember by what means or literary instrument my grandmother deepened the channel through which my frail skiff could pass with easier buoyancy.

As my rendering of minor fossils gave satisfaction to the watchful palæontologist behind the scenes, who was in fact no less a personage than the famous Edward D. Cope, I was next given the opportunity to draw the portrait of his first-born among fossils, and the heir to all his hopes.

This was rather a complete specimen, the head of an extinct ass that had roamed the plains of the Far West when they were covered with sugar-cane. Its supreme distinction as a relic lay in its having canine teeth. There they were, almost tusks, superb in size and ebon polish, and had been used in breaking the great sugar-canes for food before the period of grass.

It purported to be the only one known, up to that date. I was to do three views, one-third life-size. The fossil was by no means clear of the rock, so, besides the difficulty of reversing and the new one of reducing in size, I had to make sure of bringing out all important indications.

Before the drawing was finished, Mr. S. drove the great man out to see how it was going — a fearful ordeal for me. Dr. Cope was a tall dark man, something like Matthew Arnold, and a Quaker of few words. The strong lightning of the moment has blurred memory and deprived me of all detail, but when he had left, my lifted heart told me that all was well. He had given me a few minor directions and was satisfied with what I had developed from the long, rough fragment of brown rock. I did not myself like the idea of reduction, which was, of course, necessary. It seemed to detract from the majesty and awful forms of the original. I had never seen a Holbein drawing, but felt the lack of elimination and choice in my production, in which also the effect of the masses, in light and shade, must be ignored, and which was a description, rather than a presentment.

Next came the skull of a small camel. It was beautifully white and clean, nearly cleared of the rock, and as it took the light boldly, it was not very difficult; at least, I had now obtained relative control of the medium and had learned to prove the indications on one side of the specimen by what could be seen 'coming through' on the other.

Dr. Cope came out to see it as before, when there were still possibilities of change or accent. He sat down before the stone, and, after a short examination, pointed to a bony formation I had 'found' or thought I saw evidence of.

'What's this?' he asked, and when I explained it, he laughed and said, 'Well, Miss Beaux, if you can invent them, what need is there of our going way out West to find these specimens?'

Fortunately, it was not too late to obliterate the non-existent articulation.

But this work did not bring conviction of a *métier* found once for all, and it is true that during the 'stone age,' I began to have rebellious moments, and in one of these dashed off a fragment, which if not good poetry contained genuine passion.

> Lost hope, lost courage, lost ambition,
> What's left but shams of these to hide my true condition?
> Feigned peace and joy, feigned happy effort,
> False tongue, proclaiming, "Art's my comfort."
> Nought's left but bones, and stones and duty that's not pleasure,
> But grinding, ceaseless toil, whose end's the measure
> Of the short web of life the Fates have spun me.
> What's this... I've uttered words of treason.
> What's lost? My time, my daylight, and my reason.

* * *

I had achieved considerable mastery of the medium in the special direction of illustration by lithograph of scientific evidence. Intellectually and in the matter of research, it was far too large a field to be approached without the dedication of a lifetime, and interest would soon have been lost in repeating operations of whose meaning the mind had no conscious grasp. It was not possible to realize at the time what an immense educational opportunity the stone, to a beginner in art, and the fossils, had offered, and which luckily I had the sense, or rather the intuition, to take advantage of.

What was to be learned in dealing with obscure and reluctant form, in almost shapeless fossils, and above all the revelation of form in natural daylight, the revealer of truth without emphasis or exaggeration, came home with a force and tenacity that only the truth can apply, and being living truth and led by Nature, hand in hand, it never grew stale and was never exhausted. Having naught to do with fashion, this approach to truth cannot be *démodé*, though it may be abused and vulgarized, when of course it ceases to be the pristine element, which is truth.

Any one of the smaller fossils, even, was capable of setting forth the whole problem of what is now known as 'volume,' and in spite of contradictory evidence. Solid they certainly were, and must so appear. If they had been made of chalk, clay, or any single substance, light would have revealed their form with obvious ease; the lowest values would have been where light could not reach and *vice versa*; but these bits of bone and rock showed as little to accent the form as does the plumage of a wild bird when Nature undertakes to hide the timid creature. Dark teeth caught the highest light. A scrap of white bone was embedded in the deepest obscurity of the main shadow of the mass. So the performer, who might have been set to blunder over obvious truth, had to feel the form in spite of contradiction and develop a vision tuned to the most abstruse values in lighting.

Also, if the fossils had been merely lumps of mud or unpeeled potatoes, the necessity for proportion — in fact, measure — would have been less urgent. To this also vision must be sensitive and able to maintain the exact relation of parts to the whole, while developing detail.

It seems as if such a body of suggestion and proof, upon the subject of values in *chiaroscuro*, could not be contained in a small mass of rock and broken bone. But the universe is in every natural object, and there is rich experience in finding it in unlikely places.

Nothing the fossils taught a neophyte in art ever had to be

unlearned, for when one dwelt even upon the eternal categories of 'whence and where,' they were not second to the mountains or even the stars.

* * *

To each his own generation. It can easily be asserted that such preparation — that is, the presentment of form, by means of values, in lighting — has been superseded and surpassed, many hope forever. They have forgotten that light, with its concomitant shadow, takes an almost supreme part in our natural existence and cannot long be ignored in Art.

However, the moment for reform became needed, and did arrive. It was needed because of the vulgarization of form and lighting brought in by the misuse of photography, which could rather easily take the place, for the hastily inclined, of a real knowledge and individual perception of truth. Far be it for the recorder of a few salient memories to take up a discussion on 'Modernism.' Modernism is not an arrival or a conclusion. It is a constant state, and has always existed. Every generation finds a way to rediscover some phase of the great and ancient manifestation which Art is. The most stimulating novelty is that which the immediately preceding generation ignored, for the sake of its own pet theory.

If this theory has been developed to vulgarity, the happiest moment for reform is offered, and victory is sure to endure as long as it continues to stimulate. Are not full skirts enjoyable after a long period of scanty ones? There are many who cannot *relish* without the stimulation of astonishment. There must be a dash of the, to them, unexpected in it.

There is another large group who want only what they have always had. The groove is comfortable and padded, and in a way they are right; for is it not one of the functions of Art to soothe frazzled nerves and allow a weary brain to return and drink again at an ancient spring?

In this group are often classed, and sometimes unfairly,

active participants who have *subit*, as the French concisely put it, a veritable conversion, in youth, and whose ardor, into which has been poured a constant fuel of understanding and enthusiasm, has never cooled. Such minds think it not too much to give their little lifetime to the effulgent *culte* which has become part of themselves. In fact, the youth bound up with it never passed. These are not looking for difference, but to express their unexhausted pursuit. A life-time has not sufficed for this. They are still blunderers at it, but desire has not flagged.

* * *

The girl who tolerated a fossil as subject, and at the same time was entirely unconscious of the reason for her tolera-tion, found out much later that she had borne with her task because it contained a principle she could not then come at in its entirety; that is, the *idea* of light on an object as well as its *effect*. She began to be possessed of this principle, and much later witnessed what part it took in the drama of a hu-man presentment, and its effulgence upon the folds of a choice material. A lifetime seemed too short in which to pursue and grasp the beauty that lay around the mystery, as potent as any other, of actuality. Then, at last, idealism and vision were for her indissolubly joined, once for all.

Nevertheless, before coming to the foot of the long upward trail, she was to crawl through a broad morass, where shone only a few silver pools.

At this time and for long afterwards, I did not connect the work I was to do with *Art*, the high mystery, nor did I con-sider myself in any way an artist or even that I was ever to become one.

I remembered the Gibson Gallery. In our living-room — which we called the 'parlor,' no one considering that it stood for the formal dignity of a drawing-room — hung a fine colored print of Turner's 'Fighting Téméraire,' which my uncle had bought in London. In a volume of Rogers's

'Italy,' there were vignettes, engravings from Turner's water-colors and drawings. We had a few old pictures, which my father had brought with him from France, and which — unsigned, of course — had been part of a collection owned by a Spanish gentleman, and which my father's family had taken for debt; nothing very valuable, but the Old World and tradition were in the dark canvases.

I knew no middle ground nor any contemporary artists. The Williams collection also had brought me no nearer as a participant.

* * *

But life now began to contain in itself much that was completely outside of 'Art,' though that word was not used currently in our house, and I rarely heard it, although it was, in music and matters of living, persistently pursued by the family. Some one told me that a row of brown books on the shelves were Ruskin's 'Modern Painters.' These I read, and of course accepting all, was wafted to glorious heights by the style and enthusiasm of the author. But as far as consciously connecting this with my own life was concerned, I might as well have been busy with gardening or mending.

Although all sorts of intangibilities and uncertainties hovered about my existence, there was one rock-bottom reality. I must become independent. My grandmother's house was my home, and in it I was the youngest born, but I wished to earn my living and to be perhaps some day a contributor to the family expenses. To do this I stepped naturally into the opportunities offered, of which, for better or worse, there were many. I took a month's lessons in china painting from a French expert, in the ignoble art of over-glaze painting. How ignorant I was and how quickly mastered what could be got from it! My instructor said nothing to me of the legitimate field of this kind of work, and I at once began adapting it to portraiture. A sad confession. The results were, alas, too successful, and were much desired. For, somehow, after four firings at a remote kiln, I managed to get upon a large china plaque a nearly life-size head of a child (background, always different), full modelling, flesh color and all, that parents nearly wept over. Of course I used photographs, but was not content with 'making up' the color. I had a solar print made, going for this to a nice old man, high up many rickety stairs in an old house at Fifth and Arch Streets. The rude copy contained nothing but measurements, but the golden-haired darling was then brought to me and placed as nearly as possible in the lighting of the photograph. I then wrote all over the solar print notes on the color — 'most color,' 'least color,' greenish, pinkish, warm, cool. This was a real study in summing up and cleavage of tones, and added greatly to the much too great vitality of the head, carrying it far from the purely decorative requisitions of the china plaque.

My reputation spread. Mothers in the Far West sent with the photograph a bit of ribbon, the color of the boy's eyes, as well as a lock of hair. In such cases, of course, I never saw the child.

Without knowing why, I am glad to say that I greatly despised these productions, and would have been glad to hear that, though they would never 'wash off,' some of them had worn out their suspending wires and been dashed to pieces.

This was the lowest depth I ever reached in commercial art, and, although it was a period when youth and romance were in their first attendance on me, I remember it with gloom and record it with shame.

There were some crayon portraits, also, but these were of old friends of Mr. Edward Biddle, my uncle's father, and were from fine, old-fashioned photographs of splendid old gentlemen. The touch of chivalry and romance in these heads, as well as their actual beauty and the simplicity of the lighting, raised them far from the world of the china children, and I took pleasure in them, in spite of their being from the flat and from 'deceased' subjects.

So, also, as I stumbled through the rough country of these years, there were dark mystifying nights, too bright dawns, and puzzled searchings for the path. As was natural, I was not much alone. It was the time for love, and the little god was pretty constantly about. I got my work done, but there was not much time for meditation on the status or real value of it. Other things had to be decided. It was a thorny path, for in these matters it, unfortunately, frequently happens that youth is temperamentally indisposed toward the exceptionally eligible (who may be also categorically attractive) and drawn toward those whom it would never be finally conquered by. There was plenty of agony and some clear-cut drama, in a setting of November days, fresh and clearing skies, and the odor of violets the sad heart offered. There was always the terrible standard of what love should be that held back the romantic heart, and there were hours when if a stern voice had said, "You are to marry this man. It is not yours to refuse. Come" — the doubter would have been thankful and would have obeyed. Needless to say, the family opinion in these matters was always obvious, but was never forced upon the reserved young *première* in the cast.

In the mean time, I watched my sister float away on the happiest of marriage destinies, without a ripple to mar its certainty or one backward glance. (My sister, Aimée Ernesta Beaux, married Henry S. Drinker, the brother of Mrs. Thomas A. Janvier.) Happy is she, I thought. Shall I ever come to it? I was by no means set against marriage and had no glimmering vision of another sort of future I might have.

Let escape this period, without further comment. The time came when the next allowed opening was ready for me, and I for it.

* * *

Long before this, I would have turned toward the class-rooms of the P.A.F.A., but my uncle, to whom I owed everything that my grandmother had not done for me, was steadfastly opposed to this. There was no reason to suppose that my trend was to be serious or lasting. Certainly I had done well and was a good copyist. I was a seemly girl and would probably marry. Why should I be thrown into a rabble of untidy and indiscriminate art students and no one knew what influence? So reasoned his chivalrous and also Quaker soul, which revolted against the life-class and everything pertaining to it. He put a strong and quiet arm between me and what he judged to be a more than doubtful adventure, and before long an opportunity came of which he entirely approved.

I had one acquaintance — a schoolmate, indeed, at Miss Lyman's — who, after a year or two of social gaiety as a débutante, began seriously to turn toward painting. She organized a class and took a studio. She had none of my limitations in the way of 'ways and means.' She asked me to join the class. We were to work from a model three mornings in the week, and Mr. Sartain had consented to come over from New York once every fortnight to criticise us. My uncle entered at once into this arrangement, and with his usual generosity paid my share in the cost.

Across all the intervening years it now seems that the record of this adventure, for so it now appears to me, should be written with a pen of fire. Time and experience have given it a poignancy, a significance, only dimly felt at the moment.

There were a few, only, in the class, all young, but all respectful toward what we were undertaking. It was my first conscious contact with the high and ancient demands of Art. No kind of Art, music or other, had ever been shown to me as a toy or plaything to be taken up, trifled with, and perhaps abandoned. I already possessed the materials for oil painting, and had used them quite a little, but without advice.

But the unbroken morning hours, the companionship, and, of course above all, the model, static, silent, separated, so that the lighting and values could be seen and compared in their beautiful sequence and order, all this was the farther side of a very sharp corner I had turned, into a new world which was to be continuously mine.

When William Sartain appeared in the class as our teacher and critic, he was undoubtedly the first artist most of us had ever seen — and how far he was from the type generally described by story-writers! We had probably all read of a long limp figure with uncut hair, broad-brimmed hat, and loose tie. William Sartain was a middle-sized man, firmly built, with a strong intellectual head. He was slightly bald and wore a short dark beard. His prominent bony nose was almost divided above the bridge by a deep vertical cleft, which would have given his expression an almost fearsome intensity but for the suave influence of the long horizontal sweep of eyebrow and eyelid. His eyes were not too deep-set to show their color. It was not strange that at that time I had never seen their like, but among the many eyes noticed and studied since then, they still remain unique. They seemed drawn with a firm dark pencil, and without a vestige of sentimentality. The large iris was of a strong olive grey, much like a dark-green seal my uncle wore in a ring; not changeful as are most grey eyes, they had the tone of an old Chinese bronze, and the subtle strength of such a work of art.

At the time I had never seen his work. It was never profuse. A few quiet sea-landscapes, dune and valley; some strong heads, and small shadowy Oriental interiors. What he gave us was simple and universal, for his culture bore away all limitations of school or fashion. What I most remember was the revelation his vision gave me of the model. What he saw was *there*, but I had not observed it. His voice warmed with the perception of tones of color in the model-

SITA AND SARITA

ling of cheek and jaw in the subject, and he always insisted upon the proportions of the head, in view of its power content, the summing up, as it were, of the measure of the individual.

This ideal, the most difficult to attain in portraiture, is hidden in the large illusive forms; the stronger the head, the less obvious are these, and calling for perception and understanding in their farthest capacity.

When our critic rose from my place and passed on, he left me full of strength to spend on the search, and joy in the beauty revealed; what I had felt before in the works of the great unknown and remote now could pass, by my own heart and hands, into the beginning of conquest, the bending of the material to my desire.

* * *

Fatality is generally another name for misfortune, but Fate is an impartial agent, and may sometimes be caught in an act of beneficence. It was a strange coincidence that gave me for first master, and without any knowledge or intervention on my part, one who had long preceded me in feeling the attraction of a certain trend in Art. When I heard him mention casually, one day, the name of Couture, and found that he knew well the head in the Gibson collection, and held it in special sympathy and admiration, I felt a satisfaction far out of proportion to the incident.

William Sartain had been in Munich, with Duveneck, as a student, and had then passed to long sojourns in Paris. The Romantic School had left its charming memory upon him, as it had upon Duveneck, an exquisite aura lying about the vision of what might have been their not too fine virility; and what had been the very restrained life of a young pupil responded eagerly to what was but a reflection of an approaching sensation, the zest to be felt in the *quality* of painting, accompanying with delicate sensuousness the stern requirements of manifested form.

Even if it were worth while to do so, it would be hard to draw a line between the unsophisticated mental movements of early years, as any one's early years were then, and the developments of later and wider views. Whether for better or worse, the early beliefs remained. Planted in a soil fertilized, and not to be exhausted by use, growths bore their own novelties and extensions. They could be pruned and grafted, toiled over, and developed. Perhaps if the vines had rotted or been devoured by disease through neglect, they would have been dug up and thrown away, to make room for some advertised quick grower, but the husbandman was patient, and in hopeful love was always searching for fresh qualities in production, adding knowledge to knowledge.

* * *

The seasons of the class were short, the criticisms infrequent, though to one view, at least, sufficient. For two years they continued, and it then became inconvenient for Mr. Sartain to come to us regularly from New York. By that time, as I had been doing some portraits on the side, I was able to take a studio and the class painted there, with a model on certain days, without instruction. At this time I did a study of a friend which resulted in my making my first entrance into the doubtful field of the Exhibitions. It was well hung at the Pennsylvania Academy and was considerably noticed.

Finding myself in a large barren studio, for I soon wished to have the whole place to myself, I began to think of a picture. The room was high-studded, and in addition the top light was remote, but full. The walls were grey, a tone not bad, as it was uneven and age had treated it well.

The furniture consisted in half a dozen kitchen chairs which had been used by the class, and as many easels. My uncle had bought me an etching press at an auction which had served mainly as a hat-rack.

The picture I saw to do was a large picture, and I saw it

complete in composition, the figures, lighting, and accessories. I took an old piece of sketching-board and did the composition small, but containing all the important masses, lines, and color. The subject was to be my sister, seated, full-length, with her first-born son in her lap. The picture was to be 'landscape' in form, and the figures were to be seen as if one stood over them. The mother in black sat in a low chair, the brown-eyed boy of three almost reclining in her arms. He was to wear a short blue-and-white cotton garment, his bare legs trailing over his mother's knees. Her head was bent over him, and his hands lay upon her very white ones, which were clasped around him.

The whole picture was to be warm in tone and in an interior which did not exist, except in the mind of the designer.

Strangely enough, the presiding *dæmon* spoke French in whispering the name of the proposed work. 'Les derniers jours d'enfance.' And this title never seemed translatable or to be spoken in English.

In this scheme, the first and greatest difficulty was to gain the family's coöperation, for nothing could be accomplished without this. My sister did not live with us. She was engaged in her own first housekeeping. She had two young children, one a baby, and very limited means and assistance. With them lived her husband's grandmother, an aged lady and great friend of mine (before mentioned). She was extremely deaf, was very slight and delicate, but full of commanding energy and to be watched with tact and constancy. The family would be sure to find my demands exorbitant. I already heard their very just protest.

'Could she not do the picture in Irving Street? Would no one else do as a model? The big empty studio had turned Leilie's head. How large was the picture to be? Two figures, full-length, in an interior? But she had never done anything but the head. Poor Etta would have to take the boy to town, an hour's trip in the horse-cars, climb eighty-four steps, and probably do this many times, with a rather uncertain result.'

But I have no memory of any very determined opposition from the family. A mother will do anything to have her child's portrait, and the same energy and confidence burned in my sister's veins as in mine. It is a sad and halting matter, to have one's project overlooked, discussed by others, before it has taken shape, and only the most determined faith can withstand. I was either too absorbed to listen, or the elders, being artists themselves, had no mind to do more than make a few enquiries and supported my sister in her share in the undertaking.

I had pretty well arranged matters before my sitters came for the first time. None of the kitchen chairs I had would do; there would be no possibility of reaching the desired pose in any of them. There was an old steamer chair in our store-room which, of course, could be regulated, though entirely wrong in accessory and design; in fact, like all steamer chairs these qualities were entirely absent except in action, but with the aid of two flat cushions, my models could take in it exactly the desired position. Harry possessed already the garment I wished him to wear, but my sister had nothing like my design for her; but this gave little trouble. Her frock was to be entirely black with slight variation in textures. An old black jersey of mine did very well for this, and, as the picture was to show only one arm fully, I made one black satin sleeve, fitting closely, with a little rich lace at the wrist. Around my sister's knees and lap, and exactly taking the lines of a skirt, we draped a canton crêpe shawl of my grandmother's. It had been dyed black, and had a rich, hanging texture, though delicate, and taking the form.

* * *

The family allowed me to have one of the best of our rugs for the floor, and my sister lent me one of the Drinker heirlooms, a small and charming table, which was to stand near her with a few objects to be chosen later. It took some time to place the figures in precisely the right position on the canvas and to find precisely the right size and proportion for it.

The 'less than life' conception of the figures, as they sat, back in the picture, with no absolute foreground to 'place' them, would have usually required more experience than I possessed. But I had never heard of discouragement. Even after the picture was started, I changed the canvas and stretcher twice, and of course leaned heavily upon the original sketch, which contained every essential mass.

In the background, I followed the tones the sketch suggested. I felt the need of a strong horizontal mass across the canvas behind the group, and lower in value than the section above it, against which my sister's head and a little of the chair were to show.

I found a piece of panelling in a carpenter's shop — only a small piece, but I dyed it to look like mahogany, and it posed, by moving on, for a low wainscotting, uniting floor and wall. The labor, the difficulties, I remember perhaps as little as a mother does her hours of travail. My sister bore her part with her usual gallantry. The boy was extremely amused by the novelty of the scene in which he found himself. His mother's lap was comfortable, his head leaned upon her breast and her voice was close to his ear, and in the rests he enjoyed running out into the hall with me to get a distant view of the canvas through the open door.

To me, nearly the highest point of interest lay in the group of four hands which occupied the very centre of the composition, the boy's fingers showing a little dark upon the back of the mother's white hand. The arm and back of the steamer chair I had to ignore and forget, as nothing was to be found that in the main would 'fit,' and I was obliged to invent a chair 'to taste.'

* * *

The top floor rear of 1334 Chestnut Street accommodated two large studios. My next-door neighbor, when I first occupied one of these, was Stephen Parrish, the etcher and landscape painter and the father of Maxfield Parrish. Mr. Parrish was a charming man, and his talent was the expression of his exquisite perception of quality in things seen. He was by heredity a Friend (in Philadelphia 'Quakers' are the 'Society of Friends'), and all their long exercised repression of beauty, as seen by the artist in Nature, had struggled for expression in him and triumphed. 'Friends' have always been Nature-lovers. No one could better appreciate than they a sunset, waterfall, wing of butterfly, or curve and color in a shell. But Stephen Parrish's freed æsthetic soul desired something more, and was a participant in every touch of his pencil, every rich line of his etched plates, and in the slightest indicative sketch in oil, or water-color.

He had to pass my door to reach his own, and, although my studio was large, my door was always open for a longer line of vision as I was pushing forward into the unknown, with plenty of courage to act on my purposes, but little confidence in what they might really amount to. It is impossible to estimate the value to me of Mr. Parrish's presence as a neighbor. Except William Sartain, he was the only artist I had known. He had little time for visiting, and respected, as a real friend, my open door, but when he passed it, he waved approval with lifted arms, and sometimes a shout. No captain leading his troop with upstretched sword could have more gallantly beckoned to the field. Forward! ...*En avant!*... No talk, no question, no negation. Bigger my heart...firmer my step up and down...Onward!...

* * *

But when the work was pretty far under way, my invaluable neighbor went abroad and rented his studio to two young women. They were not workers, and I then had my

first view of art as an accompaniment to life, and was for retiring into a closed arena.

But, after all, all was for the best. One of the girls, pitying
my sister's heavy rôle, volunteered as a model, posed for the
draped knees, and put her pretty feet into the plain black
slippers. Then I tasted the joy to be found in the drawing
of a woman's foot, although the long dress allowed to be
seen less than I would have chosen to do.

* * *

Miss B. was extremely anxious that Anschutz, of the
Academy of Fine Arts, should see the picture. Anschutz had
been a pupil of Thomas Eakins, and I had heard of him
as an instructor at the Academy. I thought his coming
would be too great a favor, as I had not been a pupil of the
P.A.F.A. But Miss B. was unafraid and persuaded him to
come. Both of us were shy. I was frightened, and he was by
nature inarticulate, but extremely impressive in his somehow conveyed force of feeling. For what seemed an interminable time to me, he walked up and down in front of the
canvas, examined it from far and near, rubbed his chin and
forehead, and seemed to struggle for speech.

Finally, almost writhing with the effort, he said, pointing
to the child: 'What did you think about when you were doing those legs?' I, entirely unaware of known methods in
the search for truth, could think of nothing to say but, 'Why,
I thought of *them*.'

This was baffling and, alas, Anschutz's next query, if
he offered one, is not recorded. I did not know how to question him and dared not press for an opinion. He remained
for some time looking and rubbing his chin. I suppose I
must have tried to fill the space with some kind of utterance.
Alas, I cannot recall any further words of his. It seemed
afterwards as if he had felt a sort of puzzled interest, which
later, when I came to know more of Eakins's work and influence, I understood. As a master, Thomas Eakins, in the

— 95 —

life-class, was supreme, and his teaching was profoundly valuable. From his pupils I heard of 'points of support,' 'weight,' and 'balance.' The integral harmony of parts, whether in action or static, I believed in, even when getting only at third hand his general reasoning.

Thomas Eakins's formidable personality held unrivalled sway over the students of the P.A.F.A. during his long directorship there. No one who studied under him ever forgot his precepts, or could be interested in any principles of Art that did not include his. They were rock-bottom, fundamental, but somehow reached regions, by research, that others could not gain by flight.

Eakins's father was a writing-master. He is said to have hesitated in his youth in the choice of a profession. Should he be a surgeon or an artist? He decided on the latter. But it was years after, and I believe only once, that the strong tendency that had almost won him showed in actual choice of subject. His portrait of Dr. Gross at the operating clinic horrified Philadelphia Exhibition-goers as a gory spectacle. It is now held to be one of the greatest works ever produced in this country.

Eakins found so much in bony structure, articulations, and balanced weight that could be expressed by Art, and Art only, that his finding and expressing these truths became a unique and precious revelation. He relished with high zest what he found, and in his hands it became Art, although he closed his eyes to all other pleasures of vision and other equally veritable truths.

In 1917, some time after his death, a retrospective exhibition of his work was held at the Metropolitan Museum in New York. It was opportune in those troubled times, for Eakins was an American of deep steadfastness and sanity. The value of his work was seen to be permanent. It had nothing to do with evanescent art moods. It was outside of fad or fashion, the hectic desires of degeneracy, and the ebullitions of artistic anarchy.

Force was never squandered or lacking, and emanated from his canvases with an almost physical stimulation, which, coming from nearly colorless and dusky painting, seemed strange to those whose idea (just at that moment) was that color-vitality must be served up straight from the tube (that is, from the factory). As color is the child of light, Eakins's deep scrutiny took light first and with it, of course, shadow. He never undertook to reveal form without these elements, even out-of-doors. The essential and broad meanings which he sought were clothed with light, not brilliantly, but half hidden in the moted atmosphere of the quiet workroom. His appetite was so natural and strong that the dusky daylight of the studio was glamour enough for him, and in his outdoor studies he is seeking action and energy rather than the color values which are known as 'joyous.'

Color, however, in Eakins's work is far from being absent. In one of the choicest numbers in the exhibition, 'No. 1, Pair-Oared Shell,' a picture of modest size, a strong puller in the sliding seat looms out of the ember mists of a hot evening on the Schuylkill. Vital human action and the fascination of an August sun's last effort in vaporous twilight meet without friction, and the full sweep of Eakins's silent emotion reaches us.

Eakins was not much concerned with pattern, and was far from Oriental influence. His talent stood solidly upon the foundation of his inheritance from Western Art and civilization. His sense of mass and balance, however, were instinctive, and corresponded with the rugged surety of his insight.

In and from his retired home in Philadelphia, Eakins saw what he wished to render intimately. He did not go far afield. The inhabited body was his chief concern, and his pursuit of this theme never lost its zest.

He had an unerring eye for the ultimate instant in action, and in the drama of a head. Eakins never troubled himself as to originality. He was in a way a chief of cave-men, and was as unconscious of having historic significance. He need never have signed his pictures, for the slightest of them can never be mistaken for the work of any other man. Which is, of course, the surest mark of an original mind, in Art.

* * *

It was well, perhaps, for the isolated wrestler with just discovered opportunities that personal contact with the giant did not take place. I got strong food from my gleanings from his vividly impressed students, and was out of reach of the obsession of his personality, which I would have been sure to succumb to, and this might have resulted in my being a poor imitation of what was in some ways deeply alien to my nature. A curious instinct of self-preservation kept me outside the magic circle. I watched him from behind staircases, and corners, at the Academy, and my visit from his apostle Anschutz did not give me as much as did the morsels loosely dropped by his pupils.

There are curious airholes in memory, which I will not attempt to fill. Such are those which occurred in regard to the circumstances and opinions which must have accompanied the last work upon the picture. Who saw it, what they said, what the family verdict was — all is a blank; even what I thought myself. It has lasted well, and its virtues, such as they were, remain; as do its crass youthfulness, and the naïveté of its composition.

It was first seen at the Pennsylvania Academy, where it had the luck to capture one of the corner panels in the big room, the North Gallery. I do not remember its going elsewhere at that time, but oddly enough it got to France before its author did.

After some time had elapsed, it was seen by one of my girl friends, Margaret Lesley, who had been a student in France. She was bent on returning, and was filled with determination to take the picture back with her to Paris. She would take it herself, generous soul, and send it to the Salon.

'The Salon!' I screamed. What insanity it was! But she

persisted. After all, the issue was not serious. She would take it by hand, rolled up, in her stateroom. I gave in, of course, but without hope.

Her letter brought me the news of her stretching it and carrying it on top of a cab to the studio of Jean Paul Laurens, to get his criticism and advice as to entering it for the Spring Salon. Alas, I have no record of the words of the actual interview, but the great man strongly favored her sending it, so she got an impromptu frame and offered it to Fate.

It had no allies; I was no one's pupil, or protégée; it was the work of an unheard-of American. It was accepted, and well hung on a centre wall. No flattering press notices were sent me, and I have no recorded news of it. After months it came back to me, bearing the French labels and number, in the French manner, so fraught with emotion to many hearts. I sat endlessly before it, longing for some revelation of the scenes through which it had passed; the drive under the sky of Paris, the studio of the great French artist, where his eye had actually rested on it, and observed it. The handling by employés; their French voices and speech; the *propos* of those who decided its placing; the Gallery, the French crowd, which later I was to know so well; but there were not many Americans in France then, and we were not setting the idol of our wealth before them, for worship.

But there was no voice, no imprint. The prodigal would never reveal the fiercely longed-for mysteries. Perhaps it was better so, and it is probable that before the canvas, dumb as a granite door, was formed the purpose to go myself as soon as possible.

V

EUROPE

I DID not have to wait long. I had accumulated some earnings, and planned to be very economical. My uncle was now convinced that I must not be advised against what I saw clearly should be my next step. The next for him, as usual, was to aid me in every way possible. I needed no other help. Besides the matter of necessary revenue, he saw to everything in the way of settling up my studio affairs and the details of the journey — steamer passage, passport, letter of credit, etc., and, most important, a companion for the trip. A cousin temporarily visiting in the West was persuaded to change her plans and come from Montana to sail with me on the Red Star steamer, the Nordland, to Antwerp. It would be a winter voyage and not short.

My accoutrements were warm clothes — some of them my sister's cast-offs — and the 'Ancient Masters of Belgium and Holland,' Fromentin's incomparable work. An artist friend, Henry Thouron, well acquainted with Munich, Paris, and the Galleries, made monochrome drawings on oil sketch-boards, of convenient size, to be used in making color studies in the Louvre and elsewhere, thus avoiding the delay of setting up the composition and lighting. I had an eight by ten of Titian's 'Entombment' and the same of the 'Madonna with the Rabbit'; also an Infanta Marguerite, of larger size, and a head of Rubens, besides several of the more modern Masters. The value of such *préparatifs*, which might flippantly be called 'Springboards for the Galleries,' has not diminished with the years. I had to wait a whole winter for a place before the 'Entombment,' but I made a rather creditable copy of the Infanta, and learned volumes from it, though it was many years before I was to see Velasquez in Madrid.

The fifteenth of January is not a propitious day for embarking on an Atlantic voyage, particularly for one to whom the sea is unknown. But the unpropitious season furnished me with the most interesting and memorable of all my fourteen crossings. At the fateful hour, no gay, noisy, noonday crowd pushed and clamored. Of the few cabins occupied on the Nordland, none burgeoned with flowers, bonbon boxes, and grocers' baskets of fruit. On a dark, stormy winter night, we found the dock where the two relatives, one for each of us, waited for greetings, messages, and farewells. When they left us at nearly midnight, we found ourselves on a wet, not much lighted, deck, where a few almost invisible figures moved about. One silhouette occasionally showed against an uncertain light. It differed from the rest in what outline we could see, a fur collar, and something in the walk. Feminine instinct also showed us that we were from time to time discreetly observed. The Nordland was not a small boat, but we soon found that we had a whole corridor to ourselves. The cheeriest of stewardesses actually awaited us. We could have the adjoining stateroom for our luggage and overflow, if we wished. I thought of the historic 'Mantelpiece,' commanded by the worthy Captain Reece, in the 'Bab Ballads.' But all was soon explained. Mrs. —— I cannot remember her name, although I can think of many others that I would sooner have forgotten, could tell off the passenger list to us on her comfortable-looking fingers. There was the 'Captain's lady and sister-in-law,' who, of course, occupied remote and special quarters. I may say here that we never saw either of these ladies, and it was reported to us later that they came near to dying of seasickness. Besides these, there was an old German fräulein, with her maid. Here our friend gently touched her forehead. Melancholy she was, from homesickness, and was returning for good. This concluded the list of lady passengers, besides ourselves. There were eight business gentlemen, whose quarters were near the smoking-room. She said nothing in regard to the fur overcoat, and we did not ask if they were much worn on board. We would sit at the Captain's table, an honor I learned, in later voyages, not to covet. In this case there was no other. But it was my fate not to appear at it for a number of the most wretched days of my life.

* * *

Our course took us at once out into what was probably the worst weather to be found upon the 'Banks,' but we did not get all the way into it until the second night out. In the mean time I suffered all the torments, or thought I did, of which soul and body, and that mysterious agent called 'morale,' were capable. How I hated all those who had aided and abetted my going, especially those who knew all about it. Imagination furnished forth a complete and detailed account of the foundering of our plunging vessel. Die if I must, let me not sink into black cold abysses, in which lay the bones of the drowned among tangled slime; or I might float halfway down, where it was too deep for light to penetrate, lipped by hideous, grey-white monsters. From the dissolving fabric of the central pivot of my physical being, all hope of support, or endurance, vanished. Oh! yes, I would die easily enough, but how about consciousness? That was supremely active still. Was I not continuously in a state of clammy dissolution? Thus I appealed indignantly, as so many had before, to the grinning fiends who had somehow got me into their power. What a fool I had been to believe that Milton had settled all that! The good stewardess stood by, with all the help she could supply, and her cheerful nonchalance was the only point of hope for me.

* * *

In the middle of the second night, making unimportant other howlings, plunges, and crashes, the world itself and all its rocks and mountains seemed to fall upon the deck over my head.

It was not yet day, by even the least glimmer of the port-hole, which fell into blackness and rose dizzily to where sky must have been, when Mrs. —— came in, in her wrapper, wanting to know how I was. She seemed fixedly cheerful, but she did not lie to me; she confessed to me that the weather was bad. The ship was entirely coated with ice. I ought to see it. 'What had fallen on the deck?' I persisted, 'Was it coal? Where had it come from?'

'Oh, no. We had been within water. We'd been entirely under, smokestack and all, rolled under, you know, quite unusual, and wouldn't happen again.'

The drama of this episode and our proof of ability to re-cover from it stimulated me sufficiently to disperse all but my bodily misery. At least memory furnishes no more de-tails of the moment, and I suppose I slept.

* * *

Our voyage did not promise to be less than twelve days long. We were to sail up the Scheldt to Antwerp, and more than four of these days had to be endured before I could be dragged up to the ladies' saloon. But neither fresh air nor change of scene has much effect while the attack is still on. There was no sun, but as I lay in dark flannel wrapper (let travellers imagine that, now!) on the green velvet divan, my eyes, seeking the perpendicular, were not much stimulated by the huge, short, slanting column of the mast, which filled a large proportion of the cabin. It was covered with matched boards and was painted in ochre, so that the stirring idea that an actual portion of the ship's stem and strength was before me was not granted until after I had made my escape from confinement. Moreover, on the other side of the great obstruction, and always partly in view, sat the German lady and her maid. I believe it is true that the mentally deranged are immune from seasickness. Such seemed to be the case with our fellow-passenger. Not so, however, her sound little attendant, who was an intrepid sufferer, entirely devoted to her charge, and her knitting; or was it lace crochet? She never gave out except to rush to the deck at frequent intervals, and when huge trays of food were set before the impassive nostalgic, she managed to persuade her by cries of 'Essen, essen, sie muss essen,' to swallow a few mouthfuls. I thought of the fixed 'thimble-eyes' of the inmates of the asylum in Stockton's story. The same were turned on me, with a constant gaze, from around the slope of the mast. Even less to be believed by an ocean traveller of to-day, the comforting little stewardess brought a large basket of mending — stockings and garments of all sizes, worn but saveable — for the group of boys and girls at home, whose bread she was earning on the sea. She sat by me, so occupied, for hours, only broken by ministrations in my behalf.

My cousin, who had no more experience of the sea than I — that is, none at all — proved invulnerable. What were the elements to her, or her solar plexus? I might have hated her for this, but I did not, and accepted the diversion she furnished by her adventures on the heaving and slippery deck, where her passing was in view. She did not walk or slide alone. The ship's doctor accompanied her. He was a Belgian of pure Dutch type, short and extremely blond, and had, even from a distance, very thin pale whiskers, and pink eyes.

They appeared to be speaking as they jostled along, but when I enquired of M., in one of her dashes into the cabin, what had been their conversation, she told me that she had said, 'J'ai peur de parler Français,' to which he had replied, 'J'ai peur de parler Anglais.' The rest is silence.

Sometimes our great bearded Chief Officer passed the cabin window, and I was restored by the thought that we were in the hands of such a man. The stewardess told me that he was from Heligoland, a bold islander.

Later, in the sunny days we spent on the spotless deck, we sometimes had a polite word from the giant. Once I ventured a foolish question as to what was the best time to go to sea.

ON THE TERRACE

'When your trunk is packed,' he replied; so I knew we had been right.

* * *

But there came a day when the ship's heaving and plunging were no more to me than the swing of a bird on a bough. Rested from all the worry and work of departure, I took the slanting deck with a bound, catching at the rail now and then. I did not know that my opportunity was unique. I believed that on all ocean liners, two girls might have, by night and day, the whole deck to themselves. The Nordland was our Yacht, where we were not even encumbered by guests or servants, though we had a private stewardess, below. True, if we happened to have spread ourselves on the warm, sweet-smelling deck, at the place and hour when the Quartermaster let down his rope and bucket, and drew it up full, sparkling, and dripping, we might watch him attach the rope in a very special manner to the rail. We were very kindly admitted to the Bridge, where the Officer of the hour, whose cap was visible as he walked up and down behind the canvas screen, in the so innocent sunshine.

Once I asked another foolish question: 'Did the Quartermaster really always tie the rope the same way?'

The answer was ready and decisive.

'There *is* only one way, and that's the right one.'

So the matter was settled once for all, and I found later that many other queries could be solved by the same formula.

Of course, our chairs were the only ones to be found on the Nordland, and we placed them where we chose, changing with sun and wind. If we went far enough down the long deck, we might look over and down into the steerage. One could see at a distance, now and then, a sailor climbing on or adjusting something. Dark objects were suspended upon the huge yellow smokestacks, which we found to be other sailors cleaning the same with a rag and two fingers. We began a new chapter on the day when we bravely descended to the Captain's table. We were the only 'ladies,' and were received with much politeness. The eight business gentlemen were there. They seemed to emerge from the invisible smoking-room for food only, as seals come up to breathe, and there was another whom we recognized, even without his furs, as the differing silhouette of our embarkation.

As his seat was directly opposite our places, he immediately took the opportunity to offer us something from across the table, and this was accomplished with exactly the right manner and smile. Whatever it was, was accepted with, I trust, equal propriety.

We had not been lonely before, but after this we had a guest on our Yacht. There were now three to ride the waves on deck. The sunniest corners were discovered for us, the rugs spread, even the fur coat, when it was not being very becomingly worn. We were all young, and the gayest voices and laughter might have been heard, even in the mysterious distances where the powers that were getting us there faithfully carried on. Our new companion would have been delightful, even if he had not been handsome and elegant. He was a Belgian and had a name I subsequently heard often. Few details return to me. I remember sunshine, happiness, and freedom. Our Nordland had an auxiliary sailing character, and big grey canvas was spread before favorable wind. There were nights when, under a sky of darkest blue velvet, our mast and rigging rose dizzily toward the wheeling stars, while we three raced, arm in arm, the full length of the swaying deck. Joyous children, not masters or enemies of the elements.

Passion is often lost to recollection in its own murk, but the peak of happy comradeship remains, like the dawn star, clear, unforgettable, in memory.

We were now approaching the English Channel; we should be a whole day or more, passing up the Scheldt to

Antwerp. The thought of England, and of being now actually near to her, moved me far more deeply than I had anticipated. The bond I was unconscious of vibrated and shook the fount of unshed tears, which leaving home, and of course the terrors of the sea, had been powerless to disturb.

England — England! My heart spoke the word in silence, not understanding what it felt. But we approached at night. The Lizard, they said, we should soon pass. Before dark the sun had been lost in a grey mantle. We sat at dinner. It was about eight o'clock. Suddenly the fog-horn began to groan. The Captain threw down his knife and fork, and we saw him no more. 'Oscar' took us on deck, which had suddenly become populous. We moved slowly, bells and horns sounding all around us. There seemed to be a wall of impenetrable grey substance, hanging a few feet beyond the rail, over dark, still water. Looking up was cheerful, for one could see the stars, though dimly. Cold and damp as it was, we did not care to go below to our cosy stateroom, but consented, seeing that it was expected of us, and I well knew the loyalty of our little stewardess. We should hear whatever news there was, and the porthole revealed nothing less than the deck.

There was no change of scene, and in the morning, which came at last as mornings do, and was without sun, the water began to be a different color, a pale, thick greyish green.

On deck, all sense of our bold, solitary voyaging disappeared. Our Nordland had become as ordinary as were to be all the other boats I was subsequently to cross on. We moved steadily on a surface which was impressive only in having changed its color fundamentally. We had not seen England, and should not do so, but even this much of the Old World was entirely new. Queer, that no one had told me that this would happen. As a whole, sky and water were harmonized in tones devoid of the slightest hint of magenta or madder. No thin, skimmed milk of color, here. The grey of the low-hanging sky had been somehow achieved by the simplest use of ivory-black, ochre, and cream. True, the small tossing waves had a tinge in their curve of the yellowish side of a green summer apple, and the cloud's underside, of a blue plum's dark moulding.

Ha!...I almost chuckled to myself — *this* is what they had to learn color from. I had not yet seen the result, but it was all assured to me.

A nondescript group of men hung over the rail. Shouts came up from below. We were stopping. Some one said, 'The pilot,' and I, too, looked over. A heavy rowboat rolled about on the small waves. To me it was nothing less than a vision of all the color that would ever be needed by eyes long blind. But it was no vision. Seven or eight huge men in oilskins were crowded into the small space of the massive tub, and with long, stout oars were deploying it as if it had been an eggshell. Their big blond beards and ruddy faces glistened in the soaking atmosphere on every rich curve. Where could all the color be? The oilskins were tarnished, deep ochre, shifting to a fresher hue in the less worn. The darkest resonant green found place somewhere, and that red, shading from purple to russet, I had been expecting to see in their painting. Of course, lines and touches of vigorous black were not missing — I remember no white. Its place was perhaps taken by shining surfaces that showed points of light, or the composer intended to depend for a high value on the small creamy crests of surrounding waves. A splendid majesty imbued the spectacle with a truly Biblical significance, caused chiefly by the suppression of all tonal garishness. Never could color carry further, with a richer weight, luminous in profundity.

All that Fromentin had described in the volume I had been poring over was before me. Rubens needed no further commentary. So momentous was this occurrence to me that it has always occupied a major station in memory, and has a place among those inevitable articulations that, in life, are as certain and as resultful as are the courses of the stars. For such events the *fond* seems always to be cunningly arranged. Eyes, that for twelve days had been satisfied with the familiar cool greys, mauves, and blues of the Atlantic's ingenuous color scheme, were ready and more than ready for the glamorous manifestations of an unknown climate and history. The eyes also were young, and had been unaware of appetites that sprang to the feast prepared, partaking, with almost sacramental exaltation, of what was to be ever after, for it, the first fruit of vision.

* * *

To land in Europe for the first time, in Northern Belgium, during the last week of January, might not appear favorable, but we were *hors de saison* and outside of climate and circumstance. We had for hours turned our bows toward a painting, sometimes an etching. We had moved slowly past Flushing, at the mouth of the Scheldt, standing below its dykes, its peaked red (?) roofs nearly reached by splashing yellow waves. I had always thought the latter a fantasy of Dutch artists, who chose to paint their waters as bold yellow wavelets, interpretive treatment, it would be called now. How well, and how proportional they appeared! — with the etched black lines of distant river-banks, and of course with windmills, which, however, were not to be interesting to me until very closely approached, even so far as to fill the whole design.

The sun, as such, did not take a major part in the composition, except as a diffused luminosity. As there was little or no modelling to be revealed, this was no drawback, and when we docked, the falling of a little snow and glistening wet pavements 'went,' in our greedy vision, faultlessly well with the rich colors, old polished brass, and strongly laid-in forms of the inhabitants around shop doors, and down vistas of distant architecture.

Snow on dark pavements gave the highest value, but
could not interfere with the quality of *coiffe*, or banded
black velvet. How completely new the old, old story was!
But no painting, or illustration of peasant life or costume,
had bred a desire to see them. I had never really believed.
Partly for this reason, I would have had no desire to sketch,
even if I had had the power to do so.

We merely deposited our belongings at the hotel, and
walked out to continue our orgy, and feel old Europe under
our feet. It was impossible to keep away from the Cathedral, though the enormous green baize curtains would not
be removed from the pictures until one o'clock. Our first
cathedral did not move us at once, or rather we failed to perceive what it offered, as one of the outposts of memory.
Perhaps we were tired or a little hungry, for when we entered
the church again, after an extremely good luncheon, all
was changed. How glad I was that Fromentin had led me
by the hand! — at least, I was glad afterwards, for nothing
would have interfered, for or against the tidal wave that
swept me off my feet in the Rubens pictures. Did I think
them beautiful? Not relatively to any standard I already
had. But while I looked up at the 'Visitation,' set against its
lofty grey wall, tears, the most completely joyful I had ever
shed, blinded my vision.

Why? Well, chiefly because of blue and red, and that
majesty could be so touching, and be at one with so opposite
a force, with so incontestable a rival, as the actuality of
sensuous pigment. But I was not analyzing then, and would
have been incapable of doing so. I was in the arms of a
moment of life, epochal for me, and only feared an end, and
to awaken.

Would there have been any critical sense mingled with
my joy if I had not lately been with Fromentin, who knew it
all? Dumbly I might have been aware of débris borne

among the currents of the broad river. They could never have disputed possession with my absorbed contemplation. That the huge torrent was in places turgid only showed me depths of unspent force, a vast natural element exactly in the control of mind, and one with a master will.

No one who has not met the material opposition of pigment and its allies can gauge Rubens's power to command it. What his religious compositions lack in the subtler side of holiness, they gain in the presentment of human emotion, as it appears, humble, adoring, and abandoned to sorrow, even in the ignorant gazing upon the uncomprehended manifestations of Divinity.

The most mystic of all leading is by way of the senses to the soul, the touch of sense upon the spring of emotion. The Church has always known this and has used it at times coldly, but with what efficacy! Rubens's titanic brush wrote the story to be seen and felt from afar, without strong lighting, and from behind the paraphernalia of altars and the mists of incense. Every bending line, and even the great diagonal, reaching from corner to corner of the vast 'page,' could bear with it the prostrate soul, and with color in wide resounding areas, and passing from top to bottom of the scale, from twilight blue to scarlet and from the cream and gold of an infant's head to the glint of armor and the green of dark forests, find the chord that stretches and expands the tough fibres of the heart, and prepares it for sacrifice. Strong, locked doors must be opened before the chambers of holiness can be reached, and if there is any possible meeting-ground between Art and Conscience, if the two great 'Services' *can* be in harmony at any point, it is when Art is able, by an elemental appeal, to crumble and melt obdurate inhibitions, and lay open furrows to the sower and the rain.

* * *

Three days at most were spent in Antwerp and Brussels. There was that school in Paris. A girl's opinion is worth little in criticism and her crude sensations have a mild pathological interest only. Many months after this, I was to see the Van Eyck in the National Gallery. Years afterwards, Amsterdam and Haarlem, and the Van Dykes in the Louvre, when I got to Paris. But seen for the first time even, Rubens, Memling, and even Mabuse, could easily be believed in at the same moment. From choice they occupied different fields and did not clash. That the two latter could be achievements in what was known as painting was the miracle. But an exact method, time, preparation, system, and patience were a reasonable explanation of the result. What these artists deemed negligible accounted, however, best of all, for the miracle, and in fact did away with all thought of magic, or power superhuman. No messengers from the domain of the passions, whether human or divine, were admitted to the workroom. The quiet task proceeded hour after hour. Nothing disturbed the construction of enamelled surfaces, the complete knowledge of superimposed mediums, or the unfailing production of small jewelled areas of color.

No doubt they were too busy even to realize their own rarity. There were three brothers Van Eyck. There was only one Memling, and no more than Rembrandt did these men need to sign their pictures. They were not reformers. Theirs was the earnest desire toward perfection. Not to break down, but to build better. Sturdily they went at it. Hearts were for their own prehistoric affair. Emotion might shake a steady hand. Memling opened a magic casement far enough to see the Madonna as the most delicate and sheltered of young and noble ladies. Her robes, her tissues, were fit textures to surround her, or as foils for the lovely pallor of her translucent fingers. With Memling's predecessors, the Madonna, though robed in rich stuffs, was not above her suite or worshippers, in charm or spirituality, any more than she was a happy and proud young mother.

Other types were copied, with unswerving fidelity. I

longed to know something of the studios in which these
works were born. Surely they were not *ateliers*, and did not
need to be. A room, perhaps, in the artist's own house. The
light would be perfect, coming from the side by a high
window. The room would be quiet, of course, and reached
perhaps by a dark stairway. The artist could *sit* before a
small canvas, placing it and himself in perfect and steady
lighting. He might dispose his tools and materials on comfortable stools, within easy reach, and, bending over his
pictures, spend whole, uninterrupted days, upon the union,
edges, and modelling of small adjoining parts. The drawing
would have been perfectly accomplished first. There would
never be an impulse to alter, no second thought even on a
fold of drapery. The procedure has no margin for change or
undoing. The construction of a watch is not more exact.

* * *

The only fitting *milieu* for these works is a choice position
upon the walls of a museum, in calm, steady daylight, such
as that in which they literally 'saw the day.' They cannot
be seen in churches, or by multitudes. The best of natural
lighting and vision is their due. They will never be sub-
ordinate to the furniture, spacing, and electricity of a 'good
room.' They will disappear, leaving only a name for their
owner to boast of.

I examined these works with awe, fascinated by their
physical completeness, and above all by their style, a pre-
eminent attribute, which, when present in painting, is able
pretty well to dispense with more obviously ethical qualities.

* * *

Strangely enough, it was not until I reached Paris, and
saw in the Louvre the 'Supper at Emmaus,' that I attained
to a perception of Rembrandt. I did not and will not attempt to eliminate the influence of the narrative, to me, in

this picture. Rembrandt's imagination produced it, without doubt, rather than his Christianity, but it is an entirely Christian picture, and all that initiated the greatest of religious movements is there. The words are not spoken, nor the act repeated. The sacramental supper and the cross are already accomplished, but 'This is my Body' is the text of the picture. In its creator's approach to it, every offering of the senses has been shut out. The aid of color has been denied; line and form, as such, not permitted. What light and shadow could do for meaning is there. The picture is *small*. One must be alone with it, and very near, if one would attain communion and a true sense of its revelation.

Rembrandt must have been familiar with the simple story, in whatever text he knew. The English Version, however, could not be more strictly and poignantly reflected. The painting has the same unburdened eloquence, the same use of the essential Word, and that only.

Again we must say, Can this be painting? — and for what a different reason! Rembrandt knew that for this subject, the act of painting must be by way of fasting and sacrifice. Would this weaken its power? Not as he would use it. There stands his greatness.

Rembrandt chose life-size for portraits and for nearly all of his painting where quality was essential; for Drama, never. Other artists have practised the same procedure. William Blake is more majestic and epical in the small engravings of the 'Book of Job' than in his flaming curves of wing and body. Goya, for dramatic content, is greatest in his etchings, and our own Ryder in his small canvases. No element has been more abused, or at times more powerfully manifested, than the element of size, as an integral part, not a convenience, in Art. Raphael, Michael Angelo, Tintoretto, and Rubens used it with supreme understanding of its scope, and each with individual reservations, as the only way for each, with the given subject. More or less limiting himself to the wall space, Giotto composed a formula, for which he cut away all but the essential idea. He allowed a thin wash of pure, *de*sensualized, textureless color, but denied the services of *chiaroscuro* and modelling, as such. Strong accent of line and feature, that with united voice could reach the worshipper, was his most powerful arm.

* * *

As only a few impressions were assimilated during the two or three days I spent in Antwerp and Brussels, it is fortunate that one does not leave behind the Art of Belgium and Holland, in quitting those countries.

I left in haste, as one would carry off rich clusters from a vineyard thrown into a basket at random, an eager and fearful pillage. The flavor of what was gathered has remained, and as an experience has never been repeated with equal force.

Singularly enough, we reached Paris and entered it without any memorable foretaste. Of what Paris was to occupy in the future of my life, I was not vouchsafed a glimpse.

A tall cousin left his pleasures and engagements, even his work, which was in medicine, and met us at the Gare du Nord. Every one knows the endless journey by fiacre, or taxi, to any habitable part of Paris, from this point of descent. On a rainy night, glistening pavements in the purlieus of a great city look much the same, even though every really observed detail is strange and of *obsédant* novelty. Paris, Paris! — and I am glad that Paris, as I was to know her, did not answer, then.

Our *pension* was in the quarter of the Pont de l'Ama, but not near to the river and its beauty. All that a skimping French *pension* could mean in mid-winter was ours. Mdlle. de Villeneuve, our keeper, bore her considerable years, which had borne much skimping, too, under a brown wig and a long nose. She carried Fi-Fi, a tiny, old dog, with rattling teeth and a cracked bark, constantly under her arm. She had bony fingers, and for the first time I heard the rattle, also, of keys.

Friends were expecting us and there were others there who were to become friends. Our room was *au premier*, and was furnished in Bon-Marché imitations of Louis XV, and of course second-hand at that. We were to spend a few months in a type of French house which at that time Americans, who wished to appear respectable, and even stylish, used to frequent. Our room looked into a side street. We did not know then that we should have been thankful that in this quarter it was not a court that our windows commanded, and although the street was in itself monotonous, we soon found that on all stories our opposite neighbors were not. Probably our waterproofs and cotton gloves had already instructed our landlady in the type of art-students we represented, and she guessed that we were too *sérieuse* even to recognize the character of the tenants *en face*. They were much on the balconies, *au quatrième*, and one of them (it will hardly be believed to-day) used to come out and water her flowers, of a morning, in a red flannel petticoat. As spring approached, an exquisite victoria, with two servants in livery and the daintiest pair of blacks in shining harness, stood most of the day in front of the door, and I had the immense pleasure of seeing, on the Grand Prix, the loveliest creature I ever beheld, in the most ravishing of toilettes, emerge, glide past the waiting footman with haughty grace, put up a parasol which I had never dreamed possible, and drive away.

* * *

The visit of our *blanchisseuse* was one of our pleasures. She had apparently been forgotten in the gathering at the Judgment Seat of the Tricoteuses, left over from the Terror. She was huge, and had an immense head with bold pompadour, and a beard. Her every word was oracular, and one day she peeped between the curtains and scanned the opposite side of the street.

'Ce ne sont pas des duchesses,' she said.

Our room was, of course, unheated, though it had a pretty chimney-piece and a clock, and what heat the previous summer had left behind had died long since between the closed windows and door. I was not pampered, and of course steam heat was unknown to me at home. Our house had a small furnace, whose efforts were entirely devoted to the aged, the invalid, or the very young, but I had never known the damp, penetrating chill of never-heated houses in winter. Of course, a wood fire was impossible for us, but they wheeled us in a Schoubersky, a black charcoal stove, which could travel from room to room and never demand a chimney. Our chimney was a very retiring one, but with the Schoubersky approximately near it, we might avoid suffocation.

Snow fell incessantly and never froze, or remained, except as a kind of cold especially designed for penetration. A muff was indispensable or one would come in whining, or worse.

Until May, we never saw the sun, but I had started immediately at the Julien Cours in the rue de Berry, and my good circulation did the rest, for a polite little French woman in the adjoining room used to borrow our Schoubersky in the morning and forget to return it.

The *cours* was an easy walk by way of the monotonous streets in our quarter, but the Arc de Triomphe was never in sight. In spite of the relishable novelty of the *cours*, and the new world I had expected and found, in the Life-Class, I had to sustain a grand *déception*. More even than on the instruction, I had counted on an association of superiority.

I had worked alone, and fully believed that, in Paris, I should be among brilliant and advanced students, far ahead of a practically untaught American. I was to learn that the Académie Julien was a business enterprise, and could not be maintained for gifted students only. The personnel was heterogeneous. The class was composed of Russians, Poles, English, and French. Among these the Russians were the most prominent, the English were serious and determined, and one of them, who happened to be Irish, did the best heads ever drawn in the class. As I have frequently described her to my own class, 'She made the paper model.' One or two of the French girls were charming, but not eminent in the *cours*.

The English girls upheld the valued characteristics of their race, sincere, steady, and reaching a high average in their work. To my surprise they were all original types. Later, I accounted for this by the fact that at that time few English women broke away from custom and tradition. Most of them were clergymen's daughters who had decided against gardening, tea-parties, and the old women of the parish. This had required energy, and also that they should have had a pretty good start already.

Some had worked at the Slade. Some had to concentrate on a very short stay in Paris. How friendly, how generous they were!

I began, of course, with an 'Academy,' a full-length drawing. 'Tony' — that is Tony Robert Fleury — was to criticise that week, and at the hour entered a young-middle-aged and very handsome man, with a face in which there were deep marks of disappointment; his eyes, grey and deeply set, smouldered with burnt-out fires. How un-American they were! As I observed him from behind my easel, I felt that I had touched for the first time the confines of that which made France and Paris a place of pilgrimage. Into the room with him came something, not perhaps a quality of his own, but of what he had come from and lived in. The class, although accustomed to him, was in a flutter. I was still and icy with terror, fearing among other qualms that I might not understand him and blunder hideously.

My turn approached. He sat down. I knew only enough French to stammer out, as my defence, that it was my first attempt in Life-Class. He muttered something in a deep voice that sounded like an oath, and plunged me deeper in woe. The class, which understood better, looked around. I began to hear that he was quoting Corneille. He asked me where I had studied, and my story did not seem to account for my drawing. He rose, not having given me any advice, but bent his cavernous eyes on me with a penetrating but very reserved smile and turned to the next. The class had gathered round by this time, the English to the fore, and when le Maître had left, they rushed to me, and, if it had been the practice of the day in *cours* like ours, would have borne me on their shoulders.

Of course, I listened to all the criticism I could get wind of, and was to learn that analytical methods were not used in the French *cours*.

* * *

M. Julien, the organizer and director of the *cours*, had been a prize-fighter by profession, and whatever the turn of fate or necessity that directed his ambitions toward the realm of the Fine Arts, he was certainly an example of the versatility of the French mind. He had never attempted to become an artist, but he had frequented the *milieus* and haunts of artists. The lobbies of the Salons and the Exhibitions were familiar to him.

He had haunted the sittings of juries, in one capacity or another, listened, in cafés and on the Boulevards, to the heated discussions of the newcomer, and the Grands Maîtres, on the *pavés*, through spring nights. All was familiar to him and he to all. Most of all he had lived in Paris and had for years not stirred outside of her most characteristic circle. As he was French, neither his origin nor his eye for business

stood in the way of culture in the Fine Arts, far in advance
of his opportunities. He was a big, handsome man, who
never for a moment forgot his position of manager only, and
held the masters who came to criticise the class in high reverence. Nevertheless, he had an eye on every pupil, and would
appear unexpectedly in the class, a serious and observant
figure, decidedly on the watch.

I do not remember what our *abonnement* was, but I know it
was a paltry sum, and I am sure that the stipend received by
the artists who criticised us would appear laughable to
present-day estimates here.

True, we had no luxuries. The room was kept warm by a
stove, on the models' account. But for that, I fancy we
should often have drawn with numb fingers. The patience
and fidelity of the models to their job was pitiful. There
were so many others to take their place, if they failed. One
poor thing, who had the face of a worn-out provider, and,
with her ageing countenance and shabby clothes, would
never have been noticed by any one, had a slender and perfect form, with exquisite articulations. Like our little
stewardess on the Nordland, she used to fetch a large basket
of mending from behind the screen, during the rests, and,
drawing a forlorn skirt about her shoulders, fall to with
French zeal upon small ragged stockings and patched under-
wear. I heard that she was a favorite model for the 'Prin-
temps,' 'Sources,' and 'Jeunesses' that we were to admire in
the Salon before long.

It had been, and still was, customary for the artists whose
advanced pupils had aspirations toward appearing in the
Salon, to spend the day before 'sending in' in visiting the
studios of their former disciples.

Boulanger and Gérome had had each a great following.
Their influence was immense, and deservedly, for their personal view was never imposed. They inspired their stu-

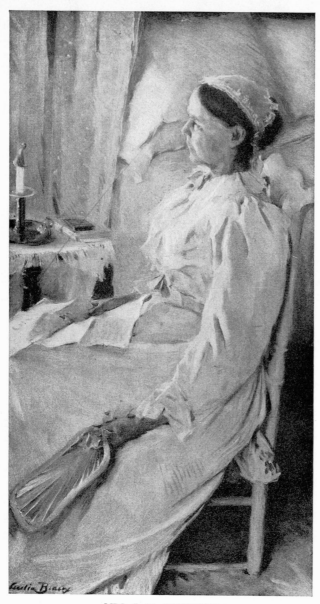

MRS. J. H. RICHARDS

dents without bending them in any direction, and their most grateful pupils 'arrived' without a trace of their master's style upon their canvases, and ready to undertake freshly individual subjects, and treatment. The legend was that Boulanger and Gérome were severe, and never spared their pupils' feelings. Gérome is said to have visited an ambitious American aspirant who had done a huge canvas for the Salon. It contained nine American Indians over lifesize. Gérôme examined the canvas, asked the artist why he didn't draw his moon with a compass, and left the studio. Boulanger was asked to criticise a picture whose subject was the mounted cuirassiers of the Opera.

'Dans ce tableau,' he said, 'tout est en fer, excepté les cuirasses.'

* * *

M. Julien had two allies in the class, the *massière* Mdlle. C., and Marie the *bonne*. Marie, strong and amiable, could be counted on for any service, and her name was constantly shouted across the class. She 'found' materials that had been forgotten, tabourets and easels when desired, but most of all at twelve-thirty, when the model retired, she became our loyal *commissaire*. Marie wore a black crocheted cape on her broad shoulders, and a black alpaca apron, and of course came and went on errands in the Quartier, in rain and snow, as she was, hat and coat being needless.

As many of us 'déjeunéed' at the *cours*, abundant were Marie's commissions at this hour, but she never forgot or confused any of them. 'Un sou de pain, deux sous de beurre, cinq sous de galantine, pour Mademoiselle.' 'Un petit pain, deux sous de beurre, et une cuisse pour Madame,' etc. 'Une cuisse' was the leg and thigh of cold chicken and was too great an extravagance for most of us. My choice was nearly always for 'galantine,' a *pâté* made of veal and other solid but creamy substances, and showing beautiful black accents of truffle, sagaciously inserted in the shapely, well-carved slice. The butter, of course, was a small white paper parcel, like all the rest, and they were all drawn from Marie's net bag with gracious alacrity. 'Pour vous, Mademoiselle,' as if it had been a token.

Mdlle. C. marshalled us, saw fair play, and displayed much tact in so doing. No advertising was done for the *cours*; it would have been thought shocking. The room was always filled 'to capacity' as we say, and it was necessary to mark each easel and chair with white chalk and to look out for encroachments. We had scarcely elbow-room. 'Enterprise' was not the idea. Great effort was made to raise the standard of work, but it did not seem to occur to the ex-prize-fighter that he might be a richer man and secure an increasing membership by publicity. No Exhibitions were held of students' work, and, if they continued their struggle, it was not with any immediate hope of public notice, though the time might come when a word from M. Julien might be the opening wedge that would lead to candidature for the Salon. Every week subjects for composition were given out. The compositions were handed in on a Saturday, and the student who had produced the best in the opinion of 'le Maître' had the privilege of first choice of place on Monday morning, for the new pose. This, in such a crowded room, was an immense advantage, but punctuality was also the price, for without it one's chance was given to the next. I had the good luck to win it pretty often. The subjects were frequently Biblical, and when the 'Supper at Emmaus' was given out, I had already visited the Salon Carré. Of course, what I produced was inevitably an imitation of Rembrandt, though not in design. I had no models and had to bring forth the same by means of inward vision, which I was beginning to practise. The compositions were shown on the wall and, summoned by Mdlle. C., we all stood behind Fleury, or whoever the critic of the month might have been. He stood growling before them with folded arms. Pointing to mine, he said savagely, 'Qui est-ce qui a fait ça?' Mdlle.

C. dragged me out and thrust me, quaking, before him, for he was often bitterly ironical. 'Humph,' he said, 'c'est vous? Je n'ai pas vu les autres, mais je sais bien que c'est la meilleure.'

The next day Julien came to the class. He held up my composition, which was in size about eight by ten inches and looked at me smiling. It was to be *accrochée sur le mur*. This was the highest honor the work of a student could hope for, and the wall showed a meagre collection of examples, charcoal studies from the model, and a few paintings, and once there, it was *pour toujours*. They were never to yield their place. Once worthy, always worthy—a record of the Cours. What simple faith in an everlasting standard! Glorious reward, where are you now? But it can truly be confessed that no subsequent award or distinction that Fate thought good to bestow on me had power to seem such a gift as this.

M. Julien had a few words with me, very serious, and with some emotion, to which my beating heart, of course, responded. 'Mademoiselle,' he urged, 'you must devote yourself to the expression of feeling. Do not waste your time upon trivial subjects' — or words to that effect. I always felt that he looked upon me with a kind of anxiety, as if he feared that I would go astray, wander, exaggerate, not adhere to the noble 'truth only' which was the ideal held before us by 'les maîtres'; and one day, a year after, when I was working in a little studio I had taken in the rue Notre Dame des Champs, he suddenly appeared there, to my great astonishment.

'Mademoiselle,' he said, with intense and solemn earnestness (and then followed the estimate of my 'talent' as shown in the Cours, and which may be omitted here). 'Mais, Mademoiselle, *mais*, je crains pour vous, je *crains* pour vous!' I think I must have sworn adherence to 'La vérité' and to that only, and it was an adherence that I was already, if not vowed to, making daily practice of, with all that within me was.

Where were we just then? Some believe, plodding along stupidly on a beaten track. I am glad that my long hours in the Life-Class were untroubled by doubt. I was working my way into the mystery of Nature, like a chipmunk storing up what could be used later, every step revealing secrets of vision I burned to express; to cease from blundering and begin to conquer, to state what I saw as being a salvage of the best; discovery of integral truth, discovery of means to report it that would mate with my emotion. My powers, such as they were, were too occupied for self-analysis or self-estimate. There was no virtue in this; I was simply too busy with what crowded the moments before me to think even of what I should do with my accumulation. I made one or two attempts at painting and found that, without space and power to move, I got nowhere. I could neither see nor feel, and I felt smothered among the canvases about me. I decided to give up painting in the class, and devoted all my time to drawing, the difference of scale taking the place of space. I tried only to learn the figure, amazing enough in the pose, but when the rest came, and I could see what movement revealed, I attempted only to get it by heart, to store up passages, articulations, weight. What I saw of color quality, surface light, which painting would express, I could not do violence to. I could not destroy my vision, turn it into leaden, meaningless pigment. I must *wait* for painting.

What peace, what space for deliberation, there was *in being a student!* I did not have to think of exhibition, or any of the sordid growths that flourish about student life when permitted, and in fact are planted by their directors in many schools now. It was all between the fascinating object and myself. Not even the Master would come between. He would say little. If I felt that my work did not interest him, something was wrong, blind, in it, and I was goaded into greater effort. If I felt sympathy in his 'vous êtes dans une très bonne voie,' I could go on with a happy sigh. How untrammelled I was! How satisfied, in my unimportance, that

Life made no demand! Time enough ahead for Life, for friends, lovers, and all other complications, perhaps because I had already tasted of these in their promiscuity. How far away it all seemed! — even the picture which got to Paris before me had faded, and I was not dreaming of others, nor of what it might all be leading to.

The world of Art in Paris was in no wise opened to me, and in fact was too far out of sight to be even longed for. I saw its reflection only in the Exhibitions. Bastien le Page was being worshipped. Dagnan also, for less reason. The polished sentimentalists had lost ground. L'Hermitte was enormously admired and respected, and, indeed, it was something to have recorded the scent of hay, and summer noon and toiling bodies, resting in the stubble, themselves part of the field and drying their sweat in the spices of earth and the hot sun.

I had an aunt in Paris who was working in Carolus' Studio, and brought word of his sayings. One remains in memory, a watchword for painters: 'Cherchez le demi-teinte général.' But as I saw his work, I did not care for it, and in fact was not captivated by any of the contemporary artists, although I envied their attainments and obvious ability to set forth what, or how, they wished. It was a period of Peace. The Salon drew crowds of all kinds. To *Vernissage* flocked the élite of Paris, the aristocracy of Society, of the Stage, of Music, and Literature, as well as of the Plastic Arts: in other words, the French Crowd, always intelligent, always amused, always disputive. How new to me to see a group of forceful, middle-aged, or old men, masters in some field without doubt, stooping over a small picture, arguing with heated insistence, denouncing, eulogizing! Never had I seen assembled so many men of 'parts' — real men, I would have said — so absorbed, so oblivious, greeting *each other* warmly, and with absolutely no general curiosity; pausing a moment, with great deference, before some quiet lady, or obvious beauty, but really there through profound interest in contemporary art. I longed to get closer — not to meet them, but to hear their talk, their dispute about the supreme Subject.

* * *

Into the gallery one day, as our obscure party moved about, there entered a Personage; a charming figure, with a following of worshippers. The lady was dressed in black lace, strangely fashioned. Though she was small, her step and carriage, slow and gracious as she moved and spoke, were queenly. She was a dazzling blonde, somewhat restored and not beautiful, as one saw her nearer. The striking point in her costume — and there was but one — was that the upper part of her corsage, or yoke, was made entirely of fresh violets, bringing their perfume with them. Every one, artists and their friends, ceased their examination of the pictures, and openly gazed, murmuring their pride and joy in their idol, Sarah Bernhardt.

* * *

Numerous, of course, in the crowd were the artists themselves. Many of them were men of sixty or seventy, with fine intellectual heads, sometimes with a quiet little woman beside them, 'Madame,' or 'Ma fille,' radiant, and *toute dévouée*. Puvis might have been there in his black silk cap, venerated, full of honors, or Jean Paul Laurens, Raffaelli, or Renoir even.

Every one was there, from the little old man, loved and respected for his lifelong devotion to the *cher métier*, to the young aspirant, long-haired and loose-cravated, and of course accompanied by his *petite amie*; and the flamboyant *bel homme*, trying to be satisfied with what he could get of notice. Sometimes I thought, 'I have been here before, this is the place. Where did it hang? Or did it never happen?'

I felt like one born out of due time, or reincarnate from previous existence. But generally I remained ready to progress noiselessly, and without importance.

* * *

Youth is not conscious of predilections, tendencies, even while beginning to follow them; but it is hypnotized by personalities, and above all will turn to leadership, which, among other fascinations, has the supreme one of being mysterious, a problem youth cannot solve, deeper than youth's short plummet, or with a veil that seems like depth. Such leaders draw like magnets. Contact with them may be accidental, but once established it is inescapable. No one would have been more open to such contact than I, but Fate withheld me from it. Schools, novelties, trends, were known to me only in the Exhibitions and Galleries, and all the time I was choosing a direction without knowing it, and without personal influence. For in the *cours* there was none of this. Was it wisdom or negligence? Until I went for a month's criticism to Charles Lazar, no word of theory ever was spoken to me by any of the masters who criticised me at the Julien Cours. I spent much more time in the Galleries, and chiefly in the Louvre, than at the Exhibitions of modern painting, for in the nineties there were 'we moderns,' as well as now.

To begin with, the Old Masters were a much greater revelation to me and a much greater novelty than the new. A good many of the latter I was familiar with in the Gibson Gallery and elsewhere, and I turned to what moved me most. Generally this was a purely subjective influence, unapplied to myself, curiosity, or my doings, and was the same with both old and new. I rejected, albeit with admiration, trends and subjects, as a nesting bird turns from all but what is fitting for its building. But though instinct denied, it could not blind. The enthusiasm I felt for Monet's iridescent pigments, his divided rays to reach the light of Nature by means of color only, left me with no desire to follow. Landscape, *genre*, I could pore over with no desire to take a white umbrella into the sun. Light, the sun, I desired these as joined with their logical mate, shadow, which indeed seemed as worthy to be treated by an artist as any other theme: the universal sequence always present, with vast variations, Nature's Trinity: the Sun or Light, the Object, and its Shadow. Out of the union of these three emerged Form. Form made Flesh and dwelling among us, intimate and divine at the same time. I did not have the pain of knowing that this comprehensive union as a subject for artists, which practically was the sequence of values, would ever be threatened or impeached. One would as soon expect to see the moon abolished, the moon, a conspicuous instance of the logical performances of Light and Shade, a logic which has been founder and partner in her reign as queen of fantasy. 'Imaginative interpretation' — I did not know the term, but I felt the evidence all around me of the union of reason and imagination in what moved me most.

Weary of nothing, it was not boredom that had me, but an instinctive sense of having no proprietary right in many aspects of Art. Why does a musician choose piano, violin, 'cello, or flute, and remain attached to it? Is it because such or such an instrument has been handed to him in youth? Sometimes, but not always. If there was anything that could have drawn me off my feet entirely, and divorced me from painting, it was to be found in the lower galleries of the Louvre, on some of the upper landings and among the isolated examples of Greek and Italian Renaissance sculptures. Mystery again. Sculpture for me was surrounded by the never really comprehended glamour of its creative act, as well as the absolute power of its beauty, on emotion. But although I sat down before it to shed comfortable tears, disguised as a cold, I never dreamed of running after, of a stumbling and falling pursuit of the god, casting his mighty shadow upon the hither side of the clouds.

At that time the Salon Carré contained, not an educational series as now, but a collection of what might be called 'preferable examples' of Titian, Rembrandt, Holbein, Veronese, and others. The magnificence of the Gallery itself, majestic in height, not too large for perfect presentation of both large and small works and superbly (and of course, naturally) lighted, it should never have been chosen to contain any work that had not attained to deserve the best that could be done for it, regardless of school or origin. In later years, it was heart-breaking to find the 'Supper at Emmaus' relegated to a side gallery of the Dutch School, where, although honorably placed officially, it became 'paint only' in a light that showed only its surface. On the other hand, when I visited the Salon Carré years later, I was glad to find the Murillo Madonna had accepted an invitation to come down with her crescent, and retire to the 'School' to which she belonged. The 'Entombment' may now also be better seen, needing not to be sought for.

The Veronese had never been really visible before its change of place, but as passages, I missed the cool notes of the Murillo and the 'Mona Lisa.' The place seemed rather brown and of unmingled richness without them in spite of the pale greys and blues in the upper spaces of the 'Supper in the House of Simon,' but from the beginning, as a *festa* which seemed at once as being spread for me, and my cravings and predilections, Titian's 'Man with a Glove' held first place in personal appropriation. I knew after that pretty well what I wanted, though not, of course, why I wanted it. Its rich, serious intensity, its entirely unsentimental attitude toward voluptuous browns and reds; the mysterious simplicity of its facture, which one could never probe; the limitless drama of young manhood — what were the specific indications and where? No answer, though so integrally present in the size of the canvas even, the placing

— 129 —

of the mass. When I approached the portrait, it was not in recognition. I had never seen a copy or photograph of it, nor even heard it spoken of. The 'Mona Lisa' was infinitely more remote and inapplicable, but I was familiar with photographs and chromos of this picture, and was chiefly concerned with the limited account they had given me of it. Now I am glad that I had not done my 'sums' beneath copies of these or other *Anciens Maîtres* on the walls of Miss Lyman's school.

* * *

During the months that remained of cold and damp, surface life between *cours* and *pension* was not vivid. Far different would it have been if we could have gone first to the *quartier* where we spent the precious winter months of the following year, in the old rue de Vaugirard, near the Sénat.

We were far from touching the high elegance that existed near us. We wore shabby clothes, *démodée*, and prim, and until spring came and we did a little shopping, we were invisible in the street. Our complexions always proved that we were English, our ulsters bore out this fact, and the *cochers* shouted *Anglaise!* when they wanted to be rude.

But in spite of the protection our mere appearance gave us, the American aunt and cousins who were living in Paris felt responsible for our never forgetting the conventions. My cousin Constance never went out without Adèle, their incomparable Breton maid, and her brother, who was studying medicine at the 'École' and who I am sure relished the display of his superior experience, tried to persuade me that I should be quite *déclassée* if I accepted the invitation of an American friend to escort me to the Salon; but greatly would we have missed the guidance of our relatives in many of our excursions in Paris. Especially were they helpful in the mazes of the museums, which they knew well, and in the churches for the processions and fêtes, and the rest that was possible after working hours, and on Sundays.

Unforgettable the first tiny *pâtisserie* to which my aunt led us, and where, at an exhausted moment, I was restored by my first 'Ba-Ba.'

* * *

The winter wore away, but to the vulgar and uncomfortable *pension*, and the dismal monotony of the quarter, I was to owe one of my choicest memories of Spring in Paris. Spring in Paris; I ask only for language equivalent to one aspect of the miracle.

We were many blocks from the Champs Élysées, but on a night in May, when it was mild enough to set our *croissée* wide open, as I lay stretched out in my cool bed, and there was no sound save footfalls in the street of horse or man, there stole in (it was inconceivable from so far) the perfume of the gardens in the Champs Élysées.

The lilacs, rhododendrons, acacias, were all out, perhaps lilies-of-the-valley. There had been a light shower. The exhalation reached my keen senses by way of Paris street and boulevard, yet unsullied, pristine, tender.

How could it be? The answer is 'Spring in Paris.' What else?

* * *

In February and March, the snow had fallen sparsely and melted. It never lay upon the pavements of Paris, and I learned what it was to leave a chill house for the bitter chill of outdoors. Not once did we see the sun, and perhaps this had something to do with another moment of ecstasy.

One morning in early April, we met, and saw, the first of Spring in Paris. All of youth, hope, and joy seemed to be in those shafts of sunshine, pouring through virgin leaf and violet shadow, and in the voices that called this and that from cleverly manipulated push-carts, heaped with flowers, vegetables, fruit, whose fresh moisture the sun touched with rainbow hues.

Every French heart bounded with the hour's happiness, and I knew that my heart was French, too. Fate was kind, for none of this should we have had at its best if it had not been a day when we left the rue Boccador and the *cours*, and 'descended' to what I always felt to be the real Paris, where heads *en cheveux* and stout figures in small, black, crocheted capes were frequent, all moving briskly — except the butcher's boy in his long white apron, who seemed touched by Spring's languor.

We saw the French sky for the first time; a Heaven not too high to be mixed with Earth's quality. Tender blue and white lifting large forms over, but in perfect unison with, wall and verdure, and the sumptuous greys of Paris.

During the winter we had had one glimpse of the best that that anomalous company, the 'American Colony,' could provide. We had letters to a lady, who, being *sui generis*, could not be claimed by the group, except by the outstanding eminence of birth and fortune. Immediately after sending my letter, I received from Mrs. Green, 12 rue de Bassano, a *petit bleu*, in which my cousin and I were asked to call upon her at '3.15 on Thursday.'

Number 12 rue de Bassano was one of the distinguished apartments near the Étoile. Of course, our destiny was *au premier*, and we were aware that the broad low stairs, richly carpeted and graced by a delicate iron balustrade, were lifting us to another world from the one we knew — at least, in Paris.

All that a French butler could possess of perfection admitted us, and left us a moment in just such a salon as he would naturally preside over. (How well he knew just what we were!)

'Madame would see us.' Only the pulling aside of a pale blue brocade *portière*, and the opening of a door, and we were within a Louis Quinze boudoir; birds, flowers, lace and blue satin, and upon a richly furnished bed, of the same period, under a canopy of gold and blue, reclined Mrs. Green, an exquisite old lady, of a waxen delicacy and softness, which creamy satin and old lace were the natural setting for. A *fichu* of the same filmy lace confined her lovely white hair, which lay in curls against her cheeks, and was fastened with diamonds under her fine pointed chin.

But I saw only her eyes at first, large, blue, and tender, and her hands, in long loose white kid gloves, held out in welcome.

All was ready to receive the two young art students. Tea, when I first knew the true *gâteau de Paris*, and, best of all, a chair beside the bed, which she pointed to for me, and before I was aware, I was pouring out my life history, the story of my work, my little nephews and the rest with very near to tearful joy. Her eyes, her smile, her questions, drew it all from me. How little she needed to be told about my grandmother and aunts and the uncle who had brought me up! She knew it all, recognizing something that I was hardly aware of. She saw us alone, but in about half an hour another guest was announced, whose hour was probably a fixed moment as ours had been, and I rose at once to yield my place, and receive Mrs. Green's parting salutation.

She never forgot to summon us, and we never missed an opportunity. She was not an invalid, but she had found, years before, that she could enjoy her friends without fatigue in this way. But when I had a little studio, the next winter, in the rue Notre Dame des Champs, a very fine carriage drove up to Number 15 one day, and our concierge conducted, through our snowy, dripping courtyard, a great lady in rich furs and black lace, and I had the joy of a visit, in my shabby little *atelier*, from our adored friend of the rue de Bassano. I never knew why Mrs. Green chose to spend her life in Paris. She received, did not offer, confidences. Perhaps, though, she was a Shaw of Boston, and, a 'loyal subject,' she found that, having once tasted, she could not do without the 'milk of Paradise' which many feel is to be found where she elected to remain. A grandson lived with her. She never returned to America and, when we parted the following spring, I felt that I should never see her again. Alas, it was to be so. But it was from her, in all the glamour of her noble, gracious beauty and sympathy, that I received in Paris the accolade, the salutation and blessing, upon my opening life.

VI

INCIDENTS AND EPISODES

ON a beautiful afternoon in late June, four travellers descended from the Paris train at Vitré. They were *en route* for Concarneau; had risen at three-thirty in broad daylight; being four, had had a compartment to themselves (second-class, of course); had lunched comfortably from their own basket, and spent a day which for joyous novelty and liberation was unprecedented for all of them. The French country and sky seemed to be something they had waited for, and which soothed a secret and heretofore unrecognized, *malaise.* I am sure we all whispered 'At last!' to ourselves, but one of the party, who had suddenly come across her birthright and inheritance, would have cried, if she had known the words, 'Where hast thou stayed so long?'

In all her letters home loyalty forbade her being more than frankly descriptive. 'The little rivers,' she wrote, 'run through fields, winding, like this [illustration] and have no rocky, shelving banks, and the grass finishes them off a few inches above their surface, and they are bordered by poplars, like this [illustration]. There are thatched and tiled cottages, and often a lovely old church that looks almost like a cathedral, for only a little village.'

Two of the party were particularly care-free, because they had been persuaded by the others, a mother and daughter, to throw in their lot with them for the summer at Concarneau. These ladies were Americans — one hundred per cent the type is called now — new friends, but staunch; first known at the *pension* Villeneuve, and who proved to be all that the cousins were most in need of, in economy and management complete, the rarity being that the daughter, a delicate, brilliant girl, struggling, against ill-health and imperfect eyesight, to become the artist she was born to be, was fully seconded by her guardian mother, in the enthusiasm, said, mistakenly, to belong to youth. The daughter had superabundant humanity, and almost outdid me in instantaneous and warm interest in passing individuals, as well as in every sight and sound and color. To both of us, the element of style, always present in the French scene, was a continual *festa*. Her humor was ready to be caught and flash a sign, at every point. No, there was no 'dampener' in our party. We were not looking for 'spectacle,' but endlessly enjoying the ordinary.

We would have insisted, however, that there was nothing of the 'ordinary' to be found in Vitré. Our first French town, after Paris, was, we had learned, 'the second mediæval town in France.' Little trouble, we might be sure, had the Ducs de Tremouille taken to make it what it was to us. 'The château, which of course dominates everything, even the church,' my letters says, 'stands on the edge of a precipice almost, which the town clusters against. It is the same beautiful grey stone, and over the part that is ruined, a rock-lilac, pink clusters of flowers, is growing. It has round towers, with pointed roofs, and dates back to 1100.'

It had been raining, I remember, and everything had all the color that moisture and a breaking sky, full of light, not sunshine, gives. When we looked up or down the steep little winding streets of mossy, grey, toppling houses, there was always a burning spot of red, a geranium in an upper window, or a white-coiffed woman, in a deep blue or green skirt, knitting in a doorway, coppers shining inside, or an old woman in sabots clattering down toward us over the rough stone pavement, or a tiny cherub in grown-up garments supping its bowl of *pot au feu* on a doorstep, and three children's heads in a narrow window under the eaves, looking down at us.

CECILIA BEAUX
From a photograph

Remembering what is the due of justice in regard to travelogue, let me explain that we had been prepared for none of this by either the advertisements of Tourism or Automobiles. So strong upon us were the reports of our greedy eyes that they can scarcely be called 'impressions.' They became inherent, like the veins in marble, or color in rose petals, dissolvent and permeable in abiding consciousness.

And here shone the Spartan virtue of our friends. Result, a bargain with the powers at the little Hôtel de France, and the choice of a room that would 'do' (it was to hold all four of us) for a price too small for memory to register. Two large beds were draped in brilliant calico; it had small windows, with curtains of the same, at each end of the room, which looked on street and court, and was *au premier*. One saw, too, that the hero of many a novel had entered it with fearless stride, thrown hat and cloak upon the table, and awaited the suspicious-looking stranger, who had requested a private interview, below. We did not order supper to be sent up, as he had done, but, after a little informal attention to the minuscule hand-basin and pitcher, descended to the *salle à manger*, and enjoyed one of those unrecorded, humble, but satisfying repasts, for which small provincial hotels in France used to be famous.

But prior to this comfortable consummation of our day, we had climbed up to the château, and down into the church. Looking from a window in one of the turrets, the roseate tiles of many roofs sloped up toward us upon the mystic grey of their walls, and became a more violet rose and grey as they joined the not distant fields and sky. Small trees, in a clear pattern of greenish blue, reminded me of the Boldini in the Gibson Gallery, never forgotten in its loveliness of truth. Below us, far below in the fortress's foundations, were the *oubliettes*, real ones. Queer forms of wood and iron hung in some of the stone passages, and down there, History, in detail almost obliterated, was plainly conveyed, even if it had been by the horror of great darkness only, and the whole constructive system of defence, starting probably from a Roman camp, or vantage-ground of rocky eminence, had passed through from the urge of ambition and holy war in a few minds, every period necessary to its existence as a stronghold.

The rock in the woods had become a nest, where heavy labor, courage, death, tyranny, torture, and love had made place for their conduct and desires.

At a narrow window high up could not one hear a silken rustle, catch a glimpse of a fold of rich fur or even a flowing veil?

Out of what is beauty made? Here, it seemed, from the strong passions of covetousness, pride, and bigotry unto death. There had been chastity sometimes, courage constantly, faith and honor occasionally, and even clemency, as flickering spiritual quickeners. In the physical structure there had been plenty of cunning to build for strength to hold, below and above. These were the impulses and materials that had found a way permanent and cumulative, that was to result, finally, in something utterly unimagined or desired by its creators. A charm had been born from violence and its allies that was to provide and offer to the thirst of young minds and unspent hearts moments of the best they were ever to have of the joy of seeing. One could examine the lichen on grey stone, and could find tiny black spots in the pale yellow texture uniting it, cold, and moistened to richness of hue, to the mellowed surface it clung to; masonry, meticulously welded in a broad curve, where one's bare palm found no evidence of rude purposes, even when nought intervened upon the wall, between stretched fingertips, and the valley far below.

The church dated with the fortress or near it, and like it had gained steadily on all its original simple beauty. My letter says: 'They had had a great funeral for the head priest that afternoon, and the church was draped in black, which a nun was helping to take down. After dinner we went back to see the carved stone pulpit, in the wall outside, for preaching here in the old days. We went in by a little side door near the altar. They were having evening prayer; a priest was playing on the organ and a choir of priests and boys were chanting the service. The church was full of white-coiffed women and nuns, from the convent near by. They, with the incense-bearers, made the only light, yet it was not dark, a harmony in half-tones for spirit and sense. As we went out, a group of women in a doorway were talking, evidently about the funeral that had just taken place. "Le Cortège était très beau," one of them said, as if something else had failed and they looked mournful over it.'

* * *

The fact that a 'spider in sabots' brought us hot water and towels is the only other record of our night at Vitré. The journey to the coast occupied most of the next day. The sky lowered in horizontal lines, as the hours went on, the country, darkening under the overhanging grey of the clouds, became a grim olive streaked with chalky and sandy soil. It grew cold; the exaltation of the day died down within us, and we approached our destination without much hope, a chill drizzle adding to our depression.

At a station shortly before we reached Concarneau, a big capable woman got into our compartment, who turned out to be Madame Julia, the landlady of the hotel at Pont Aven. She knew many of our friends, her inn being well known, and could boast of walls covered with sketches and studies by the men who had lodged with her. Her generous personality instantly forged a strong link of promise for our summer, and gave us an idea of the persistence and solid energy of the Breton people, whom we were to watch and live with for many months.

* * *

Of course, we drove at once to Les Voyageurs, with

which we were already acquainted in a novel, 'Guenn,' then at the height of its popularity. The famous Madame came out to meet us. As per my letter, 'She is a beauty, and exactly like the description,' a superb figure in sombre cloth with touches of black velvet, jet-black hair under a small winged *coiffe*, gold earrings, a handsome, strong-colored face, and gay black eyes. She could have been counted on to command and vivify a whole community, as well as a hotel, which was a toy in her hands. The hotel in the place faced the whole scene of Concarneau; the fortress in the distance, the sea and the quays, prickling with masts, and ruddy with the sails of the fishing fleet, at anchor, or tied up to their dock. Lights were beginning to show from lantern and lamp-post and moving spots of white — or what one called white — were present everywhere in the circulating crowds. The hotel was warm and populous; dinner was served; our friends hastened to meet us; every window contained a spectacle. Every line and movement of the *bonnes* who served us at the table was a detaining composition. Even the thoroughly bourgeois appointments of the dining-room, where no trace of primitive beauty could be seen, outside of Madame and the servants, was toned and massed by the not too generous lighting. The quality of generosity was in the unctuous exhalations of the cuisine, the steaming soup tureen (we had a tureen at home), the great fish lying brown and rich on its huge platter, which easily accommodated head, tail, and every natural accessory, and the subtle underlying constant of cheese, knotty apples, and wine.

* * *

But we were not tempted by either Madame or Les Voyageurs, in any meaning of the term, to linger, and with the help of a friend we sought lodgings in the town. On one of the streets, or rather roads, where Concarneau joins the open country, an old couple — Papa and Maman Valdinaire, they were called — owned a small *propriété*, a house

and garden with an eight- or nine-foot wall entirely enclosing the estate, which was about an acre, and was in fact a
garden full of flowers only. The walls were covered with
carefully trained fruit, pears and apricots, and a number of
small trees, perhaps for blossom only, cast flickering light
and shade over the flower-beds. Pigeons circled overhead;
privacy reigned. I nearly stepped upon an old turtle con-
fidently crossing the path. But our hosts to be were not
hedonists, but florists, the only ones in town. How little
disturbing were *les affaires*. Small groups of children or their
elders, awed by some event of death or marriage, or a
première communion, I sometimes saw from our window on the
garden, considering long, and finally passing out with a
bouquet, usually of stock and poppies, with one pink rose in
the centre, a ravishing and indispensable addition. Although we had been somewhat discouraged by the entrance
and hall, where Madame Valdinaire's chickens casually
walked and could easily have been met on the stairs, we
were all, even the most practical, for immediate settling
with Madame, who of course conducted the business of the
establishment. There were other and almost more important drawbacks, such as that Madame V. had no personality,
and was without race; above all wore no *coiffe*. She and
Monsieur inhabited the lower story, which connected directly with everything, the road, as the front door opened
directly from it, and it was the only access to the garden,
tant mieux. But a goat also kept house with them, as well as
the chickens, and had the freedom of the hall and stairs; as a
matter of fact it never took advantage of the opportunity,
although climbing was by way of being within its primeval
nature. The house was one room deep, and we were offered
the two rooms on the second floor; also an attic for our
kitchen. This had a large dormer window with lovely view
toward the sea and a *brasier* for cooking on the hearth, really
perfect in our eyes — but the fact that only one of the bed-
rooms was for the moment habitable was temporarily dis-

couraging. They were at the top of the bare stairway, on —
I called it — the second floor. There were windows on both
sides, the sunny ones looking on the garden and within easy
sight of the pigeons, and the garden, which was, with all its
varied charms, to be our painting ground and studio. Both
old people were instantaneous in accepting even our guardian's idea of the value of the premises to us, the main difficulty being that the room which was to be ours had for wall
decoration only lath and plaster, the furniture was a pyra-
mid in the midst, and dust and spiders had possession, but
wall-paper had already been bought. There, indeed, were all
the clean rolls of it. Papa Valdinaire, with his brown *béret*
jauntily topping his grey curls, was prepared with hammer
and tacks to put it up. No filthy glue or sour paste was to
defile our virgin bower. Our landlord nailed up *clichés* first,
and upon these the paper was literally hung, revealing to
me the first steps of this class of wall decoration in the past.
True, that by this method the paper was not married to the
wall. It had freedom and nonchalance, and would not give
a sign if spiders and even mice made their homes behind it.
However, we thought, if it were tapestry, one might have
rats as well as conspirators behind it. As we were in great
haste to be settled (we and our unpacked trunks had spent
two nights in our friends' room), it was pleasant to know
that no drying would be needed in our chamber. A perfectly bare floor is easily cleaned. In French beds one may
always have confidence, and it was very soon after Papa
Valdinaire had picked up his last tack and Madame V.
had gone off with her bucket that our room had a comfortable, even cosy, allure. 'Our two windows have curtains,'
my letter says, 'white lace and chintz. One bed is a lounge
by day, the other contrives by means of its position and arrangements to look like the wall of another room. We have
a big fireplace and medium high chimney-piece, painted
black, on which is a large gilt clock, in a glass case, the pride
of our landlord, who has now added a brass candlestick that

he made himself. There is a large table, and we have a lamp of our own brought from Paris. When this with its pink paper shade is lighted at twilight (it is never quite dark here), it is all that there is of the most homelike. Also there is quite a large mirror on the mantel, meant to be upright, but we laid it on its side and made a "landscape." Yesterday we had a big branch of Easter lilies from the garden on the mantel, and a native bowl of yellow (could they be prim-roses?) from the same on our little nightstand. There is a big chintz-covered chair, a large armoire, and a closet with shelves; in fact more than metropolitan conveniences. It would be more fun for you to hear that we had a stone floor, an old carved bedstead with doors, and had to wash our faces at the well, but we would just as lief peep into other people's houses for these luxuries. The only really pictur-esque and native-looking thing we possess is our big earthen *cruche*, for water. Madame brings us a *bouillotte* with our *eau chaud* in the morning, but this is only temporarily ours, and considered very valuable.'

'Mrs. C. and her daughter, pursuant to the arrangement that they should undertake the whole *ménage*, went every day to market, and I now lament the scruples that withheld me from joining in this rite.' I was determined to remain consistently *hors concours*, and they had obvious pleasure in relating their adventures with the natives on their return. In about a week Lucy had become fluent in all of the Breton language that she needed to express enquiry, astonishment, admiration, and strong objection to price; also she was expressive in repudiation of alleged values. Large heavy coppers, which were still in circulation, were usually suffi-cient, after argument, for most of the outlay. They came home rejoicing over their *trois sous de pommes, cinq sous de tamates*, etc. The price of butter and chops was fixed accord-ing to every shade of well-known value, and our guardians were too appreciative of superlative worth to attempt a bargain where it would have been useless.

Also we acquired a *bonne*, a lovely young creature, a bride of only eight days, who satisfied every desire in the way of costume, which was complete, and which it was a joy to watch in action, and examine in repose. We had hopes, too, of using Marguerite as a model, later.

* * *

The innumerable and generally amusing details that life now presented on every side promised to be entirely absorbing, unless resisted, but I very soon became conscious that free absorption might be admitted for 'getting' the scene, and even appropriating it as something to be made one's own, forever.

Not, however, in view of painting it. There were certainly essentials in it that sketching would never yield up, neither would even a serious approach by a more searching plastic medium, especially by a newcomer, who was aware that nothing she knew or could accomplish would serve her in expressing what she might discern. But if one did not 'draw' it or attempt to approach it plastically at all, how could one be sure of getting anything?

Some groping instinct averred that I couldn't really watch anything, without (it being so much stronger than I was) being somewhat possessed by what was deepest and oldest in it. Later, much later, I learned that especially in the case of Brittany, 'deepest and oldest,' and the long line of evolution, starting at climate, and necessity, had worked out a school in which a complete æsthetic concept could be observed. It could not only be observed but absorbed, and applied to the great need of one who was open to the allure of multifarious attraction, and to whom what she felt to be a whole universe of opportunity was more broad than deep.

Proud, indifferent Brittany, indifferent to all her admirers could give her, except the *petit sous* she was so much in need of — of what small importance to her were her worshippers except the few who were her sons! The *paysanne* and the *femme de pêcheur*, apparently neither envied nor imitated the *petite bourgeoise*, who sometimes was a relative and who went in high heels and her *cheveux*. How profound had been the process — how inevitable the result!

It seemed, to at least one observer, that no matter where travel might take her, she would always think of Brittany, in *ensemble*, as the masterpiece of the Great Designer, at least as the one that has survived, or had at that time. It is one of those fortunate compositions whose initial *raison d'être* is germinal from the remotest, purely natural causes. Individuals have had nought to do with it. The sea, the Gulf Stream, and a rocky shore which was France, and where a few fishermen and farmers struggled to live, are the materials. As a design, nothing has succeeded better in being simple and homogeneous, the background laid in first, and all the rest enclosed in the *cadre*, physically, ethically, and æsthetically, flawless in unity down to the remotest protoplasm, fibre, grain of sand, and aqueous particle. There could be no other way. Conviction of this is an experience sobering in its mystery. To Brittany nothing may be added nor may anything be eliminated. Poor, rude, suffering, even dirty, from the low olive background, touched with the russet of the chief occupation, inland to the poorest *chaumière* and its inhabitants, hidden in a muddy *chemin creux*, Brittany is perfect in style. The reserve, almost the solemnity, of the landscape may be found in the lines of the dark costume, and the white *coiffe* mingles with tints of sunlit cloud. Figures battling with the wind in full heavy cloth have their base in the strong lines of the sabot, and its making visible strong tones of ochre. How about Holland? Unified, yes, but by much greater outlay of material, and in Brittany, the intrinsic evidences are of a purer, choicer flavor, a starker residuum of essential design. The young Breton girls have faces whose forms have as good a reason for being what they

are as has the modelling of the perfect wild creature of unmixed strain. Beauty is an unpopular word now, but a face
that halts the passing stranger, by its pure cool perfection of
line and proportion, its color and texture like the inward
slope of a seashell — well — if 'beauty' will not do, what
will? She is *paysanne* — where did she get those facial lines
that mean high race in the selective sense of the word?
And the design of her head-dress, which so perfectly sets off
this very type, purifying purity, enhancing the absence of
woman's major triumph, her hair — there is not a lock in
sight; a high black bodice, tightly binding in her form, as
she goes in her heavy skirt and sabots, with her long boyish
stride.

This girl passed my window several times, generally
alone, and I decided that I would abandon my idea of not
'doing' the peasants, not blundering over what had been
done already many times, and as well as might be, and I
wanted a better chance to enjoy her beauty and know it
better. I thought of various views, various lightings for the
serious, unsmiling face, generally slightly bowed, which
brought out the elemental simplicity of the lines. I described her, with reticence, to Madame Valdinaire. Oh,
yes, she knew them, they had a girl. Did Madame think she
would pose for me? Madame's face changed a little; she was
non-committal. There was no certainty. I might enquire.
She pointed down the road toward the country. 'Quelque
distance,' and then one must 'tourner à gauche dans le
chemin creux.'

Full of hope and confidence, two of us followed these directions. It was a good walk to the lowest and loneliest of
chaumières, almost invisible in its protective coloration of ivied
wall and pollard oak. Although furnished with our best
manners and modest allure, we had hardly got within the
low doorway, and perceived figures in the half darkness,
everything seen being beautiful, when we became seriously
conscious that we had not been asked to call. *She* was not

there. The two parents in full and sombre regalia made little more than monosyllabic replies to the proposal which we politely led up to. Negation was steady, and increasingly cold. Our being ladies and tenants of Madame Valdinaire, whose acquaintance they acknowledged, altered their view not a bit. Still less did the very liberal remuneration I offered, nor the added assurance that the posing would take place in the Valdinaires' house. They were stony, and we turned away humiliated by the consciousness that we were in some way suspect.

By the time we emerged from the *chemin creux*, in spite of my disappointment the idea that we, so obviously prim and shabby, should be rejected as unsafe associates for their daughter became highly amusing. But we found that the people, especially the country folk, did not really like *les artistes. Les galopins* might *porter les affaires*, and earn anything that was coming; but for the rest, an ironical shrug was the answer. For praise of their interior they cared little, undoubtedly considering it insincere, although, when it came to proposed purchase, they apparently had been informed as to value. The most ordinary — and there were differences — would smile when the baby, in costume a reproduction of its mother's, received compliments. Of course, the mystery of our defeat was never solved. Madam V. heard our lamentation with a very small smile, which said that she knew as much; so one illusion remained perfect, and the fact that the girl was unattainable seemed to explain somewhat the line and proportions of her face, which, although it was an abstract of Beauty, was original.

I settled down then to my chief effort, a three-quarter portrait of Mrs. C. in the garden under the dwarf trees, with their firmly drawn spreading branches. Mrs. C. had waxen features, grandly arranged, and as she sat in black, with touches of white, among the shadows, filtering light, and green leaves, I forgot everything else I might have been doing. The garden studio was of itself worth our choice for the summer. We were envied by every one, and I was also getting my lesson from Brittany, without rough-handling my enjoyment of it. Alexander Harrison and Charles Lazar each had a studio in the neighborhood. In fact, their presence had been an important factor in drawing us to Concarneau. A. H. never gave criticism, but Lazar came, approved, and counselled. 'The lost and found' was his slogan at this time and his perfect honesty and humorous illustration gave zest to all his opinions. It was a period of minute research for values and their perfect sequence, and I believe that for this direction (driven as all 'directions' are) nothing could have been more balancing than the opportunity to have always in sight the simplicity, line, in fact, the *style* of the Breton ideal. Such influence, silent and without emphasis, 'falls upon the place beneath' and reaches interior fibres closely adjacent to the very source of life and energy; reaches with lasting and increasing force.

I did not, however, eschew all dealings with '*col* and *coiffe*.' I attempted two life-size heads, at dusk, on the beach; two girls of the merely robust type in conference or gossip — the tones of *coiffe* and *col* mingling with the pale blue, rose, and celadon of the evening sky. Shorty said, in his vernacular, that I had 'bit off more than I could chew' — an expression I had never heard before and to me very potent. I knew he was right, but the great A. H. came in, considered it thoughtfully, and left me feeling that I had done well to try, pointing out some false color values which his peerless vision and experience could easily detect, and also as easily describe the tones that should be in their place.

Harrison, now at the apex of his strength, had already met the 'Dæmon' and thrown him, in his two big pictures 'Arcady' and 'The Wave.' His method was of a type now nearly obsolete, and interesting as being in direct opposition to what his viewed personality would have expected. He

would have seemed to follow pleasure chiefly, and its concomitant beauties and elegancies. Tall, *lancé*, and superbly
handsome, he easily won all he appeared to care for, and
much that he didn't want; but he had a religion — it was his
art; an industry — it was his painting; and he had an untiring faith toward these. He could not be called a Nature-
lover, for he loved Nature perhaps only when married to
Art. He saw large and wished to paint large. He desired to
make the sensation coming from Nature felt as real stimulant
and bestowal, and in its passage through the mind as Art to
gather momentum and power. He was enamoured of the
successive opaline surfaces of low incoming waves and strove
for the Sea's gift as it comes to one facing it on long beaches.
His method was searching, and had the quality of science,
perhaps because he had been trained as an engineer, which
profession he abandoned for painting. His attack began
with a small study, only a few tones of the choicest, an
ébauche for a certain effect, at a certain hour, but whose sign
and substance was to last and be the key to all future development of the work. From the five by ten inches to the
great canvas measured by feet (or metres in France), he
passed by means of six or seven graded sizes, each containing accumulated truth, until the next to the last, which
would be a not distant approach to the final. Neither desire
nor purpose ever faltered or grew stale. Sensation increased,
and charm found a better place on broad spaces.

* * *

To one who feels color, it is a simple matter to find it on
the palette. A small palette yields accidental bits, fortuitous
touches, for what used to be called a 'gem.' But to prepare
individual color on a large scale, and with truth of relation
on a large canvas, is another matter. Resting upon his
supersensitive vision, this was Harrison's strong point, and
his big pictures had the fresh, resounding spontaneity of
sketches. Then, too, he had with him the sympathy and the

'moment' among his confrères, and the critics as well as the artists enjoyed what they might have called 'inhaling' his pictures, as well as viewing them. Harrison may be said to have 'flowered' not many times, and with immense labor, which his strength bore gladly. 'Arcady' followed 'The Wave' and 'Crépuscule.' The subject called 'Arcady' was a lush dell, with small trees and several nude figures of wo-men about to bathe in the river near by, unseen, but felt in the color, growths, texture of moist grass, and the humidity of a hot summer noon in the shade. The figures, about half life-size — as the scene was large and they were back in the middle plan — were incidental, only values, and far from faultless in drawing, but giving the final sensation of pre-sence in such a place, and the luxury of the moment. Here annotation stops, for, as in all plastic art that is of value, something has been shown that words cannot convey, or, if used, fatigue instead of refreshing the mind.

Toward the end of the summer, some one left and a studio in the loft where Harrison, Hoeber, and Lazar were in-stalled became vacant, and I at once took possession, a move memorable for me in that one day a step was taken into the 'next square' as Alice so aptly puts it. Arthur Hoeber would pose; there was gay talk and much laughter, but something came of it for the performer that was the turning-point toward what she has more or less sought ever since. There was no other way. Not that this was known to her or any one else, at the time, but applause was warm, and surprise evident. It is so that changes come. Growth from unsensed sources, generally so opposite as to be entirely unsuspected. What one got from sober Britanny fed psychic fibres that had been perhaps unready to receive before, and new shoots sprang forth. Art and Nature were shown in this place to be more one and interchangeable than I had ever imagined they could be. How easily and naturally I followed the magnet, for it was the way I wished to go, and how welcome is the consciousness of being fortified in one's desires, desires that took me toward the intimate union of Art and Nature, as it might be, as it had been, in portraiture, renewed in every subject in every fresh personality, not always, perhaps, with the austerity of the Breton example; it was sometimes exuberance, in youth, its style governed by each subject, 'according to his kind.'

* * *

We lingered in Concarneau until every one else (including the Conants) had left, except Harrison and Hoeber. Harrison, in fact, outstayed every one, and was rude enough to aver that it was the best time of the year, though he later confessed that he was lonely and had 'varnished out old Maurice.'

There had been, however, two rather late comers, one of these a Miss W., who 'joined' us and was our constant companion and able supporter. Not much occupied herself, she was one of those comfortable people who find their life in the troublous atmosphere of those of the struggling, beating wing, always intelligently ready and never in the path of the wind. The other was a young English officer, on leave from India and fever, to walk in the strong air of Brittany and recover. Harrison had seemed separate, but infinitely more remote was the civilization that this young son of Britain's choicest rearing had sprung from. We began to notice the unusual figure in brogues and homespun, striding along the roads in all weathers. We also heard of him at the hotel as one of those Englishmen who never 'saw' any one. But one day the 'shy' stranger mounted the steps of the granary, and called on Harrison. Quite a long visit he made, and when he had again strode past my door on leaving, Arthur Hoeber appeared, bearing a card, 'Lieutenant C. D.-R., 28th Connaught Rangers, has just called on us,' Hoeber said, in his best imitation. After this Lieutenant D.-

R. often dropped in at tea-time. 'I'm stoker,' he said, dealing with our very inefficient lamp. In him the usual naïve approach to Art, which we expect from his compatriots who are not among the especially initiated, seemed to be a rather pathetic craving for participation; at least for being an observer of what he had humbly but very persistently undertaken to penetrate, alone and in a completely alien existence. 'Spare time' was all he had ever given or could ever give to his predilection, and one day he showed me his sketch-book. His drawings were done with a fine lead pencil, washed in with a little water-color; vignettes reminding one of Rogers's Italy. The first was a high battlemented fortress, surmounting a wooded hill. I asked if it was an illustration for a poem; whereupon he became slightly embarrassed, and stammered, 'Oh, no, that's my father's castle in Scotland.' And then, to explain that he was not Scotch, he admitted that there were three other houses in England. I said I thought Tychefield Abbey a nice name for a place. Alas, I was to learn long after this that the Abbey, park, and woodland had been requisitioned by the Government after the war, and is now a barracks for soldiers.

So clear-cut was the personality of our so-eager-to-be comrade, so unrelated at any viewed angle, that although he had an ambition *de coté* to be an actual participant in painting, and took some of us more seriously in sight of future eminence than we did ourselves, we met in space, poised for observation. *We* could have been seen *en bloc*, or in an unaccented pattern of interwoven parts, upon which the *chiffre*, or blazon, which might have been *his* designation, had been struck, not really joining the integral design, but, by its placing, giving the composition zest and concentration. Some of us would have been satisfied with finding him charming, but to others, suggestion in regard to him was almost limitless, there being so much more of him than was confined within his slight, vigorous young person, though

MRS. ROBERT CHAPIN AND CHILD
An oil drawing

forcibly evident in his spare countenance, which sometimes became fixed and impenetrable.

He had more grace than beauty; fine proportion, rather than size. If one could see him apart from his invariable homespun, it would never have been as a scarlet and beaver dandy of the Horse Guards, or even in the English hunting field, or tracking man-eaters in the jungle, though either or all of these would be his natural setting. He brought with him a period much more distant; a casque and full suit of steel would have suited him well and the visor would have matched the straight setting of his remote grey eyes.

His sketch-book brought out the suggestion of *autres temps, autres mœurs*. Sometimes it seemed as if History and flawlessly developed Tradition were more visible around him to us than he was himself. And how unaware he was of this! The serious realities of the Staff College, from which few emerge with honors if at all, related to this; his first year in India, his mission to the Interior (with the necessary equipment of twenty Hindoo dialects, as well as the rest of it), and the almost limitless sphere open to him by tradition and education. The world of society, both in England and the colonies, with which at twenty-six he was entirely familiar, were the immediate and near to him. Nearer than all, perhaps, in his interests was the adventure of hunting in India, and with this he entertained us by the hour when he became thoroughly domesticated.

The year in India brought him promotion, and soon after he left us he wrote me joyfully, in his beautiful English hand, that he had got the rank of Captain and had been put in command of the garrison at Malta.

Such a view of the material that England has the means of forming to her mind for service could never have been perceived by us in a visit to England. He was compact of it all, which for the type had done away with all waste, and the choice and value of the elimination were clear, present, though not presented.

I recognized something I had seen in the elders at home, a serious, easy poise that would be unaltered by any situation. In them I had taken it for something that belonged to years and experience. I had never seen it in so young a person, with so boyish an allure. Some one said, 'He looks younger than he is, and *is* older than his years.' I saw the operation in him of a great and exigent Society, which had chosen and perfected points and surfaces, a few only; elimination did for the unimportant, the selected residuum would be adequate for all and any of the infinitely varied contacts such a sphere as his would present.

For one who attempts to pursue a *métier* for which his whole reserve of time, strength, and opportunity seems insufficient, there is a continual contest between what may be called 'ventilation' and interruption, masquerading as the former. The latter, which jars sediment that has just settled and left the element clear for use, is like the planet with exterior rings, which, though they may be only gas, enormously increase its bulk, and perhaps its influence. A message brought to the studio, in mid-morning, to know whether —— has no engagement for Thursday evening, and will dine, etc., will probably shatter an indispensable period, pull off tentacles which have strengthily fastened in the prey, and perhaps injure a passage beyond repair. But an interlude — outside of working hours, of course — which throws open a magic casement and lets in a wind from the unknown or unrealized, fresh from far-off peaks, whether of mountains or minds, does more than directly stimulate. The performer is drawn away from his place *into* distances, from which he can discern his production (and that of his contemporaries) and give it its true measure, both as project and expression. Sometimes it may be a personality which has approached from a completely other scene, other past, other future. The ideas, the life courses, the habits of another society have come with him, and are effective in the *enlèvement*, effective in the manifestation of placement, value, ponderation, and continuant worth.

* * *

Between the synthetic economy of the Breton idea as an æsthetic unit, shown in all aspects of the original creation, and a young British soldier, whom England seemed to have sent to us as a manifestation of the same idea, at the extreme other end of the scale, there was a deep similarity, though all the obvious difference in the world. To one of us the leading of both was the same, though unrecognized until years afterwards. It was 'too deep for sound or foam.' But to a nature whose impulses were increasingly for the presentment of *life*, vivid and permeating, an influence, joining with her New England inheritance, saw to it that there should be stout fibre and reserve.

* * *

A few days before our departure, we became quite prankish and gave a supper-party in our attic. The *pièce de résistance* for this was to be a chicken salad. Madame Valdinaire proposed providing the *poulet*, and we consented, without even bargaining, in which we fell quite away from the precepts of the C.'s. The chickens looked quite large walking about in their feathers, and although the thought of an execution was almost prohibitive, reflecting on the amount of chicken we had already consumed as life went on, we could not logically withdraw, and felt that an absence of several hours, and at a distance, would place the matter in its normal light, and that, on our return, we should find the chickens trussed neatly in their tidy skin, and looking like all the others we had seen and whose breast-bones I had consented to test, on market days, in West Philadelphia.

Alas, this was not to be. When we returned at night, Madame Valdinaire reminded us that we had not yet *choisi le poulet.*' It was a dark night in October. The chickens had retired early, and it was my lot to follow Madame V. and her lantern to the sleeping-quarters of her brood. Of course they had heard us coming, and when the door was opened and the lantern shone upon a row of dusky, perching bundles of feathers, a dilated, circular eye scintillated with terror in each sideways-turned head. A few sleepy, guttural croakings came from the back row, but those in front were silent and fixed. Madame Valdinaire, with cruel liberality, asked me if I preferred the brown or the speckled, or both, and seized one at random by its yellow legs, holding it upside down for me to *palper* its shrinking body, the one eye always turned up and fixed in the struggling bunch of squawks.

Here I turned and fled, bidding Madame V. *choisir* herself, and stumbled into the house and up to our room, where my cousin sat placidly writing a letter.

* * *

The next day, the day of the feast, which was to be a supper-party, Madame '*monté*'d' the carcasses, extremities all in the air, boiled and '*tout préparé, Mademoiselle.*' But it was at once evident that, under the ragged skin of the poor victims, there was not enough 'chicken' for even half of our party. The closest scraping of their very obvious bones would not suffice. It was pouring, had been since early morning, and it was much too late for further depredations in the hen roost, even if our nerves could have borne it. Some one, not I, had heard that veal had often been used as a *dernier ressort* in cases of salad that had been given up as hopeless, and, when jollity ran high, white morsels of veal, we hoped (and is it not true that a calf is a nobler and purer animal than a hen?) would naïvely be swallowed by our three male guests, two of whom had not tasted the real thing for years, and the third probably never.

I remembered a shabby window, the only one of the kind

in town, where I had seen and turned from cold roasted fowl, portions of beef and sausages, etc. I went forth, glad of the umbrella which would shelter my guilt. The rain was torrential, but as I reached the shop and stood at gaze, recognizing the blessed solid square of cold cooked veal, Harrison passed on the other side of the street, head in air as usual. If it had been Hoeber...But Harrison was only thinking of the clouds, and whether the sun would be out to-morrow at four-fifteen. Miss W. made a magnificent mayonnaise, and the pale richness of the final result would have deceived even Augustine himself, and I spent a residuum of relieved tension on a full set of rhymed verse, *à propos* of each guest.

The *rôti* — I mean by this our hot dish — was to be scrambled eggs and fried potatoes, which could not be prepared beforehand, so it was not till the guests began to be heard downstairs, staggering into the dark hallway out of the downpour, that we found that our chimney fairy had another engagement, and that the draught had decided to come to the party instead of passing up and out as was expected. They all wanted to come up and help, but Harrison and the Lieutenant were commanded to content themselves in the salon with the illustrated papers of ancient date. Hoeber, whose virtues we well knew, was not only invited but conjured to intervene, and when I had seen him take off his cuffs and begin getting black, I took the frying-pan and the potatoes *nature* down the dark stairway and knocked at the Valdinaires' door. They and their whole menagerie were *chez eux*; the goat, the chickens (who appeared unaware of their bereavement), and the old dog, all sheltered and warm, for there was, as I had hoped, a fire. How welcoming, how friendly they all were! Immediately, with cheered and mounting imagination, I sprang to the thought that I might not only fry the potatoes, but that the Valdinaires might have an onion. The dish that descended plain might reappear as *lyonnaise*. Madame Valdinaire remembered that there was an onion and began looking for it. The old desk revealed nothing of the kind, but Madame hastily drew out the drawers of the work-table, for such it appeared to be, and, rummaging about among old spools, rusty buttons, and the remains of Papa Valdinaire's suspenders, found at least three examples of the cook's indispensable friend. Time, neglect, and strange company had done nothing to injure their quality (onions are born with a shell as protective as that of the egg), and soon the true, appetizing aroma was mounting with me to the attic, where Hoeber had, of course, triumphed over the fire, and the eggs, which were *'juste à la pointe.'*

Such are the feasts of Bohemia, and good old France is always ready, even in her remotest poverty, with wine, delicious butter, bread, and fruit. To Hoeber, after what he had done, anything would have been permitted, and when he rose from the table, peered about in dark corners, and finally lifted a corner of the cloth and searched under the table, his answer to the astonished enquiries of his hostess was, 'I'm only looking for the butter.' Then, taking upon himself to place the superbly decorated 'Urne Funéraire' upon the board, he shouted,

'And we can all be sure that there's no veal in *this* salad!'

Letters from home and other circumstances at last fixed our date and plans for our Italian trip, for which we had been waiting. Before leaving America I had had a present of a visit to Florence from an old family friend. This was to be our next move. Neither of us spoke or knew any Italian, which was a matter of more importance then than now. But I had been gathering *renseignements*, and not a small part of the benefit to us of the Conants' guardianship lay in their being fully equipped with exactly the type of information needed by us. We placed our hesitant feet in their footsteps, and made as few blunders as could have been expected, considering the devitalized intelligence of imitators.

Their economy was ours, and we could not have followed a worthier model. With hand luggage only, mine largely filled with data which were not much used, though much was added, we took our round trip *deuxième* and *troisième classe*, but to our credit never skimped when it came to coppers for the porter. I was not very eager. I knew I was not ready for Italy, and was only going to have a look and expect the real thing later. But ignorance may have sensations. For us, only Paris lay between Brittany and the rocky door of Italy, for we travelled by night in the ordinary *voiture, dames seules*. I watched the night by the window, most of the time vastly entertained by the small happenings at stations, the toy whistle of the train, and the silhouettes of the guards. But toward morning, exhaustion took the place of every other sensation and the bowl of hot *café au lait* and Swiss roll, on the platform at Basle, was one of the supreme sensations of our journey.

Another sensation, of quite an opposite nature, was at Lucerne, for which the bed linen and the Swiss breakfast even did not console me. We had arrived in the afternoon by a grey flat daylight. The Lake, leaden and monotonous, stretched toward a shore which was plainly the opposite bank of the Delaware at Riverton, New Jersey. There was no fog and there were no mountains, so I did not believe them when they told me that Mont Blanc was there, and the rest. I am glad now that it was so, and that the best possible Alpine spectacle was reserved for a supreme impression. We left Lucerne in the morning of a day, the whitest, bluest, and greenest. Immense clouds and dazzling sunshine interchanged their powers. There was no so-called view. The train passed through a tunnel and gorge, where mountain walls rose out of sight just beyond the window of the train. An oyster-white torrent dashed along on the other side where the sun was. Peering out of the window and up the rocky wall, I could see the zenith, the very centre of the monstrous dome, whose centre only was exposed. In it, and for a moment only, the shifting masses opened and a new light flashed, a dazzling slope (ice, was it?) glittered in the very peak of heaven, poised, hanging there on its bed of vapor. It could not be earth, not the rock the train was moving over, not the ground I was chained to. — I was heart-struck, as I was to be in the transept at Beauvais, but no other sight of Nature ever did for me what was bestowed in that brief moment of the awful *nought* between.

**

We went over by the St. Gothard, arriving at the little station standing in snow and ice among black rocks. It was high noon, and the sun blazed through the sparkling, freezing, but quiet atmosphere. How we longed to stay, to walk about in the thin snow, to see purple shadows cleaving grey rock, and fill our lungs with cold purity.

Equally novel was the peace of the great valleys, where Nature and man agree that tidiness is best, and the cows enjoy the result. What could be happier, greener, brighter, cleaner! If there had been a scrap of paper in the world or a chip of wood — they had been used for the morning fire, or a bag had been made of the precious 'journal' to serve many uses. The 'inhabitants,' as seen by the roadside, or conducting donkeys over torrents by low stone bridges, were without the style and reticence we had left behind, and were not to see again. Unlike Brittany also, the people had nothing intrinsically to do with the landscape, except to cultivate it, and we have all heard that at heart they are inseparable from it. How I longed for the 'diligence' and its wide prospect, but at least there was no collection of high-powered cars at the Pass. Tourism had not yet come.

We were above all fortunate (for certainly we planned for no such sophisticated sensation) in the hour of our arrival at choice stages in our advance. We reached Venice at seven P.M., but November 1 is a short day anywhere, and it was a night of low rising moon and high stars, and after the right signification on the right cap-band had joined us, and care had fallen away, we passed into the story without jar or dissonance.

For the true dramatic impression of Venice, short cuts through retired waterways, below great windowless walls, by night, is best; soundless but for the warning call of the boatmen from around dark turns and under low bridges. For our emergence there were the palaces, ghostly over black water, and under the red moon.

* * *

From our German *pension* on the Riva, I wrote home the next day:

Of course the photos of Venice don't look like it, and only a few of the paintings, B.'s water-colors most, though they are too thin and not big enough. The color of it is tea-rose; that is, it goes from a creamy white touched with grey into the softest salmon, and pale yellow with the relief of bits of dark or clear green and intense, no, tender, black.

This morning the sky was a luminous grey almost white. In the afternoon we saw it in sunshine, and I like the white light almost best, because then you have color only, no light and shade. We haven't done anything but walk about and go to the Cathedral. The Doge's Palace isn't the brick-dust color it is generally painted, but the palest ivory, I might say flesh color, with enough black discoloration to make it beyond anything refined and elegant (black discoloration doesn't always do this, does it?); as for San Marco, it seemed to almost bend under its weight of richness. It seems to have been made by a people who loved delicate harmonies of color and understood them as well as any really Oriental people, but would at the same time have exuberant form. Inside, one's first impression is a deep, inexhaustible, golden richness, and you find it to be far richer than you thought. You see what apparently is a fine oak, openwork, carved railing of a superb arabesque design, and you find on feeling it that it is not oak, but a lovely waxy deep yellow *marble*. It is all marble, where it is not gold mosaic and fresco. No, the frescoes are mosaic, too, up in their misty heights, but marble sounds like coldness, and this is warm and deep and not shiny, but like old wood, worn by the hand of many generations.

— 161 —

It is clear that the term *patine* was unknown to the writer, who also before the great outer staircase of the Doge's Palace found it to be 'most like a delicate old lace fan with mother-of-pearl sticks, almost ready to fall apart in its mellow fragility.'

* * *

The afternoon we gondola'd to Murano with the Powells differed from every other, though the *décor* had the same *fond* washed in with cool, pale tones. But the lighting was of the rich, harvest-color of August. It was summer, heavy with indolence, warmth, and silence, as we floated and heard only faint water-sounds. Our shadow was Rubens green when we got upon the Lagoon, but in the canal, the sun, beating in long hot rays on melons, oranges, tomatoes, and cabbages, both in and out of the canal, turned strong faces and limbs russet, and their modelling purple, and flaunting itself around the traditional dyed sails, and laying a sapphire shadow beside every projection, showed us what it could do in Venice.

Murano, when we approached, seemed even more deeply steeped in color and indolence, but the glass factory which we entered, as if it had been a cave, directly from the Lagoon, was, though after all only a large barn — its wall-sized entrance opening upon the Lagoon — a scene of persistent production by magicians in white paper caps, who stood behind long tables, manipulating with easy grace their simple tools and small furnaces. There were trays, of course, holding beads of all kinds, and a few shelves with examples of fairy substance and color, familiar even to us, and we could watch the miracle being performed without interrupting it, as could also any passer-by, as if it had been a blacksmith's shop. The difference being that the inhabitants being Italian and having knowledge, however vagabond, of the arts, and respecting the great fame of the industry of their island as well as extreme pride in it, would never have committed any indiscretion within the great portal.

I knew for the rest of my life then, as we floated away at an even richer hour, that I had been witnessing the only way of producing the best things of their kind, in what are unjustly called the 'lesser arts.' A few skilled workmen, in an appropriate and natural environment, working upon individual pieces, with always the possibility of even small individual invention, is the true, the right, productive group. There is no other way to carry on the union of brain and hand, of which the storehouse of the ages attests the value.

* * *

Not only because it would have been practically impossible, in so short a visit, but because I had no inclination, I did not work, not even sketching, in Italy. I felt that if any absorption were to take place, it must be in some other way. For tapping the crust of my ignorance, the good Powells (our at once discovered English friends), because so restrained, one might almost say, so determinedly sure in a certain direction, were far better for me than up-to-date expertism would have been. Mr. P., who was a musician, in fact organist at the Canterbury Cathedral, was an emotionalist, like me, and 'got it,' one might have said, by breathing. He did not care much, back of his big black beard, for being interrupted in his joy by even the same type of rapture in others. Mrs. Powell stood behind us with her book, ready for any sudden reversion to the purely mental that might occur to the hedonists, in regard to a name or date. When with them, I abandoned myself to the Carpaccios, Bellinis, and others of their worship.

When Mr. P. found that I admired Rubens, his face fell, much as if I had confessed to being the Scarlet Woman. His æsthetic sensitiveness was extreme; my appetite was voracious. They came every year for their holiday to Italy, as do many of the English. They knew exactly what they wanted; I was a little like a spaniel who wished to investigate the whole garden. The garden, I knew, although walled by the sea, had no bounds. Its extent was both vertical and horizontal. Rich layers of the harvest of creative minds had been gathering for a thousand, fifteen hundred years. Every type, every direction, was supported by its own technical will to express. Italy had been 'nursed upon the broad lap of Nature.' All the idealism, as well as all the materialism of two great systems of religion, had inspired her. The same sun shone upon me, perhaps would do so for the six days that were my portion.

I must take away all I could carry, all, I might say, that was portable, for me, and I have never really lost anything that I made mine in those six days in Venice.

***

We spent two weeks in Florence. I would not go to Rome, to 'have a look.' I must have that at another time and way. But Florence was ungrateful for our favor. A bitter, draughty wind laid me up in a damp chilly *pension* for most of the time, for it was November, though Venice had mistaken the date. I carried away from Florence a smaller *recolte*. It was to have more for me later, but I learned of another and austerer aspect of Italy's universal genius. Without either a Fromentin or a Powell, I walked and stood in the galleries. My very bones seemed to acquire a firmer fibre, as I looked at the Renaissance sculpture and the Bronze Boar and knew what I needed; that inner fibrous force, which in Nature I did not spontaneously perceive, but which in Art I could not do without. Yet in the work I above all and constantly returned to, Titian's portrait of a 'Young Florentine Gentleman, Unknown,' there was only sufficient body to convey the spirit. From the wall where it then hung, one could not approach it very near, and I am sure that its author intended its domination to come from afar and a high position. I believe that the drama of mind in an individual has never been presented before or since as it is potent in this portrait, and with less elaboration of means. It shows a young man disdainful of being 'painted,' a mentally lonely mind, born at the wrong date, and conscious of the anachronism. Perhaps an Englishman, or of other mixed parentage. This theory exists. At all events, in the thin reddish hair and veiled grey eyes, a Mediterranean strain seems possible. Remembering this example, one may be sure of what the ideal of portraiture should be; one can learn what *must* be present and what may be ignored. Alas, this implies a subject to which such an ideal of treatment may be applied. But the broad opportunity which portraiture offers lies in the fact that, when personality is lacking, treatment, on its own account, design, color, much that is independent of character, is ready and waiting to be used. Titian at his best, whether he merges himself — unconsciously, of course — in a fascinating personality, and cuts out, as in the instance in hand, all else, as encumbrance, or finds his pleasure and satisfies his taste in sensuous, external qualities, is always Titian.

What I brought away from Italy is only valuable as one instance of what a young observer may keep and return to as a permanent possession, applicable to any future effort. It is like the health one stores up in a two months' outing in the mountains, a many-sided well-being which shows itself in some result of the following winter's effort, and shows it against all odds of adverse circumstances. That first short glimpse of Italy has never ceased to warm my mental vision; its sunlit particles are still glowing in the dark corners of consciousness: the energy of its age-long production; its long, long summer; the weight of its immense harvest, has set a standard with which other peoples, if they are honest, other periods, must compare themselves and the volume and vitality of their productions in Art. But a humble mind may also be an undiscouraged one, and the multiple splendor of the feast may be absorbed by a very crude participant, who, even after a very brief admission, will have got, once for all, the knowledge that in art, values in any direction of their period and setting are absolute, as is history, to whoever has the power to discover them; the narrow shadows of less richly endowed periods will be powerless to obscure them, and they will emerge between the mists of change as long as their physical survival is able to support their message.

Art has its vintages, like wine, whose qualities no one disputes, which are always supported by precious reality, and of which the causes, however obscure, are as absolute as the course of the stars. But more than all that which remains, and always in relation to the most vital examples, is a rather clear sense of the unconscious state of mind in the creator. It emanates as a sort of childlike integrity, a state of being in the practice of his art, and in painting actually radiating from the canvas, it takes an important part in the magnetism, the attraction, the work projects. This, of course, had many variations. The artist might be the pet or tool of sovereigns, or of a school. He was in any case a humble individual in his relation to Pope or patron, by whom it was expected that he would do his best. True the gods were with him. Nervous energy was above par. Everything got itself done often better than might have been expected even by the artist himself. Yet no one found the picture nearer to perfection than it ought to be. An unusual degree of the power to express drama and emotion was sure to be admired, and the group of fur-trimmed connoisseurs who came to congratulate the artist's employer may be pretty well counted on to have been especially struck by a bit of advanced realism, the shadow of a fly's leg, or the coursing tear upon the virgin's cheek, or even a new type of busy devil, made up of a greater than usual variety of bestial attributes.

The artist's position toward his art, and himself in regard to it, seems to have been, in those happy centuries, the best ever. Whatever his domestic troubles, his debts or disappointments in regard to his pay, however powerfully self may have obtruded its demands when work stopped, during the long hours of performance he was free of everything but It, and he awoke from it and returned to life and himself, as from sleep. How he would have stared if friend or patron had whispered to him of 'self-expression,' though all the time the obscure stamp of what was himself was slowly appearing upon the work, never to be obscured!

* * *

Turning northward, by the Riviera, with a memorable détour to Siena, our six weeks was about spent when we again turned aside, to 'lay a wreath' upon the altar whence had been brought living embers, treasured by one of us. Avignon in Provence, my father's native city, though he saw the light first in Nîmes near by, must be visited. If this was filial duty, what an urgently welcome one it was! — and only the first of several pilgrimages thither. My father had always wanted me to see it first when 'les Amandiers' were in blossom, but even November and the whistling cold of the Mistral, which visited Avignon at the same time we did, could not destroy the picture. Grey rocks, olive trees of slightly lighter shade, and a steady, brilliant sun remained what they always had been, and at Arles, Les Alychamps, the day we walked there, was a golden arbor dropping flakes upon the lines of empty sarcophagi. But in all these little cities, History and the humble homes of unimportant life were mingled. There was no middle ground (except that at any time from one of these 'humble homes' might emerge the child bearing what would be one of the great names of France), but Greece and Rome at their grandest were present always. At our little hotel, a charming classic column — remaining from a temple, of course — was embedded in, and perhaps supported, the corner of the house, just outside our window. Christianity made its appearance, near by, in Romanesque, in the church of Saint Trophème, and of course within the museum, which was an ancient palace of the Castellane. At Nîmes, Les Arènes and the Maison Carrée were close to the pretty public garden, where French people and their babies sat and played in the sun.

The Rhone, grey and white from its snowy source, had permitted the deep Gothic thrust, which, as always, had left, with its depredations, the endurance and projectile strength of the Northern race.

The people — the women especially, tall, *lancées*, with proud carriage, and faces more sculptured than are to be found now, in either Greece or Italy. Where was one? What time was it? In the composite that had survived, there was a romantic, an imaginative *résumé*, like the photographs that were made some years ago of perhaps twenty superimposed heads and which, registering faintly only the eccentricities of each, presented finally only the large forms, the general, and therefore, to every one's surprise, something more noble than any one of the heads that had taken part in the composite. From a group of average people emerged a head that might have been a poet's idea of Saint John, or Dante's Beatrice. For whatever reason, the grand sort of beauty of the Arlesian women, and which is to be found in the whole region, is a definite fact, and might easily have had a bearing upon the Courts of Love and the Birth of Chivalry; the placing of woman as a being to be adored, and in mentality the equal of the men of the period. Precious elements had been brought from Greece and Rome, not in material things, but in the blood, in fire and energy and idealism, which, transplanted, were a precious seed for France, and have not lost their germinating power; and that they have been met and sustained by the infusion of the Nordic strain accounts for the fair skin, dark blue eyes, and strong features, often seen. My father was a striking example of this, not at all the predominating type of

FLORA WHITNEY

homme du midi, who is dark, sprightly, and often insignificant, Ligurian — that is, aboriginal — and 'Mittel Europa.'

* * *

The museum and even Saint Trophème yielded us only groping sensations of pleasure, as we knew nothing of Romanesque. From eggs-on-end cobblestones and absence of sidewalk in Arles, we soon learned to save our bruised feet by leaping from one doorstep to another. To the Pont d'Avignon we, of course, gave full heed. But the Papal Palace was, above all, after the Greek and Roman remains, impressive to me in its bold, severe upwardness. Alas, how often I am reminded of it in the streets of New York, but it is the Godolphin Arabian of the new architecture, for it has bred a type where windows — those acres of perforation in a thin surface which has no *apparent* strength — are partly concealed by endless verticals of construction. Inside, the Papal Palace at that time was a barracks for soldiers, who swarmed in its whitewashed halls. I knew I should return to Provence, as I did several times. Paris was beckoning, as it had in Belgium. Work, a studio, for these I was bound, and to it I went as a needle to the Pole.

* * *

It may be of passing interest to present-day tourists to know that in our six weeks' journey we were only by way of second- and third-class, by train; and *pension*, never hotel; we spent just $107 apiece and had no sense of being penurious.

As we drew near Paris, our anxiety as to our next settled lodging obscured nearly everything else for a time; and I give thanks that, although our final choice was humble, it was entirely free from the vulgarity that had so sullied the months at the *pension* Villeneuve. As we climbed the waxed stairs of '30 rue Vaugirard, *maison meublé*,' we might easily have met Balzac, Flaubert, or even Madame Bovary herself.

There were five flights for us, but easy, broad, spotless, and without taint of late decades. I would like to boast openly that I have lived in an attic in Paris, a tiny chamber in the mansard, with a dormer window opening its *croissée* eastward and sunward. The window would hold a plant or two, and outside was the leaden ledge that took the rain on stormy days. Leaning out one could look down upon the Senate, grey and dignified, and the Luxembourg Gallery was very near. The iron railing of the garden was across the way.

There was a small white-panelled chimney-piece, just where the long slope of the dormer permitted, and a tiny cupboard in the wall space between. Nothing had been even touched by late nineteenth century. The bed, against the end wall, was the purest bourgeois, plain and bunchy, of course, with dark green cotton curtains, scanty, for which I was thankful. The sheets were of a grey *toile* I might have painted on, but they had known strenuous lavage. At my first plunge into them they seemed harsh, but though robust were somehow good, and when I had to leave them for others, I missed their force and tang. The carpet, very old and patched, had once been velvet, and in the not quite fitting corners, one saw that it covered a tiled parquet. It was a place where anything that was purely French, or that was possible in an attic in the Quartier Latin, of the bourgeois provincial order, might have taken place. It might have been the first stand before greater poverty intervened of any of those ambitious youths of the nineteenth, who left their obscure provincial birthplace, to starve, or nearly, in the hard years of their way to fame in Paris.

It was a house of silence. The other occupants of lower *étages* had not the same hours, and we met no one on the stairs. We saw Jean, the valet, only once during the day, if we happened to be in at his regular call. After that, there being no bell, he was as lost to us as yesterday's dew.

Without our youth and health, there would have been serious drawbacks. No food of any kind was served in the house. We made our own chocolate by lamplight on dark winter mornings. Other meals we 'found' outside. We might have a tiny wood fire, for the chill was great, but counting Jean's services for this it would have been a hideous extravagance. But there was a damp cold we had felt before, and soon I had bought a stove for four francs, about as large as a quart pot, on the *pavé*. For this we carried in our own fuel from the *épicerie* near by. It was never a large parcel, and I learned the fire recipe for comfort of this size: a morsel of *feu diabolique*, bits of charcoal, a few splinters of wood, and two or three lumps of coal. How many of my home letters were written under the lamp on the table *à tout faire*, within easy reach of the stove and supplies, which were called for every five minutes! Very often after our early departure we did not come in until after eight P.M. Then it was that the chill mustiness of innumerable Paris winters met us when we unlocked our doors.

No fuel in the cupboard, and often we earned our bit of comfort by a long descent to the street, on a cold December night, in pouring rain, returning with our newspaper parcel, dripping, but content, though very weary.

Sometimes for these sallies, when I went alone, I threw a shawl over my head in true *paysanne*, a perfect disguise, and such get nothing but respect from the passer-by. The rain felt good on my face, as I hurried along. One night when we went out together on the same errand in the steady downpour, and were perhaps chattering as we went, an upholsterer's boy in his long blouse, carrying an armchair in the white, legs upward, on his head, stopped before us and said with mischievous deference, 'Voulez-vous vous asseoir, Mademoiselle?'

Not far below us, at Number 36, there was a high gateway opening into a *caserne*, a big courtyard with rough cobblestones and low white buildings with peaked roofs, and an air of the *dix-septième*. It was the quarters of the 'Cuirassiers de l'Opéra.' Horses' hoofs have a very special sound on the asphalt, on wet nights, and often, lying awake in my rough comfortable bed, with the tiny glow of our small fire glimmering on the ceiling, I have heard the cuirassiers returning from their guardianship of the *grande monde*, at two A.M., and, turning the corner of the rue Tournon, the rich irregularity of the big deliberate tread pounding the *pavé* with rhythmic majesty. Often I had to leap from my warm nest to lean far over the wet window-sill and gaze down at gleaming helmets and cuirasses beaten by long streams of black horsehair; at the sheen of the rain on the great horses, and the straight, indifferent backs of the riders; the turn in at the *caserne*, and the dying resonance of the hoofbeats.

Fascinating nocturnal spectacle — lost finally in night and storm, one of the bold salients of memory, complete, unspoiled, and unforgettable.

* * *

During this winter, daily work at the Passage des Panorames was my program. The 'Passage' was the downtown Julien Cours. Entrance was from the Boulevard. The place might have been called 'ripe to richness.' Its flavor was much less dilettante than the rue de Berri, but not much more talent was evident. It had a rougher *ensemble*. What one got was chiefly practice. I continued to draw, as there was even less elbow-room than at the rue de Berri.

My persistence at the Julien Cours during my second winter in Paris was owing to its general, non-specific nature. I might have delivered myself, of course, to an individual master. There were several of high repute who admitted disciples. By an instinct I could not resist, I shrank from the committal, although there would have been contacts resulting from it of high value and interest. I saw no special direction in any exhibited work (I fear to say it), among the living, that I felt like joining. At Julien's one had not to think of adherence, and I held in abhorrence the habit of floating about from one *atelier* to another, by which procedure many had the hope of stumbling upon the precious 'key.'

The criticism, as such, was small, and, as in the rue de Berri, there was no theory. What came to me from overhearing did not apply to me, and what I got was chiefly encouragement to keep on as I was going. I am not sure that there is not a good deal to be said for silent treatment in Art. All special direction and theory are liable — almost certain — to be in error, sooner or later. In Art as in Religion, Faith is necessary — indispensable, in fact. What the student above all needs is to have his resources increased by the presence of a master whom he believes in, not perhaps as a prophet or adopted divinity, but one who is in unison with a living world, of various views, all of whose roots are deep, tried, and nourished by the truth, or rather the truths that Nature will reveal to the seeker. He is the present embodiment of performance in art, better called the one sent, representing all. He is serious, quiet, a personality that has striven. Nothing breaks the sobriety of his visit. There is never the least social or offhand intercourse. His thoughtful consideration of your drawing will be impartial. He will do you justice and will be gracious toward your earnestness, but it will be a simple matter for him to probe your weakness. He is a Parisian, though probably of provincial origin. He is one of the esteemed of his day and generation in the world of French Art. How much he has seen! How great is his experience! How great his reverence! If his interest is slight, you suffer. If he seems to recognize in you some evidence of power to come, you will feel it in his few concise words as he passes on. Courage and persistence to perceive the truth flame up and stronger, quicker pulses feed subconscious force.

The men who criticised at Julien's were not great, but they had beliefs. Their work was personal and unmistakable, but they laid down no laws of their own invention. Never did the least sign of a desire to teach their personal view impinge upon their delivery of the 'message' to students. The great effect of this large general method, if method it was, was in the faith one had in it, or it might be said in the High Priest who served it. I venerated his consecration, his office, and this veneration opened the breach toward those, however small, creeping conquests I might achieve, in power to express the truth which renewed vision could directly pursue. The 'message' was the incoming tide upon which any species of seaworthy craft could be lifted over the bar.

Fortunate is the pupil whose master brings with him far more than he personally contains or is aware of, as something communicated. A student's first conceptions of Art should not be delivered to him in small packages. He should find in his masters more than is given to him. Or, let him feel only a sense of his relation to Art, to the Subject, his preceptors only liberating him upon the road, warming his desire toward what he is attempting to do, not showing him the overmuch and the myriad possibilities of it, but the simplest solution. He must find out the secrets for himself later, if ever.

The immense value to the student, in Paris, lies in the place itself. He cannot step out of the *cours* without having his crass judgments in regard to art developed, adjusted, poised. Everything is there. It is his own fault if he does not perceive. The rapid, constant invention of the World Magician is always going on; she eventually casts away many of her experiments, and is perfectly aware that she *may* do so even when in the very heat of creation. But she is loyal; she preserves; she has thousands of pigeon-holes where are kept fragments of changes and novelties, never despised by *l'histoire de l'art française*, and of the rest of the world. She will show you, if you take the trouble to look, the long series in which your decade will take part, a brick of more or less

value, as will be proved by time. The student may get, once
for all, in Paris, an inescapable sense of relation, not to be
found elsewhere, and Idealism has never been less sentimental, except perhaps in Greece.

* * *

From one student in the *cours* that winter, I received light
and leading, though not in any word she ever spoke. She
was an American from California. Her story, when I heard
it, was that she had worked in an Art School there; that her
father, having business in France, had brought her with him
for a limited chance of studying in Paris. It was clear that
neither of them knew anything of this but the name. Her
father had deposited her in a *pension* and left. She knew no
one, and not one word of French. She was rough, silent,
and difficult of approach. She had plain, coarse features
and buffalo manners to hide her extreme sensitiveness.
She hated Paris and everything French. This I learned
later when I persuaded her to go out to lunch with me. I
saw her first making her way to her place in the front row
among the low stools, close to the model stand. 'Maree,
Maree, où est mon taberay de pal? Où est mon taberay de
pal?' she shouted. She would use no wooden-seated substi-
tute, and I soon saw why this persistence was required.
The 'tabouret de paille' was flexible, elastic, one could sway
about on it, a means to an end necessary to her production,
but causing great clamor in the *cours*, especially among the
French, who hated her. Cries of 'Oh, Mees Braddy!... Oh,
Mees Brad-dy!' could be heard, but were entirely unnoticed
by her. When settled, her progress was *infime*. She drew,
only using a sheet of rich white paper, and a stick of broken,
not sharpened, charcoal (broken charcoal has an edge finer
than can be made with a knife). She held her charcoal
lightly in her very extraordinary fingers. There was complete diversity between her hands, her harsh features, and
whole remaining person. Her hands were soft, pulpy,

tender, with long, full fingers, seeming to be ready to melt with a kind of refined sensuousness. Nothing ever seemed right in her arrangements. She would not approach the paper when the model was out of the pose so little that no one else noticed it. She must have the whole, the perfect rhythm, for the slightest touch, and how long her travail was before the charcoal was permitted to reach the paper! She crouched on her tabouret, struggling toward the slightest visible performance. But that touch was magical and never anything else. Her drawings were living breath upon the paper, which, for her, also modelled. How could form, flesh, be expressed by those occasional erratic trails, so powerful as leaders of the eye toward what she felt. The masters groaned joyfully over them, with true French seizure of any form of superiority. 'Mais...mais...ce sont les desseins de Maître.' Some said she drew like Leonardo (not a line of whom she had ever seen), and looked at her, wondering, amazed, at the rude branch from which the rich fruit hung. When she attempted to paint, the power and obstinacy of the medium were entirely beyond her control, and as *she* would not give in, much time would have been required to conquer it, her desire, or her conception, being mature and exorbitant.

I was obliged to leave the *cours* for a few days and when I returned her place was empty, and I never saw her again or could find any trace of her. I have always hoped that some catalogue, some list, would bring her again into knowledgeable distance, but she was one of the gifted who have no sense of their own value, so far do their dreams carry them beyond what they do, and discouragement, with such, may submerge effort. So the rarest appears and floats away while the ordinary we have always with us.

* * *

A student in Art must never expect regular progress or to 'acquire' systematically. The gods will send him messages from strange places and at unexpected times. Long periods of apparent stagnation will occur, and, after what he has lamented as time lost, 'the fruitful hours of still increase' will find him suddenly on a new elevation.

A studio, even a poor one, is indispensable for *recueillement*, even if little gets done in it. At Number 15 rue Notre Dame des Champs, a long winding street in our quarter, was found a small working place, literally on the ground floor, for its two-leaved and very insecure door opened immediately from the snow and puddles of the court. It was nothing, in fact, but a one-story lean-to with a window in the roof, into which it would have been easy for more favored neighbors to peer if they had been interested in either me or my blunders. But all of us were of the same *culte*. All poor and all striving. No one interfered with me for even a little teasing (waterproof and cotton gloves again, perhaps). They had other hours than mine, and I seldom met any one in the court. The concierge was obliging and sympathetic. It is well to have a friend at the portal, which always maintains its dignity in France, no matter what it opens upon.

One must be more than a beginner to be able to refuse the lure of the picturesque, and when it is found in a person of great beauty, it is irresistible. Every one envied me who heard that Louise Kinsella would pose for me. She was one of two charming sisters of the colony at Concarneau. They were of Irish origin and might have been inheritors of what the Spanish Armada left upon the fatal shores of the Island. Louise, however, was the palest of blondes. I had not yet heard of Kathleen O'Houlihan, or I should have seen that she was incarnate of that magic being. Any name, except Deirdré, from the long lists of Irish poetry, would have suited her. She wore a loose, flowing gown of brown cloth and a cloak of the same, into the hood of which flowed the flossy strands of her light golden hair. Without being large, her face had almost sibylline grandeur and a luminous pallor shone upon it, lifted as it generally was, and as I had often seen her gliding alone over the roads at Concarneau. Her eyes were pure Irish, grey, long, superbly drawn, and wide apart. In spite of her appearance of other-worldness, the sibyl was prompt, patient, and never weary. What was weather to her? She lifted her long skirts and came through the grey mud of Paris, as she would have come through the Glen in a storm, on some errand of warning.

I soon found that she was an *œuvre* already, and not to be much disposed by me, though she would have been ready for any manipulation. I did her standing, her grand, pale countenance lifted toward the light, in profile, a pearl against the shadowy suggestions of her dark costume and the darker background. No easy matter to solve the 'simple' problem, and although I got the sense of her beauty and of light upon it, and taught myself a good deal about a pearl's passage into darkness where its so-called edge meets it, a brown picture, with a light spot in the midst, is not a good picture, nor satisfying, and I was surprised when it was accepted and given a centre wall at the Salon, though if it had any other notice I never knew of it. Of course I gave her the portrait.

After I left Paris, I did not hear of my lovely model for years, and when I did, it was to learn that she had passed from her own shadow to a deeper one, or perhaps to Light. I could not have imagined her growing old or changing. She was a poem and the best of these are never very long.

VII

AN ENGLISH VISIT

UPON the dual origin which was the birthright Nature had awarded me, France had absorbed and fixed a pursuing lover, but one who remembered the keen onset of an unexpected emotion felt on her approach during a night of fog on her other parent shore. Hidden by night, and a heavy veil besides, the name if not the sight of England had sounded — one of those oracular messages straight from the sources of destiny that pierce and settle in the heart and are never withdrawn from it. Lost as I was in the very present claims of the *cours*, and my abandonment to the magic of even the little I then knew of France, the name had caught me a second time when an English girl at the *cours*, half demented with homesickness, had cried out, in a broken voice, 'England!... England!...' The others had laughed, and teased her; I did not. I seemed to know her pain and love, and what caused it.

* * *

During the early spring days of our second year in Paris, I heard from an old friend in Cambridge, an American girl who had married George, the eldest of the sons of Charles Darwin. She demanded a visit, and soon, as the gay season in Cambridge was approaching. Her husband was at that time Plumian Professor of Mathematical Astronomy, Fellow of Trinity, and as I had always known, one of the leading men in the University. They, with their four children, lived at Newnham Grange, through whose garden the Cam, hidden by high banks and big trees, pursued its quiet and narrow way. But I knew nought of this, nor of the other joys I was about to taste. It would be my first adventure alone, and the prospect of the Channel and the various changes to be made were almost prohibitive. But go I must — I knew that. Preparation, too, was necessary, and exactly for what, I did not know. I was invited for an indefinite visit, but decided to return in a week or ten days, at most.

We had much anxiety as to the summer, and I knew that I was leaving the attic in the rue Vaugirard, probably forever, as pressure for my return home was beginning to be urgent. Ended were those days, which with all their privations and discomforts I felt, and rightly, would never be mine again. I did not know then, what I have since learned, that the best days are those which are both busy and carefree, and such were these. 'Busy' must mean the work of one's choice, planned and accomplished, friendship, and the open road.

I was to return to Paris, but to what? My cousin had persuaded me to undertake our living in the studio. 'Other people live in their studios, why should not we in mine? Beds could be hired, etc....' I had consented reluctantly, but without realizing how much worse it was to be than my fears. The Channel crossing on a bad night I had thought I knew how to dread, but it was hideous far beyond my feeble imagination. Sleepless misery, in a revolting scene of suffering, endless delays of debarkation which seem to an exasperated memory to have been without food or drink, and which are recorded only to give emphasis to the sweetness of an opening scene.

Crossing from Dieppe to New Haven is rather a countrified way of leaping the ramparts of Empire, but it holds the inestimable privilege of coming at once upon the English landscape and especial characteristics. I saw it without the interference of even the quiet English way of being a busy port and town. At least, memory has it that I might as well have been rowed across, pushing prow upon a beach from which soft, pale green lawns rolled skyward, not too steeply to bear majestic groups of great trees, sometimes leaning slightly, to form faultless composition. The weather was mild; sun breaking mistily through, presenting fresh unaccented aspects of form, and so discarding all monotony. The 'difference' lay in the infinitely greater number of leaves the branches bore than I had ever seen upon an American tree. They hung in huge moulded masses, the leaves being generally small and compactly placed to form broad shadow and relief. I remembered Harding's drawings, which I had considered to be imaginative rendering for effect; but Nature it was to whom they were owing, and climate, Nature's most potent tool. Harding had only bestowed admiration and fidelity, and the power to express these emotions.

I passed through London without looking her way, not wishing to take an unconsidered, casual glance at her, knowing that I would soon have a better chance, and longing only to see my friend's face upon the platform at Cambridge.

* * *

My first waking in the big, chintz-hung guest-room at Newnham Grange is one of the jewel-set markers of memory. It was a near-by cuckoo-clock that woke me (I found out later that it was the fellow himself), and a pink-calico-clad houri came next, pulling aside curtains and arranging the bath. The sun poured in, and through its beams I could see across a meadow and under huge trees. Another window was hung, without, by a rich drapery of lilac wistaria, in full bloom, and when I sprang from my bed and put my head out, there was a cherry tree full of 'ripe ones,' just outside, also bird song; and a robin, making the best of the feast, superseded the cuckoo, and children of English voice and speech were in the garden below.

My friend Maud had discovered that for brittle-nerved

Americans the day began too soon if it opened by family breakfast downstairs. She did not ask me if I shared her opinion, and, although her husband had a slightly contemptuous smile on the subject, we, in our separate nests, had trays with full English menus, and descended when we pleased before luncheon: a life-saving plan. Workers, by nature, cannot be agreeable all day, even when they have been kindly presented with the luxury of idleness. One must be a professional visitor to have a steady appetite for conversation. The English manage, by becoming monosyllabic, and without reproach. I watched the very nice-looking little wife of one of the most agreeable of the young professors, and saw that she did not speak at all during the whole evening (it was a dinner). She fell to my lot before the men came in, and I could glean nothing but 'yes' and 'no,' even by varied effort; but she did not seem either shy or embarrassed, or to feel that she was failing in an obligation.

I soon gave up trying to express all I felt. I knew myself to be a plant whose roots were expanding in a deep warm soil, its own, but never felt before. Beauty, native and homogeneous — not a jarring or irrelevant passage anywhere — was always present. Mr. Darwin left his protected study and library, where I soon observed that he was steadily concealed, and led me about great courts, and by charming bridges over the still waters where undergraduates floated with dog and book. Strange that, under the stately towers, gateways, and walls of Gothic elegance, the England I already knew could circulate and look at home. Was this because it was all a slowly accumulated inheritance, without break, from a germ literally prehistoric? To one nurtured on the intimate account (it seemed to be almost contemporaneous) of Thackeray, Leech, and Du Maurier, a familiar figure was to be met at every corner. But in the general summing-up of what one might call essential England, in such a place, especially in silent, deep-shaded courts and alleys, Tennyson was above all present. His lines they were that kept rising in my mind, and I continually heard also fragments of Matthew Arnold's deep-toned elegies. From the old bells of Great Saint Mary's, I heard the Westminster chimes (that is, they are so called) for the first time, and have suffered in hearing them, since then, calling for such different reason, from the many stories of commerce.

*_**

As these fragments of experience are those of a light-hearted young person, perhaps she may be pardoned for a few impressions *sur place* ——

They have had people to dine both evenings. For the first, there were two men only, both very distinguished scholars; Mr. Robertson Smith, the Librarian who contains the whole British Encyclopædia, and a Mr. Middleton of Middleton, a Professor and Lecturer on the Fine Arts. They look middle-aged, but are not. Mr. R. S. is like a little Scotch terrier, with every hair of him a telephone wire into storehouses full of facts. You only have to take off the receiver, and it comes pouring out in a monotonous voice, nothing about him moving but his lower jaw. Mr. M. is long, narrow, gentle, bald, and has much more temperament and no less 'larnin'.' I wore my blue dress, and had my gold combs in my hair, otherwise 'no jewels.' I looked rather nice. Mr. Middleton knew it and observed me furtively during dinner. But Mr. R. S. would just as leave I had been bound in calf.

Luncheon to-day with Mr. Middleton. Mr. Darwin went with us. Maud appeared in white muslin and lace, white hat and feathers — an English beauty, if she *is* American, with her grand braids of golden hair and splendid blue eyes. I was sorry for her that her visiting friend had nothing effective to wear. In a corner of the Great Court of Kings, we found Mr. M.'s rooms. There was one other man, a Mr. Wilfrid Blunt, well known in politics here; had much to do with Araby Bey in the East; great Home-Ruler, has been in prison for four months for having been thought to have stirred up insurrection in Ireland. His meekness, Mr. M., received us very graciously, in his little rooms full of early Italian and Renaissance reproductions, etc. The luncheon was very informal, the men guests and host waiting on the table. They put the finished dishes on the hearth-rug, with the elegance of established custom in a refined *milieu*. (By these simplifications, 'Fellows,' who are never well off are able to entertain in their rooms very delightfully.)

After luncheon Mr. M. showed us his collection, and we all talked very learnedly. Mr. W. B. thought he knew something about Art, too, and condescended to a remark now and then. Then we all went to King's Chapel.

Here my feeble pen refused to lisp platitudes, and does still. It was the custom at Newnham to go to King's Chapel for Sunday morning service, and to Trinity for evensong. This made Sunday for me the best of days at all points. I had heard scarcely any music since leaving America, and this in itself would have fixed my happiness, even without the satisfaction of all the rest. Our party was Maud, the three older children, and myself, Mr. D. accompanying, but, as a Fellow and much besides, occupying a different throne. But we, too, as his family and adherents, were also among the chosen — we might pass under the great dividing Gothic screen where was the organ (or part of it), leaving the congregation in the *anti-chambre* of the chapel. The *élite*, who were about the number to fill the choir-stalls, might take their places in these, under high black-oaken canopies, behind reading-desks of the same, and turn the leaves of enormous in-folio prayer-books which lay upon them. But the most lofty and beautiful of all Gothic in England, and the succession of nearly as lofty windows, with glass, not brilliant, but satisfying to the limit of desire in design and tone, were subduant to any pride of place an interloper might feel in finding herself as near to occupying a Bishop's throne as she would ever come.

How delightful the walk home, joined by one's new friends among the Fellows, to be escorted to the Backs, and the Fellows' Garden of Trinity. How seldom are Peace and Novelty found hand in hand, especially when both are wrapt in beauty. At Newnham there was no retirement after this, for the rest of the day. Guests to luncheon, callers all the afternoon. Tea, in such weather, in the garden, under the

MRS. JAMES B. DRINKER AND SON

copper beech, which hung over the river. Having come directly from an *atelier* in Paris, and being rather full of all which this implied, I began by expanding upon what, even in new and fascinating scenes, I could not forget. But I soon found that a polite silence followed any mention of French Art, and the Lecturer on the Fine Arts had never heard of Bastien Le Page, or any other contemporary artist just across the Channel. But I had little time for any but instant impressions. I had expected to find a kind of static calm in England, but every one, including myself, seemed to be busy. In spite of the telephone, Maud was constantly writing and posting notes. They would be delivered in an hour or two. Bicycles continually flew by the windows which gave on the road, and were generally pedalled by undergraduates, but bulging scholastic gowns, mortar boards, and flying grey beards were to be seen as often, and were equally fearless and hurried: and, of course, there were all the girls from Girton and Newnham Colleges, whom one should honor for their preoccupation with matters more important than the fit of skirts and shirt-waists.

Even old ladies going out to tea might be met wheeling steadily in black lace and floating veils. Another swift goer was the butcher's cart. The pony never trotted other than briskly, and I enjoyed the sharp patter of his hoofs on Silverton Bridge. Pedestrians also stepped forth eagerly, as if just starting on a ten-mile walk, and were generally in pairs and very importantly conversing.

Noteworthy functions followed each other swiftly. The dinner at the Vice-Chancellor's Lodge soon occurred. The D.'s said it would be dull, but that I should see one of this kind. The Vice-Chancellor's 'Lodge' was Pembroke College, historic with a poignant significance, for Bishop Ridley had been led from it to the fires of Smithfield.

It was a big house; dark carved oak, everywhere. Many menservants were standing about, but not in livery, and before I had time to notice this, I observed a *distingué*-looking young person at the top of the staircase, saying to myself, 'At least, there is one young one, and I hope he will fall to my lot.' But, alas, as we passed him, he murmured to Mr. Darwin, 'This way please, sir.' Our host and hostess were a nice, comfortable-looking couple, the Vice-Chancellor a small, stout, elderly gentleman, with a high collar and wearing bands with his otherwise worldly, evening coat.

Every one [my letter says] looked very proper, and there were no frumps, though some of the coiffures were very queer. The men were mostly elderly, but they gave me the only youngish one, a Scotchman, very clever and talkable, and as I had on my other side an eccentric and jolly professor of anatomy, I had a 'monstrous good time.' Of course, it was a huge table (Maud told me there were thirty-seven guests), and covered with massive silver and flowers. Among other fruits, one muskmelon was offered with the faintest shade of importance. Its seeds remained as Nature had made them, but it did not blush for this informality, and had a very delicate flavor. When the 'cloth' (which means long strips of damask linen laid along the edge of the table) was removed, the rich dark mahogany shone out, with resplendent age-old *patine*. Two servants then carried about a massive silver ewer, and a basin of equal proportion and richness, one of the men assisting with a long damask napkin. Each guest held a corner of his own serviette in the trickling stream from the ewer, and wiped his hands and lips, but the male guests also dipped their fingers in the basin, and touched the backs of their ears. This was far more picturesque than finger-bowls, and more delicate than the French *rinse-bouche*. I made as if it was no more a novelty to me than to the other guests, whose conversation flowed on uninterruptedly, but soon I could not refrain from asking Mr. Neil what it meant. 'An old custom,' he said, 'only surviving at formal functions at Pembroke, and dating from times when, in order to continue drinking, men were glad to cool their blood by external applications of cold water.' This was being 'Wet,' indeed, and a suggestion for Anti-Prohibitionists.

* * *

An English garden-party differs from all others especially in the domain of the University. The Master of Trinity, who is the King of Cambridge, has a garden which occupies one bank of the river for a long distance. Acacias in full bloom hang over the wall during May week, tall dark yews associating as background. The Master himself, large, brown-bearded, and urbane, looked his part to perfection, and I was proud to have a share of his gracious attention. He walked with me for some time. My letter says, 'My mouth is dry with talking, and stiff with smiling, but the strawberries and Devonshire cream! — neither of these should or indeed can be found in perfection out of England. As in King's Chapel, one halts before attempting description. I longed to retire behind a yew and enjoy alone, but talk and smile I must, and they kindly forgave my "vurrys" and "Amurricas."'

A very notable call was one we made upon Professor and Mrs. Adams, at the Observatory. 'He is one of the greatest living astronomers and mathematicians, and the discoverer of the planet Neptune. He and his wife are two old dears, simple and childlike. They have been to America and stayed at Swarthmore with the Magills. The great man told me that they had been invited by American friends to visit them in Florida, and hoped to go there for a week-end. Something had interfered, and they had had to give up this jaunt. His face, when I told him, and explained why it would have been a formidable undertaking for a week-end, was a study. He had not had the slightest idea of the distance.' How unimportant was the geography of the 'States' in those days!

Also, I was very proud in being taken to call on Mrs. Darwin, the wife of Charles, and mother of many sons, of whom my host was the senior. She was very old and received me in a wheeled chair, but had lost nothing of what had made her a fitting mate for such a man. She instantly reminded me of my own grandmother, and I realized how straight the line was of my English birthright, and how close. She had the same grand sort of sweetness, and the long lines of forehead and nose, accented by the same bands of hair, and even a similar bonnet, though it must be admitted that Mrs. Leavitt's *chapeau* was a little more elegant than Mrs. Darwin would have concerned herself with. She inquired if I had done any sketching in England, and would have been surprised if I had told her that I had not thought of it, being too much occupied with *looking*. Every one expected that I would have drawings to show, and could not believe that I had brought no 'examples' with me, but soon I had done a little something, and vindicated in some degree this omission. I did a pastel of Maud in the garden, in her white hat, under the copper beech. What charming mornings we spent! George Duckworth, a beautiful and fascinating youth, and an adherent of Maud's, sat by us, reading aloud, while I stood working on the little picture. I also did a drawing of Billy, the youngest boy. All this prolonged my visit, but brought demands that I should return and undertake commissions, which I was fain to do.

Much restored by a little work, I entered with renewed vivacity into the functions and gaieties of the short Cambridge season. Maud urged me to come back for the 'Long' if I must return to Paris. I had begun to feel the reality of opening friendships, and the work I might do was full of allure to me. Work and play seemed here at their best — how could I resist them!

The circumstances of my return to Paris should be mentioned only by way of warning and contrast, and I shall always regret that I returned to the adored place, by way of my own blunder and a very squalid experiment. When I entered the shaky door of the studio, I found it filled with a helter-skelter collection of our belongings. There had been no preparatory cleaning or arranging. A bed had been put in. The toilet arrangements were simple, but for use required a complicated process. A tin basin, which I had used for washing brushes, was uncertainly disposed on the corner of the bookshelf, the soap saucer scarcely holding on beside it. A chair-back was all there was for towels, and, if one wished to sit down, books and dresses had to be put somewhere else. It had become scorching hot. I insisted in rigging up some sort of screen under the skylight for decency's sake. Squalor, wretchedness, into which no gleam of fun entered; I sympathized with royalty and was 'not amused.' Beware, young student, how far you go in trifling with impromptu eccentricity in living, in town, for it will bear no comparison with the tent, blanket, and mountain stream of the great outdoors.

* * *

My good friends in Cambridge had made a tempting plan for my return. I was to have 'the Mill,' which was an antique structure by the water, on the edge of the garden at Newnham Grange, and far outdating it in age. This was to be my studio. Two ladies wished to pose for me, one of them being Mr. Darwin's sister-in-law, the other a Mrs. Goodheart, a neighbor and friend. I knew them both. Each, though not having actual beauty, was an exquisite type of character and grace. I longed to try what was so new to me in type, and also bearing the stamp of a remote civilization and breeding. Mrs. Goodheart was breaking through an ironclad plan in order to accomplish the sittings at all, and should begin at once. With a brimming beaker of hope and energy, I rushed back in a week, my cousin with me, sailing postponed, all plans changed. It was to be England for as much time as the work, or rather the adventure, required.

I insisted on our taking lodgings, as we were two, and this in itself turned out rather fun also. Ashton House was a small brick dwelling in a shady street, only a stone's throw from Newnham. It is difficult to refrain from recounting the details of our life in lodgings. For the pen of Dickens, it was a worthy subject, and as at Newnham, the procession which I had thought invented by him, Thomas Hardy, and Leech, passed my window continually. 'Yesterday being market day, carriers' carts full of people were abundant, also Leech's greengrocers, and the well-known butcher's boy balancing his familiar tray, and holding sweet converse with the white-capped maids opposite, who stand down in the area looking up and grasping the railings just as in the pictures.' My early intimacy with 'Punch' (which has never waned) has made me familiar with England in the social grade which has been immortalized by many of her best-writers and draughtsmen. The policeman is an old friend, Leech having *seen* him in the full-flavored essence of his humanity. The women are almost never so charming as Du Maurier made them, and I saw no queenly governesses and nursemaids, but his well-born girls from twelve to fourteen are often visible, and always lovely, and dressed with the greatest freedom and simplicity, and as unconscious as 'Alice.' The English got the start of the rest of the world in this, and girls at that age always held themselves well.

Our maid, 'Kite,' the slavey of our gentle landlady, couldn't exist out of Dickens. She is small and scared, and murmurs, 'Yes, Miss, thank you,' when we tell her she has forgotten the napkins or something else. I had a short, but acute illness, which necessitated great abstinence, in recovery, so, as my letter says, 'M., temporary commissary for food, accepted Mrs. Clark's suggestion of a gooseberry tart, with the idea that a tart was a small, round, open bit of pastry, with something sweet in it. But a gooseberry tart is a deep pudding, with a pale thick pie-crust covering, and to-day I suggested, being without pity, that she should count each day the number of scallops consumed of the edge, by way of encouraging herself to push on. Mrs. C. makes some kind of custard cream for the gooseberry tart every day, which I eat, as it is within my capacity, but M. thinks she makes more progress without it.'

To quote again from my letter to the family: 'I am in the Mill Studio. The D.'s have had it cleaned, and have put in screens and a rug. I am adding photos and some of my copy-studies at the Louvre. Mrs. Goodheart has begun to sit. An anxious time is to come, of course. I have not come to be less, but more anxious, about my work. Mr. D. has begun to submit to the first experiments in lighting, etc., but I have to give all my strength to Mrs. G., as she goes so soon. She is pastel. He will be oil.' I had just begun to experiment in pastel (as in the small study of Maud), but the portrait to be, of Mrs. Goodheart, was the first life-size composition I had attempted in this medium. I had seen two or three canvases in the Luxembourg that had made me wish to try pastel. They were life-size portrait compositions, and done *as painting*, the pastel chosen, and used, in single, unmingled strokes, as with a brush. This meant extreme care in the choice of the tone used, and a composition, in the sense of subject, textures, and lighting, that would not strain the medium or push it where its power ceased. Mrs. G. had a charming long pale face, with grey eyes and perfectly straight dark brown hair. She had great individuality of drawing, and infinite grace in the quiet movements of her long slender body and hands. The color was to be violet, some dark blue, and a little pale yellow, as I remember it, all supported and harmonized by a grey which 'went' with her pallor and dark hair. The limitation of the medium, to my regret, came in the lack of depth which I could achieve in the hair. I had not learned that that super-dark tone Nature shows at times, and which defies everything but the strength of oil or etching, is not demanded for truth of relation. Of course one cannot reach the force of light in Nature, and one should never insist on any but a corresponding dark. The gods being with me, I 'got it' within the week, and was rather more satisfied than usual. The Goodhearts called my price 'paltry' and showed their gratitude by sending in great trays of flowers, and a rich plant of growing lilies, from their small garden. As it was my first pastel portrait, I had not counted much on its value. The head of Mr. D. was soon under way. He is a delicate man, and suffers seriously and with great patience, but he buckles himself down to pose, and is so conscientious and careful to do it *right*, and be exact, that it is quite touching. He is very particular about the line of observation between us, and tells me when I have moved from my 'base,' as I frequently do. All of which is the perfectly natural conception of the operation, by a great mathematician and pioneer in the calculation of tides.

VIII

RETURN TO AMERICA

OUR voyage home on an inferior vessel of an obscure line was far from commonplace. It was harried by some hardships and much rough sea-going and cold fog. For it started from Greenock Harbor in Scotland, and we thus met all the 'weather' to be found when embarking from the northern coast of the British Isles. But on a boat, which at first seemed to have as passengers only companies of the most aggressive type of Cook's tourists, we found limited, but perfect, comradeship in a fraction of the ship's company, who were, indeed, the only ones of their kind on board, and who were there for a reason which we later found to be identical with ours — economy, of course.

At our first meal, we found ourselves at a long table and quite *de trop* among the 'Cooks' who were, or had become, during their foreign jaunt, great friends, and didn't care who knew it. At the next meal, three unexceptionable persons sat in line next us, profiles turned straight out. But soon there were small courtesies to be extended, and during the rest of the long voyage, we were an inseparable group, and one of the number, George Seymour, became a lifelong friend. Since the commonplace was entirely absent in my first two voyages, I was naturally confident in regard to future crossings, but never again, when sea-going, did Fate offer me, albeit with a rough hand, scenes and circumstances so vivid as in my first two voyages. The boat was small, and sometimes after a hard night's blow we tied our chairs in the small space at the head of one of the companionways, and watched the huge grey and silver mountains soar within a few feet of us, while our stern swept the horizon — but I am wrong, there was none.

After a separation of nearly nineteen months, the great emotion and happiness of return was in finding them all there. The little ones were larger, and — this was best of all — the older unaltered, to my perception. My uncle helped me to find a studio, and very soon I was undertaking new projects in painting, the next five years being very busy ones.

It is singular that, without having a mind consciously made up, corners may be turned and directions taken, of very strong meaning and constancy. The initial decision had not been analyzed at that time, and existed only instinctively. It was, however, so powerful that there has never been any possible turning from it. Narrow as it may seem to many, to one following it, it is boundless in scope. I never found myself happy or functioning in any *cadre* that, in varying dimensions, did not contain a type, sometimes two, as the subject of a composition. Into other aspects of Nature I could gaze and worship, without wishing to join, or to intrude with the materials of performance. In fact, so many different senses were engaged when it was external Nature that there seemed no place for anything more.

When taking part was strengthily desired, the medium might, and turned out always to be, oil-painting. Previous experiments in pastel did, however, contribute very practical aid in bridging the first of the chasms that opened in the path of a young painter, after her return from the adventure of Europe. Then it is that memory fails and the struggler longs for one more look that might have revealed the secret; one deeper examination of the means the master had found to serve him. The painter in question, alone in her unfamiliar studio, knew that she must now deal with actuality, in no way tentative. She felt much more than she knew, or had ever been told. But she did know that she had little power over her palette — that is, the color upon it, its substance, and what should be its power of connecting up with what was planned to appear on the canvas. *After all* — she had not learned to paint. She had partially found out that the course for her would be in some way by simple statement, direct and clear, of a not at all obvious matter.

Ambitious? Yes. Ambitious, but she did not know it. She only chose what she thought 'nice to do.' She knew very well, concretely and particularly, how she wanted it to look. But she had not found a method of achieving the result desired. Some way must be found to make the obstinate mess on the palette something which, lifted by the brush, *might* prove to be 'right' when placed where it belonged on the canvas. The relation between the palette and the canvas cannot be absolute, because mind is the amalgam that comes operating between. The story is too old to be repeated, but too apt here to be omitted. When some one asked Sir Joshua with what he mixed his colors, he answered, 'With brains, sir.' But without restricting the '*élans* of inspiration,' one must recognize, on the differing angle, lighting, and circumstances of the palette, what is going to serve, and as swiftly as the bird selects the nourishment, invisible to the rest of us. In the classroom, I have always found that a glance at the palette accounted for much of the failure of the study.

Chance seemed to offer a sort of approach to a simple solution. This was in trying pastel again as means to an end, differing from its use merely as a change in medium. I greatly enlarged my pastel collection, spending much time, and something else, in choosing shades which were not primary colors, which of course I already had. I found a kind which were rather large in form, like chalk, and very sympathetic in substance. To work with them, I used a light tray, covering it with a piece of white cloth, to show the tone of the pastels, and also to prevent them from mixing. The secret of the procedure lay in the fact that I must *know* the tone I desired, and then strive to find it. The value of this lay in the fact, also, that the color tried and proved to be right was generally strangely *un*like what it *appeared* to be in my hand. This, as teaching, and for developing a faculty, was far more valuable than its use as permanent means of expression. Fortunately, I knew better than to abuse it. Also, I remembered a small circumstance during my first days under the criticism of William Sartain. One day, he took my dirty little palette, and, without the slightest hesitation, picked up, on a brush, what I would have seen as a bit of mud. Laid upon the half tone, generally one of the most resistant of passages, it proved to be pure, sustaining, and perfect in sequence. *Recognition of tone on the palette* — this, the fragile medium pastel by the separateness and individuality of its already existent tones (which positively were or were not 'right'), taught me; also choice, and strict rejection.

Pastel was never a rival of oil color. It taught me only a bit of useful strategy that was an aid toward meeting the obstinate armaments of so-called 'oils.' Another virtue of pastel was that one might push a morceau and leave it half conquered, to be taken up any time later and found in absolute '*statu quo*,' a liberty never permitted by oil color, without heavy, often ruinous, taxation. This enabled one to pursue continuously, and possibly conquer, a difficulty (and there is no teacher like this) in separate 'winds,' giving it several fresh breathings, and so multiplying vigor on a single point of attack. (In oil painting, stopping, except at wisely arranged boundaries, will be taken advantage of by the enemy and defeat is nearly certain.) Painting is much like war or hunting, adding the primitive zest of the chase to quite an opposite set of emotions. I had substantial proof that my dealings with the operations of pastel put me considerably forward in painting; hence this tribute to the medium I incontinently threw aside when I had extracted from it what it could do for me, which was to be my Aladdin's lamp at a critical moment when the treasure seemed to be undiscoverable.

* * *

The next five years were busy ones, for me, and also for those who came to 'sit,' and who found that the rapid sketch in which they expected to find a compact of life was a long and laborious operation, and very exacting for them. One agreeable old bank president said that I was like a little dog who walked round and round before he 'settled.' But they always became interested in seeing it 'grow,' and were willing to fight it out to the end. But I had confrères in Paris, John Lambert and Henry McCarter, who were determined to dig me out, and who were urgent that I should send over a group for the Champs de Mars, which was the Salon of that year. This seemed at first like insanity, but later consideration convinced me that to *send* a group was no one's business but mine, and that if the jury accepted one, or possibly two pictures, I was willing to 'stand' the expense of the adventure.

Only one of the pictures was 'owned,' but it would be sad for every one concerned if it should be one of the rejected. Five pictures were shipped, a bold deed I felt it to be, and it was a good while before I knew their fate. The cable said, 'All accepted and will be hung in group.' Of course, I went over. It was time for another trip, even if the Champs de Mars had not been in question. I landed in England, and did not hasten a visit to Cambridge; indeed, I was fearful whether my offspring would behave well in Paris. (How one hates one's pictures in Exhibition when one has not hung them one's self!) I finally walked among them with the friends who were responsible for the adventure. But I should have been happier in even my not very rosy dream of the appearance of the pictures than I was in the reality. They were well placed, and together, of course, but at the morning hour in spring, of my visit, a ray of sunlight somehow penetrated, and gave a shock to the parent of their surfaces and values, on which, to her mind, all they amounted to depended. This almost carried her to the length of demanding help from le Directeur, who should see that no such sacrilege was allowed to continue. I was laughed at by John and Henry, who were happier than I was, and taken out to lunch in sunshine which no one appreciated more than I, in its right place. My debt of gratitude to these friends has never been and never could be repaid; for a result followed months after that contained the crowning satisfaction of my experience as a painter.

* * *

It was in mid-winter of the same year, and a day which 'began as other days begin' in my Philadelphia studio. I had met St. Gaudens, but could not be said to 'know him.' That morning, a letter came from him which made the day different from all other days. His friendly note contained an enclosure in French which he said I ought to see. It was part of a criticism by Paul Bion, a French writer and critic and great friend of his, and explains itself as a fragment of a full discussion on current art, in Paris, at that time. I was to return it, keeping a copy if I wished. Besides its acute interest to me, as coming from a source entirely unknown to me, the quality of its generous interest, the flavor of the especial quality of the French mind, as revealed in it, the whole letter, including his opinion of, and to, St. Gaudens, which it no doubt contained, would have been a valuable example of a current view of Art at that time, and it is regrettable that it is not in my power to transcribe the whole, as I do that which relates to my group, not having ever had the privilege of seeing it.*

Of course, I was anxious to make some acknowledgment to M. Bion, and, getting his address from St. Gaudens, sent him a copy on Jap paper of a wood-cut, which Henry Wolff had made for the 'Century,' of one of the pictures in the group. I looked in vain for a response, which I hoped might lead to further correspondence, and perhaps criticism, from Paul Bion, and to come in touch with a type of mind of which I was greatly in need and almost entirely deprived of; for, although much that was flattering was now offered me,

* See Appendix.

it contained little, if any, thoughtful or experienced perception. But, alas, there was to be no more of such precious freight coming to my shore. After many months, I one day chanced to meet St. Gaudens at an exhibition in New York, and at once inquired for Paul Bion. His face changed. 'Paul Bion' — he said, 'Paul Bion is dead' — and turned away, unable to speak. Of course I left him, the gallery, and the chattering crowd, and suffered in secret for a bright hope lost from my life in Art, and as I had at the time fully expressed my gratitude and appreciation, I never took the liberty of seeking to know more of one whom he so mourned.

* * *

St. Gaudens was well known to be a very reticent man, and it is probable that Paul Bion was one of the few to whom his mind was open. After the Adams Monument was finished and placed, every earnest beholder of it wished to penetrate deeper within it than he could go alone. But St. Gaudens would never answer. Silence followed every allusion to it, an impulsive withdrawal on his part, but perfectly accounted for in the work itself. It remains inviolable. For the subject is silence itself. St. Gaudens seems to have entered upon a mystery, and returned with the secret in bronze and granite, alone. It may be said to be one of those works — and few there have ever been of them — whose existence is part of Nature's plan. Great works, like great people, meet nothing strong enough to oppose their destiny. In the Adams monument, sculptor, subject, and patron were as one, and could not be otherwise. Their fusion may have been accompanied by 'groanings that cannot be uttered,' but the result testifies that it was too strong for opposition, too magnanimous to be disturbed by friction. Nothing would have had the power to confuse or hinder this work. Each step in its progress led straight to its existence and even placement, for the latter is one of the irresistible sequences in the drama. For drama it is. And not because of its especial and tragic causation. One sees at once that the drama has nought to do with persons. Its development would lie in the choice of evidence that would be used, not to be called 'choice' either, in every sense, for it was found, offered, to the deep, awed soundings of St. Gaudens's humanity, endeavoring to discover indubitable signs of truth.

* * *

St. Gaudens, then, one may venture to say, has been the only artist in modern times really to enter into conjunction with the ultimate unknown, beyond knowing; that is, to meet it plastically, as a sculptor, and with the strict limitation which the subject demands, technically. The density of the material, which he treated as without surface, is forced to serve, in itself, the mystery of the theme. No detail may distract, and, above all, no slightest misconception of the solitary purpose, which, although reduced to general, and to the superficial eye already accepted terms, reaches the open and watchful mind with a poignancy and conviction that only supreme oracles can command.

The small fir-surrounded hemicycle in the Rock Creek Cemetery contains the rarest exposition of thought, on Destiny, that plastic art has ever achieved. The uncommunicable is offered to human heart and intelligence, without word or gesture. I have sat there many times at wide intervals, and have come away feeling that question is ignoble, doubt paltry, and personal destiny unimportant, in the presence of the majesty of issues not upon the plane of revelation.

The upper part of the head is Greek, with all the significance of that form to us. The mouth, without any strain of contrast, is present, human, and has known the whole of sorrow, not its own, but ours. For there is no Person, here.

And what of the Public in this place?

The cemetery is a beautiful spot, and hundreds of gay little twos and threes go there on pleasant days in spring, as has been the immemorial way in the pleasant fields of the dead. While I sat there, a number of young people came up. I could hear their bright voices as they mounted the path. But once there, they whispered, gazing long, and when they at last passed out, turned back once or twice, reluctantly, with the vague desire that youth has toward eternal things.

* * *

I did not linger long on this visit. It was midsummer, the least characteristic period of the year in Paris. But before I left, one, to me, highly memorable event had occurred. Mrs. Tom Perry (Lilla Cabot Perry) was painting at Giverney, to be near Monet, and would take me to see him. No sun and weather could have been more fortunate for a visit to the specialist in light than we were blessed with. We found him in the very centre of 'a Monet,' indeed: that is, in his garden at high noon, under a blazing sky, among his poppies and delphiniums. He was in every way part of the picture, or the beginning and end of it, in his striped blue overalls, buttoned at wrists and ankles, big hat casting luminous shadow over his eyes, but 'finding,' in full volume, the strong nose and great grey beard. Geniality, welcome, health, and power radiated from his whole person. There was a sleepy river, lost in summer haze not far away. The studio, which was a barn opening on the garden, we were invited to enter, and found the large space filled with stacked canvases, many with only their backs visible. Monet pulled out his latest series, views, at differing hours and weather, of the river, announcing the full significance of summer, sun, heat, and quiet on the reedy shore. The pictures were flowing in treatment, pointillism was in abeyance, at least for these subjects. Mrs. Perry did not fear to question the change of surface, which was also a change of *donné*. 'Oh,' said the *Maître*, nonchalantly, 'la Nature n'a pas de pointes.' This at a moment when the *haute nouveauté* seekers of that summer had just learned 'how to do it,' and were covering all their canvases with small lumps of white paint touched with blue, yellow, and pink. But they had not reckoned on the non-static quality of a discoverer's mind, which, in his desire for more light, would be always moving. For Monet was never satisfied. Even the science of Clemenceau, and his zeal for his friend, did not get to the bottom of the difficulty, which was purely physical. One could push the sorry pigment far, but not where Monet's dream would have it go, imagining that by sheer force of desire and *volonté*, the *nature* of the *material* he thought to dominate would be overcome. For the moment, when actual light gleamed upon it, fresh from the tube, it had the desired effulgence, but it could not withstand time and exposure, and maintain the integral urge of Monet's idea.

* * *

My second visit abroad occurred during the passage of a decade, that, considering the ultimate purpose of this chronicle, was to be recorded as containing events and results, coming from far, and reaching, or will reach, as far as I am concerned, to the limit of consciousness.

It is needless to say that the environment of an artist, especially during the first years of struggle — for struggle is always present in one form or another — has an immense influence upon his productivity and expansion. Many a youthful proclivity, perhaps power, has gone under before family or other prejudice, or careless interruption, or a lack of belief or understanding of the 'case.' Equally pernicious is the overestimate of the beginner's promise; the parents bringing forward and exploiting their child's 'talent,' encouraging him to flutter from one art school or *atelier* to another. The world is full of the result of this method, which is a condition which has developed from the period when the young person, who at least felt himself possessed of a vocation, had to run away from home and suffer privation to pursue it. I am not sure that hardness is not better than cotton wool. It was my great good fortune not to experience either of these conditions. I sometimes think that one who is destined to be a pursuer of plastic art, in any form, cannot have a better fate than to be brought up in a family of musicians, and one that is not crowded by what George Herbert calls 'the bane of bliss and source of woe.' Of Art, such a group is always 'aware,' though they may have experience only in their own. They know what its pursuit means, and what it exacts. They do not apply other standards to other arts. My family never flattered me, to myself or others; neither did they pretend to understand an art they had not applied themselves to. They understood perfectly the spirit and the necessities of an artist's life. I never accomplished more than was expected of me. Any sign in me of an overestimate of myself or my doings would have been thought humorous, perhaps distressing.

The aunt with the sleek head (before mentioned), with her curving smile, used to quote a notice that had appeared in a penny newspaper: 'The Item does not hesitate to declare that Miss Cecilia Beaux is the best Female Portrait Painter in Philadelphia.' No wonder that I advanced with a thoroughly made-up mind on the subject of Sex in Art. But this aunt was the very one, who, in order that I might start fresh for my day's work, made my bed and 'did' my room, leaving the breakfast table — for I had to start early — to follow me to the front door, with my basket, containing a bottle of milk, and a large buttered roll that she had prepared. It was quite a long walk from our house in West Philadelphia to the trolley which bore me to town in about forty minutes. This was easy enough in the morning, and I generally reached my studio at nine. An hour was none too much for clearing the decks for action, preparing my palette, considering the canvas in progress, and my intentions concerning it, so that at ten I was no more than ready for the subject who was expected to be prompt also, and who finding me always waiting, easily got the habit.

I soon found that intensive work, for me, could not be carried over into the afternoon. Fortunately, I was aware when the moment came when there was nothing more, of the best, to give. But the later hours, though recognized not to be worthy of high pressure, could contain those operations and accumulations that characterize any studio, and upon which the golden hours should not be wasted. At this time, also, I was liable to the agreeable interruptions of friends, from some of whom I received fresh and stimulating influence.

After a struggle in the short winter days, with the weather, crowds, and long waits at street-corners at the rush hour (I rarely had a seat in the car), the walk home, on feet that had stood nearly all day, and with nerves that had spent all they had, what a refuge was mine! I need not speak to any one; I could go to my room until dinner time, and after it I frequently spent the whole evening on the parlor sofa, completely relaxed, and often asleep, or just conscious of my comfort, sometimes of my uncle's voice, reading, of quiet laughter, talk, and some challenge. Nothing was required of me. Although the life at home was or would have been monotonous, except for the mental quality of those who formed it, I was never expected to bring in life and entertainment to revive a dull evening; still less to do any of those small services that would naturally have been the part of the young, active member of the family. In all the years that followed my return from abroad, to the, alas, final breaking-up of our circle, I was never once asked to do an errand in town, some bit of shopping, or a call, that would have put the slightest pressure upon me. So well did they understand.

A heavy hand carved out the destinies of our circle during this period, on the elders never to be lifted entirely. The youngest member suffered acutely in the ordeal, the like of which had never touched her before, but was formed by it and tried as by fire, annealed for future strain.

My father's death came first. He had never been able to do for his daughters what he wished, and never realized the priceless heritage that they received from him by birth. This inheritance has become more and more a cause for gratitude to me, and I behold with joy the evidence of its value in my sister's children.

My grandmother was, and had always been, the central figure in our family life, and in her great age, her character and poise, and indeed every faculty, remained as we had always known them, humor above all. She had no sense of importance in herself, and, as her physical strength declined, yielded easily to changes which were thought to be for the general good, turning over the housekeeping and service-directing, without criticism, to less experienced authority. The active discipline of life upon her had developed new beauties all along the way, so that the care, never exacted, which constantly surrounded her, was given with the happiest devotion by every one, and she was, literally, the occupation of one of my aunts, and accepted with an understanding smile the constant intervention of her watchful guardians. Her happiness was to be with her family, observing, and consulting, in their occupations, while her own knitting went on to the music my uncle would be making downstairs, often to the reading aloud, in which she herself sometimes took part, long after such exertion would have been thought tiresome. Her health, except for occasional small maladies, was perfect, and when, suddenly, danger approached, the whole force of the family rose to ward it off. She was ninety-three, but we could not spare her, could not face our lives without her, so that the effort of the next eighteen months to save her for ourselves was the mainspring of every heart. Her only utterance on the subject of her state (when she realized what had happened) was: 'You are keeping me here when I ought to be gone.'

Yet the constancy and cheerfulness of her encircling lovers made her life almost happy, as far as she allowed us to see into her mind. We divided the twenty-four hours so that the best could be made of each unit. As I was working, yet unwilling to give up my time of being with my grandmother, we arranged that I should go to my studio as usual, returning in the late afternoon. This brought some freshness and change at a moment when it was needed. She called me her 'barber,' it being for me to brush and arrange her hair, and also to sit with her and persuade her, at supper. At eight o'clock, I went to bed, coming down at two, to relieve my aunt. At five, the nurse came on, and I slept again till seven, when my day began.

This programme never cost me either health or fatigue. My work went on as usual and without strain, for the reason that I had cut out all social engagements, saw a few of my intimate friends before coming home, doing away with all the extras and obligations of being in the 'world,' and lived a very intense, interior life, undisturbed from without.

When the time came when nothing could be done for her by any of us, her last sleep came upon the dear invalid, as we watched, ready to smile upon her, if she should raise her eyes again. But she did not. — 'She had another morn than ours!' —

One memory remains to me with peculiar vividness. During the evening of the night on which she was stricken, the family life flowed on as usual. She was walking about, as she often did, but this time it could be seen that it was necessary for her to touch the backs of chairs, etc., as she went. I was cutting out a painting apron upon the large table. She stood by me, interested, and commenting as

usual. When it was finished, we took our walk in the hall
(her shoulder exactly fitted under my encircling arm) and
we also walked upon the porch, for it was a mild November
evening. She leaned a little more heavily than usual. We
did not linger long. It was our last walk together.

**

Once, in Cambridge, in Maud's drawing-room, I was
standing with one of my friends, when an elderly but active
man, a guest I scarcely knew, muttered (what reached me
only on account of my superactive hearing), 'Oh, Langley,
it's cursèd, getting old.' To this, every one, including the
young, agrees. There is only one remedy and only one pal-
liative: to have a character that has absorbed the discipline
of life as part of its nourishment, and draws its happiness
from the reflection its environment radiates, of what itself
has bestowed. Rare, indeed, is the type that age cannot
deteriorate. These have learned to 'suffer fools gladly,' and
to suppress the story of the ills that age brings with it. My
grandmother, when pressed to give an account of one of her
nearly sleepless nights, used to say: 'There wasn't much of it,
but what there was, was a very good kind of sleep.' She was
well aware of the ravages of age, and she had been beautiful,
but even this grim fact she could recognize without a sigh.
I once heard her say as she passed a mirror — 'I don't
know that old woman.'

**

In one of the letters of a distinguished French general,*
written to his parents during his first campaign as a young
officer in the Soudan, there is a passage which expresses so
much better than is possible for me a feeling I have often
had, that I cannot refrain from citing it. I believe such feeling to be not unusual in France, where no tie is closer than
that between parents and children. I was an inheritor,

* General Charles Mangin.

from all the group who had passed on to me, their grand-child, niece, and daughter, all that she possessed:

Que je profite, au moins, de ces circonstances de nouvelle année, pour te dire ces paroles, inutiles entre nous en temps ordinaire, précisément à cause de leur vérité, pour te dire combien, morale-ment, comme physiquement je me sens ton fils: et malgré quelque fautes en plus, orgueilleux de l'être. Ce bonheur, inaccessible à l'adversité, fait que ma vie ne peut être malheureuse — et ce doit être maintenant, la recompense de la tienne, si dur par moments, que d'être prolongée par d'autres vies qui sont heureuses parce qu'elles sont issues de toi....

* * *

The decade that contained these losses and the shadows of other changes to come saw also the opening of some of the choicest of friendships, and contacts. The Gilders were old friends of the Janviers, who were at this time living in New York, and one evening they took me with them to 13 East Eighth Street, a house which was to be long memorable to me as a home, during my first protracted sojourn in New York, and always as the scene where I could witness and often take part in a life which vividly joined and dissemi-nated every form of intellectual and artistic activity, and al-ways in the interest of humanity. Richard and Helena Gilder were complete and firmly defined individuals; in what their marriage meant to the world around them, they were phenomenal. This arose largely from the extreme diversity of character, which, by the happiest operation of fate, formed a unit of truly centrifugal benefit constantly about them. Richard was dynamic; Helena, contemplative. If one could accept the theory of reincarnation, they could be taken as clearly defined examples of the *culte*. Richard (and age did not alter) was a newly born soul to whom the 'world and the fullness thereof' had just been shown. He met it with open arms and heart, and with a mind sparkling with the zest of being, hopeful of the conquest of the powers of darkness.

Helena, although she had the softest and most *caline* of smiles to bestow, always reminded me of Dürer's 'Melancholia.' Her spirit was as old, as experienced, as wise, and as enigmatic as an innumerable series of lives could make it. It was also as tolerant of the weaknesses of humanity, and even its stupidities. She accepted, but rarely explained why. The warm tones of her marvellous voice had a vibration brought from depths of what she knew, what she had suffered, and what she could give of support. One could follow her counsel unafraid. Her husband never made even a small decision without it. They were night-workers. During the winter I lived in their house, I was privileged to come to the closed door of the library, and enter unchallenged, when I came in after an evening spent out. The room, dimly lighted, except for the lamp under which Richard sat in his dressing-gown before his papers, reflected the accumulations of their rich life. Helena sat near, in her low chair by the fire, her lap full of homely work, which her hands only seemed engaged with, and which invariably came out somehow right. The tea-table was always near, and the kettle among the embers. Tea was often made at about one, but I was seldom present at that time, being a daylight worker. This was the hour when visitors of like habits dropped in, and were always generously admitted, often coming for consultation or advice. But Richard could never be held down on any topic, and the conversation would stray into almost any field, oftenest into the happenings of the day in Washington, or in municipal matters: frequently ending in a shout of laughter on one of his sallies.

It was here that I met Mrs. Schuyler Van Rensselaer, whose friendship has been one of the ties that since then have bound me to New York; Mr. Clemens (Mark Twain), William Vaughn Moody, and for the first time, St. Gaudens. To Mr. Gilder I owe, through his introduction much later, my friendship with Leila Mechlin, and the many contacts and services I owe to her constant loyalty. In the years before I knew them, Paderewski or Duse often came in after an evening's performance or concert. Fräulein Aus der Ohe was in constant attendance; it was at their house that she had played first in this country, coming unknown, as many did, with letters to 'the Gilders,' and generously welcomed by them. The Friday evenings are too well known to be described here. There was no other 'Salon' of the kind in New York while theirs was in existence, and I know of no other now. I belonged to an intermediate generation, but was classed with the children, that is, Rodman and Dorothea, my part being to assist with them, and often I did not meet the personalities who gathered round Mrs. Gilder's tea-table, finding out who they were later. One quiet old gentleman, with a kindly smile, allowed me to procure exactly the brew of tea that he could take, and I had a few words of gentle conversation with him. It was William Dean Howells.

Their intimacy with Mr. and Mrs. Cleveland was one of the major issues of the Gilders' lives. It was at Tyringham, where the Clevelands had taken a house to be near the Gilders and for the fishing, that I found myself seated beside Mr. Cleveland on a 'piazza settle' at the farm, and felt the strange emanation of power that one gets when very near to great personalities. Mr. Cleveland did not speak to me in any way to be remembered, if at all, but his great head and shoulders were in close proximity; his profile had the natural grandeur of colossal sculpture; his speech was slow; his hands heavy and solid. It seemed that nothing he was, physically, would be moved till needed. Yet Mr. Gilder used to tell us that no one was lighter, or more adroit, in a small boat, and his thick fingers were peculiarly skillful in the adjustment of flies. Another proof that, as in Nature's measurements, bulk is unimportant in itself, as it has the power of relation at either end of the scale.

RICHARD WATSON GILDER

It was Mrs. Gilder who took me to call on John La Farge in his studio, she having known him since their student days. He had returned from Samoa and the Pacific Isles, bringing water-colors and drawings. I was, of course, fascinated by his distinction, his subtlety, the controlled lightning of his temperament, which was of the gentlest and the most fearsome. He was engaged with his creations in stained glass. He was a man of parts in any field, a thinker, a leader, who chose to be an artist. One thought of Disraeli, Talleyrand; but, being first of all an artist, he would have laid the whole to taste, included all in the precious *métier*.

I once heard La Farge lecture to students, laying stress from first to last on the hand and its discipline by the mind. He was one of the members of the Carnegie jury for one of its early exhibitions. I also served, and was made happy by the attention and care that he, as *doyen*, showed me as the solitary female of the committee, sending his Japanese servant to wait on me, and making himself my friend and protector, if I had needed any. The officers of the Institute were untiring in their attentions to all of us. The weather being fine, it was proposed, on our arrival, that we should drive about and see the town, which none of us had visited before. Four barouches were drawn up at the door of our hotel, and into the first of these Mr. La Farge, Mr. Caldwell, the President of the institute, a mysterious stranger, and I were invited to ascend. I sat in the Queen's place, Mr. La Farge beside me. Opposite rode Mr. Caldwell, full of explanation and courtesy, the ambiguous person beside him. This personage I took to be a high official in the world of the Institute, or of coal or steel. He was a spare, oldish man, with a short, dark, almost unnaturally dark, moustache. Everything he wore, and even his cane, was new; gloves, necktie, hat, suit, never had been worn before, and seemed to oppress the wearer a little. He remained absolutely silent during the drive, in which the chief object to be pointed out to our attention — and it was a worthy one — was the jail. A number of years before, Pittsburgh magnates had decided that a new jail was needed, and that it should be an honor to the Commonwealth. The best architect in the country must be commissioned to build it. But, Mr. Caldwell told us, they did not know who the best architect might be. A committee was appointed to investigate. They proceeded to Boston, inquired of the authorities, and the advice was: 'Richardson, by all means.'

The great man was at once called upon, and accepted the commission. The prison, externally at all events, showed that he had given his best talent and interest to it. It is indeed a masterpiece. No ambiguous character has the mighty structure. It has a soul, just and terrible; it is the very epic of jails.

* * *

But I was still wondering about the unknown man who had driven with us. He looked, I whispered to myself, as a diamond expert might, if I had ever seen one. There was something intense, observant, in his quiet. His new clothes seemed like a disguise. I inquired of Mr. Beatty, who was the operating angel of our destiny. Mr. Beatty looked at me in wonder — 'Why, Winslow Homer, of course.' He was amazed that I did not know, had not met him. Until nearly the end of our labors, which, with the entertainment so generously provided, filled every moment of the day and a good deal of the night, Winslow Homer maintained his silent attention to duty. He came and went, voted and endured, until nearly the end, when he became restless, and finally confided to one of the men that he grudged every minute now passing. He had planted nine stands of corn (as models, of course); they would be now exactly ready — that is, just dry and ripe enough for his plan for painting. It was November. They might be ruined by a storm, or be in some way *hors concours*. He also would have liked to depart when, and how, he pleased. The greatest care was being taken to provide everything in the best manner to save us all trouble in leaving. As we walked, for I, too, was a little impatient: 'I could have bought my own ticket,' said Winslow Homer.

* * *

Years later, I was to see the joint collection of water-colors by Sargent, Dodge McKnight, and Homer, with bronzes by Manship, at the beautiful gallery in the 'rue de l'Épée l'Évêque' in Paris after the war. The Winslow Homers were as completely 'separate' as Paris is from Maine. They had brought their own atmosphere with them, without losing one breath of it. To me, they had even more than their expected zest as quintessential products of a great artist's native and unalloyed perception.

The Exhibition was not largely attended, being a war work, with tickets possible to rich Americans only; but as one lingered long, to be sure of missing nothing, it was satisfying to observe the approach of astute French visitors, their intent examination, often discussion, with a friend, those expressive signs by which the French make known wonder and admiration; to feel that in those small water-colors by Winslow Homer, almost without design, the essential value was being perfectly understood, nothing missed, in the little green and grey pictures. How crowded were the small framed spaces with the most illusive themes! A cold lake in Maine, in approaching night; its twilight, forest edge, and beyond, fatally certain in their complete loneliness; nothing, nothing there, either there, or beyond, in the chill, darkening woods. A deer... could it be... in the bushes? Gone... not there if one bent too near. A few nearly colorless masses of grey and dark green, a sky of the simplest, yet the miracle of a constant lover's conception in Nature, had been accomplished, and could be offered, and received, into the unlike, distant mind of France.

The French mind would know its rarity, would not pass it by.

* * *

Another man was the peer of Winslow Homer, as a revealer of the illusive aspects of Nature, that we have often before us and never really see. Abbott Thayer, in his 'Monadnock at Sunset,' strikes a similar chord. One may be sure that hundreds have used this subject; it is an ordinary view: but has it ever been really rendered before? Both these men lived in the presence of the desired object for years, and no one, I venture to say, knows when the final shock of insight and creation took place. Possibly there were dozens of trials, thrown away, painted over, and no doubt the revealing result we may stand before was scarcely more satisfying to the difficult lover than the rest.

It is possible that Abbott Thayer never loved but once in the world of the great outdoors, or never came, in his own mind, as near to touching it, as in the 'Monadnock.' He investigated the subject at a different angle in his book on 'Protective Coloration.' I was not fortunate enough to meet him in the early years of my efforts, but as in my 'absent' experience of the teachings of Thomas Eakins, Abbott Thayer's words were passed on to me by his pupils, who often never guessed the value to me of their gift, and when we finally met, he had no idea of having assisted me. I shall always regret, however, that I did not hear him in class, for his utterance, by word, was as fine and subtle in its simplicity as was his compelling personality.

* * *

I visited the Thayers at Dublin, and was admitted to the untrammelled, and so diverse, particularity of their living. Mrs. Thayer, who was the most cheerful of invalids, lived, slept, and cooked her own breakfast, in a piano-box on the edge of the woods. Mr. Thayer and Gladys, the only members of the family at home, at bedtime disappeared, each with a lantern, down the narrowest of paths to their forest retreats. I occupied the house alone. John, or William, the only servitor, lived in his own house down the hill. All doors and windows were open, of course. By day, the house was full of visitors; Mr. Thayer was not working at the moment, but understanding between us was complete and immediate, and, although we walked off upon the mountain-side, words were little needed. Once we were followed by two ladies, and A. T.'s efforts at flight were touching. He showed me some of his investigations in the field of the concealing power of their brilliant coloring, in birds; and the essential importance of his stripes, black and white, for the safety of the zebra, while drinking.

I was obliged to leave at an early morning hour, and Mr. Thayer cooked my breakfast, calling up to know if I liked my egg hard or soft. I longed to stay and drop off encumbering habits, but, alas, can our complicated humanity shake off one impediment without inventing another?

Abbott Thayer spent his creative years in a search which precluded his prolonged attention to other aspects of Nature, and which he found in his young daughters, Elise Pumpelly, and one or two other friends and neighbors. He was fortunate in having the material he desired so constantly near him. The remote and fundamental beauty which he found in these types alone satisfied him, was alone worthy to be sought for and expressed by him. He saw ultimate realities of structure, of a rare equity and proportion, in the young, firm, or tender, and sometimes wistful, countenances of these subjects. The material of his painting, modelling, and the surfaces of his form were rich in quality, chiefly. He could do without what is known as color. The swan's plumage in light; the *idea* of light, only, on dark objects; these were sufficient for the limits of his scale, in which not one fractional passage was out of place. His hand, his tool, was sometimes heavy; he went crashing through the *métier* to carve a tender eyelid or cheek. How stimulating is his passage from dream to substance! How commanding his vision!

Abbott Thayer's desire was toward monumental works. He saw his large pictures as balanced, static compositions. But his profound insight was intimate. It was a rare and synthetic type of beauty that he saw to do, but his expression of this was as intimate as his feeling toward it. He never sacrificed this to the generalization almost demanded by a monumental and strictly balanced group, and one is glad to let him have his way. How serious, how silent, how unconscious are these young creatures — unhandled Nature: yet something emanates from their human features which will be known to them later — which life will not spare them.

* * *

Dublin, New Hampshire, has been, for many, a summer landmark. Before it was known to me at the Thayers', Mrs. Leverett Bradley had introduced me to the Smiths at Loon Point. I knew Joseph Lindon Smith slightly, and Mrs. Bradley cast me upon their hospitality without further formality. How well she knew them! So I knew in its creation, almost, Joe's Outdoor Theatre in the woods. Many have been his imitators, in the Small Country Theatre, but few have accomplished it with the really magical use of the means at hand, as he did. Exquisite hidden spot, a flawless example of the alliance of Art with Nature, without strain. Here Harry Green's 'Theophile' was acted with Richard Cabot in the title rôle. Russell Sullivan also took part. Joe, of course, threw around the whole his constant invention and fancy, and the beautiful voices and drama-intelligence of the group sufficed, instead of impossible rehearsals.

'Staying with the Smiths' included an early dip in the Lake, and when their then guest took her way through the orchard, six Maltese kittens brushed her ankles with their softness, leaping through the long dewy grass. The lake was crystal pure, but the silt of ages had greyed the bottom where I longed to see and enjoy the shimmering pebbles, four feet down. So in our bathing-suits, Harry Green and I took the boat, he with oar and I with broom. With Herculean labor (his also, to keep the boat in place) I succeeded in bringing to view the bright floor of the lake, where I bathed. It had just the color and quality I expected to find, and is as lovely in memory as the clear eddies of Mallory Brook.

'With the Gilders at Tyringham' is a wide salient, in Memory, stretching, I am glad to say, over a number of years. Tyringham Valley is a realized version of the Twenty-Third Psalm. It is a valley one may enter and behold, lying between its hillsides and modelled by its river, far as the interrupting closure of 'Cobble,' at the farther end. So one may pass into and through it, as Christian might have done, in 'Pilgrim's Progress.' It is the *idea* of a valley in a poet's imagination, not entangled with unselected detail, showing only the broad seductive lines and slopes, where cloud-shadows move in the majesty of summer sunshine. 'Four Brooks,' the Gilders' Farm, lies upon one of the enclosing hillsides, near the upper end of the vale. The Mountain Hill hangs like a tapestry behind it, and it was upon this hill, among laurel, pine, rock, and sugar maple, that I spent most of the mornings of my summer-long visits at the farm. I was generally alone, but so steep was the hillside that I could look down upon the bright-colored specks, which were the children playing in the home-close, and into the tops of the gigantic maples of the road. Blue smoke from the chimney had for background the valley itself.

'R. W. G.,' with cloak and staff, like Wotan, walked by river and meadow, and I often walked with him, but, after they gave me the unused tobacco barn for a studio, I wandered less. It, the tobacco barn, was a huge enclosed shed on the edge of the orchard. Its walls were single upright boards, one inch apart. The ground itself was its floor, and when I took possession there was only one window at the farther end, a square opening with a heavy wooden shutter, through whose frame one could see the near surroundings of the farm, and beyond. When I entered it, the barn was more than half filled with winter and other farm-furnishings, sledges, broken farm tools, ploughs, old wagons, etc., a veritable heaven for the summer hours of children. They (*my* benefactors this time) put in a long large window on-the orchard side, at the farther end, and cleared the space there. I had already had a clear view of the painting I would do there. I saw straight through the ploughs and wagons, and when three glazed windows went into the long opening in the wall, light actually fell upon a canvas (the ghost of one) which would stand in perfect view from a deep ample corner.

The big and little sisters, Dorothea and Francesca, used to execute a dance of the simplest and all too circumscribed design, invented by themselves, and adorned by their unconscious beauty alone.

This was the subject. I built a platform with my own hands, as the girls could not move easily on the bare earth. When it rained hard, in September, the orchard let its surplus water run down the hill and under the barn-sill, so that, as my corner was rather low, I put on rubber boots and splashed in and out of my puddle, four inches deep. October was difficult, for it grew bitterly cold. But valiant posing went on, though the scenic effect of the group was changed by wraps. Summer, indeed, was over, when on a dark autumnal night, in the freezing barn, the picture was packed by the light of one or two candles and a lantern.

DOROTHEA AND FRANCESCA

One of us, Dorothea, has passed from her own remembering — but not ours. — Dorothea, dear companion and playmate —

* * *

One changes worlds when passing from north to south, in Washington Square. When a working place in New York became necessary to me, Henry McCarter, who had once before beneficently intervened in my fortunes, found me the most sympathetic studio I ever had. It was in the old Ireland house, on the corner of South Washington Square and West Broadway. Squalid as it was in its neglected elegance, I knew by the high second-story windows that it would 'do' before I entered it. The janitor was unpromising, though suave. He was a much deteriorated near-gentleman, whose solace, one might guess, was the usual, and at that time, not nominally, criminal one. My studio to be was the large high front room *au premier*, and included the hall-room, which had two windows. There was a plain marble mantel, and fireplace. A beautiful old white lay upon the doors and window-shutters; the view on Washington Square was enchanting, and the light from the high windows, what I had always dreamed of. Mr. Brownlow promised scrupulous attention, and 'Mac's' studio was near by, as well as the Gilders on Eighth Street. I resisted all temptations to 'furnish,' for the sake of space and proportion, and was rewarded. The room did itself, and a mirror, easels and canvases, a divan, and one over-mantel picture seemed to make it a place to live in as well as work. I was sensitive also to the depths of life that had been passed there, and which I was glad had left no visible trace that I could fix or be conscious of, but of which I could be sensible in the seasoned surfaces, and in the physiognomy, almost, of doors and windows.

* * *

I still had work on hand in Philadelphia, my home was

there, and my studio, but it was at '64' that a number of canvases developed, in which my interest was at high tide. As usual, the work I so enjoyed here was a varied succession of commissions, beside portraits done *con amore*. Although never feeling constrained in either project or performance, I had a sense of being more free than usual, in the two commissions. That is, they were exactly the types I would have chosen to do, in any case. 'They' were Mrs. Fred Barton, and Mrs. Alexander Sedgwick with Christina. The atmosphere of the room fitted them as if they had been born in it. The others were the picture 'At Home,' and Mr. Gilder, whom I had long desired to do. There were also two studies of Dorothea, who was always my 'constant,' as a model. Several drawings also were done at this time; Professor Graves, of New Haven, for my friend, George Seymour; and Mr. John Parsons; and I was delighted when the 'Century' asked me to do Anne Douglas Sedgwick, the author. A very slight red chalk drawing seemed the manner for this; but best of all, it led to our friendship, and to my better knowledge of her books, deepening the enjoyment, which, without knowing her, I should have had in them. I also drew for the 'Century' Admiral Sampson and Commander Wainwright (who captured Cervera), and Lieutenant Hobson's handsome head, and Dr. Weir Mitchell of Philadelphia, whom I knew well.

Ellen Emmet took the rooms below me on the drawing-room floor, made them over, and in them did some of her finest things. It was at about this time that MacMonnies made a visit to New York, and took her studio, for a time vacant. Old Mr. Silsbee, of Salem, who, in intervals of quoting Shelley and relating his personal recollections of Browning, used to repeat in a loud voice: 'MacMonnies — MacMonnies is the only sculptor of Modern Times, who can throw the figure about — throw the figure about ——' and it was indeed true. I believe he was known to have produced a sketch for a fountain, with seventeen life-size figures, in a day. But he had somehow tired of this exercise, and had taken up painting. His grasp of this medium, which was really new to him, was phenomenal. All his canvases were large and comprehensive. I met him at the Abbé's and was dazzled by his wit and vitality. One day, he went to Philadelphia, and came back with a huge canvas which he invited me to see. It was a colossal blonde nude, sprawling on a sofa. 'Think of it!' he cried. 'Think of doing that in Philadelphia!' But I disappointed him. For instead of being shocked, as he hoped, I criticised the drawing.

And speaking of virtuosity, the 'Century' commissioned me to do a sketch of Kubelik, who had just made a meteoric appearance in the New York musical world. He came to the slums on a Sunday morning, escorted by two secretaries, bearing each a double lacquered violin case, four violins *de premier marque*, of course. Only the night before, at the Metropolitan, he had won an immense ovation, but his large grey eyes were poignant in his spare young face, under the shock of dark hair. I had hoped to do him, playing, but I soon found that I was entirely incapable of production while a hailstorm was whistling about my head, or was it a rain of burning flakes from Vesuvius? It could be only practising, not playing, I learned. Managers do not permit one bar of musical composition for listeners. Half mad, I seemed to myself in the storm, and begged for rest; we would try another plan. He was quite willing and laid down his instrument. His head leaning upon his hand, he looked out with mild curiosity at the proceedings. I had started a head. Presently he said with a strong accent, but very careful English, 'Are there many picture galleries in New York?' 'Oh, yes,' I replied carelessly, searching for a better bit of charcoal, and casually naming the Museum, and one or two galleries, adding with egregious banality, 'Are you fond of pictures?' The lad, for he was little more, hesitated, his voice deepened, and he murmured; 'Yes... More than the violin.' This utterance was so unexpected and astonishing that I was for a moment speechless. And then, out of stark curiosity, and wondering if he would 'take it,' I said, 'Oh...that is because the violin is so *easy*...' I need not have doubted. His answer was despairing in its abandonment. 'Yes,' he moaned, 'it *is* — for — *me* ——'

Such are the woes of the born virtuoso. It is not he who performs, but the dæmon who lives in him, and has everything his own way. Poor Kubelik had never known the zest of conquest or the sweet agony of giving form to imagination.

* * *

One afternoon I had a call from Oliver Herford, at '64.' The canvas of the 'At Home' was leaning against the wall — Oliver Herford leaned over it, with his eyeglass. His slight stammer seemed to add zest to his speech, if that were possible.

'Why,' he cried, 'how comfortable the cat is! It — it looks as if it was the cat's — address!'

* * *

'Mrs. Barton' was one of the, to me, most highly relished portraits I ever did. Yet I never felt that her family were quite satisfied. There seemed to be in her a kind of unflinching heroism that she had never had occasion to use. A New England woman, who was also a great-granddaughter of Thomas Jefferson, might have been said to have a right to this quality, among others, but as far as I was concerned as her portrayer, I believed that to express her the firmest technique should be employed. A profile — showing the grand space between the turn of forehead and the line of the neck. But it must also be rich and tender; the way to be found for this, in color and texture, between the firm lines of the design. The range would be wide, a deep note, and a very clear-colored one, kept apart, with much detail between. The whole, in the matter of treatment, should be serene and composed; not a fervid announcement,

AT HOME

written with a flowing brush. It should have the quality of enamel, as if moulded in a *pâte*, flexible, but capable of solidification, and permanence. All this was hoped for and was a vision imperfectly realized, but not entirely defeated.

* * *

'Christina' was to have been a head only, but I was so hotly pursued by another idea that I was led to ask Mrs. Sedgwick if she would come into the picture as an accessory. She consented, also accepting consequent developments, which must have been irksome. So sustaining was her understanding and sympathy, so established the design, that, including the little Princess Christina, we moved in a sort of rhythmic union through the whole performance, and I suffered the modicum of torment, and only in details, whose importance had but one significance, that of being present but unobserved.

* * *

At about this time another trip abroad — in the summer, of course — was indicated. Three pictures had been sent over. Miss Anne Blake, of Boston, always a staunch friend and ally, was my mate on this trip, and she never allowed me to blunder; never had I to think where to get off, or on, or how; and with this inestimable quality, she joined a taste and perception *à tout épreuve* — was, in fact, an artist.

We had friends in London. The Gilders were there, and Mrs. Robert Chapin. The Chapins were living, at the time, at the house in Chelsea (on the Embankment) called 'Queen's House.' It was built for Katherine of Braganza by Sir Christopher Wren. A wonderful house, with a long drawing-room furnished in pure Jacobean, and with a magnificent chimney-piece of black-and-white marble. Here Mrs. Chapin held court, creating in her lustrous personality an atmosphere to which Mrs. Gilder brought her magical presence from time to time. Here also Dante Gabriel

Rossetti had lived and died, among his friends, Swinburne, Ford Maddox Brown, and others of the pre-Raphaelite *culte*.

There was a large square garden at the back, where one could easily imagine the members of this group in twilight colloquy on summer nights, and their talk, seasoned and richly brewed and colored, would have flowed in glistening currents, of opposition or astute argument. It is, indeed, a trial that one cannot listen at the portals of the past, and catch the very inflection of voices, discussing questions in Art and Literature, that were *then* believed to be ultimate, and which at all events gave to English poetry some of its richest and most poignant expression. At least, there was *time*. London lay outside, and around, in encircling mass. Chelsea's quiet — the river — was an unbroken silence at such hours, to men untrammelled by to-morrow's engagements. Thought had room in which to be born — to expand — and to reach its climax, as speech between friends. England's culture and England's liberty were, indeed, in ghostly presence in this house.

I had seen a good many of Sargent's paintings and had keenly felt his power. We had letters to him, and, although I had always shied at the moment of such presentation, feeling it to be a mean advantage, we sent him our 'ticket of admission.' His instant and kindly reply invited us to lunch with him at his club. His appearance was a surprise, though, of course, we had often heard him described. The fact that there was no flavor of the studio about him was no impediment for us, for we did not belong, ourselves, to the group who thought it necessary to carry about with them the labels of their profession. There were fewer cigarettes at that time, but many of the devotees of painting thought grimy velveteen, and a slouch, the proper uniform for artists, male and female.

We were gay. There was so much to talk about that we

all, for the time, forgot our calling; at least we did not dis-
cuss it, except that I remember Sargent pointed out especial
opportunities that might be ours just then, for seeing pictures, etc., outside the well-known galleries. He took us to
his studio in Tite Street, where he was at work upon the
central painted bas-relief for the 'Christianity,' in the series
of 'Religions,' destined for the Boston Library. Sargent was
apparently much puzzled as to the treatment of one part of
the design of the Cross, with figures of Adam and Eve: he
was a very shy man, and his almost stammering appeal to
me as to what I thought of the problem, and how to solve it,
was that of an eager, anxious self-doubter. I was filled with
confusion, but concealed it, and knew, of course, that I was
only a fresh eye, and that it must all be taken as the most
natural thing in the world. I said what I thought, and he
listened in exactly the same mood. I saw that his 'worldly'
appearance, manner, and speech were a sort of armor for
his sensitiveness, though not an armor put on by him, for he
was homogeneous.

There were no portraits about, and very little of any kind
of furnishing, but it was a grand large place, and somehow
good, and extremely suggestive of the style and simplicity of
all his best things. As every one knows, Sargent was not a
collector, and satisfied his beauty sense in the glamour that
for him hung about every person and object, and to which
most of the world is blind, though, of course, his high culture
and lifetime familiarity with the Art of the Old World in all
its phases had been 'always with him.' I saw him again
long afterwards, at lunch at Mrs. Gardner's, at Fenway
Court. She had given him the Dutch Room as a studio, and
he was engaged on his portrait of Mrs. Fiske Warren and
daughter, which he allowed us to see, in its unfinished state.
I regret that this was the only time I ever saw any of his
portrait painting *en passage*.

The last time I saw Sargent was at luncheon also, at the
Chilton Club in Boston. His cousin and intimate friend,

Mrs. Richard Hale, was our hostess, and he took us afterwards to see the Lunettes at the Library, which were ready
to be placed. He showed us also two landscapes, neither of
them, I thought, equal to the picture owned by Mrs. Sears,
a rocky alpine pasture, in morning sunshine, aglitter with
rain, dew, or ice, a revelation of truth, so moving that it
shook the soul, as beauty does.

During the winter that followed Sargent's death, a
memorial meeting was held at the Contemporary Club of
Philadelphia, at which Professor Weeks, of New Haven,
took the leading part. I had the honor of following him in a
short address, in which I attempted to sum up a few of
what I thought the foremost characteristics of Sargent's
painting. As this is too lengthy to be transcribed here and
in a fragment would be almost misstatement, another time
and place will, I hope, give me an opportunity for expression on a subject (which has many leadings), even though it
has already been so ably treated by others.

After the death of John Lambert — best of friends — best
of comrades, the beautiful old house in South Seventh
Street, Philadelphia, of which he had made the most charming of studio dwellings, was vacant. Our old home was
broken up and divided, and I was glad to occupy the
Seventh Street house, and that it should remain unspoiled
for a time. I lived in it for one winter, and my friend, Mrs.
John F. Lewis, posed for me there, with her son John. The
atmosphere of the place, which its owner had known so well
how to preserve, gave me instant opportunity, and life
there was an elegy on his presence — and absence. During
this and an extended period I criticised a large and interesting class at the P.A.F.A. Eakins had no follower of his
metal, but the tradition of his day remained, and much
very sincere work was done in the school. I served frequently on the juries for the Academy Exhibitions, and
have to acknowledge constant kindness and appreciation
from the Institution.

Crowded months and crowded years followed, and in this middle period much must be passed over, which, to the recorder, was of lively interest. But Mrs. Roosevelt's portrait was an episode of highly varied importance, as it brought me into close relation with her fascinating family, as well as with her charming self. A number of visits to Washington were needed for the work, and the portrait was painted in the White House. It was to have been of Mrs. Roosevelt only, but her daughter Ethel consented to literally 'jump in,' greatly enlivening, I hope, her mother's hours of attention to posing. This attention was constant and sympatic, but not static, and did not need to be. They generously devoted the Red Room to me for a studio, giving it up as a convenient breakfast-room. But it was no less a meeting-place for morning affairs of the family, since 'mother' was to be consulted by every member before beginning the day, not to say after, when desired.

I chose — and upholstered — a covering for the broad seat on which Mrs. Roosevelt and Ethel could dispose themselves easily; the warmth of the Red Room got somehow into the picture, and fortunately we proceeded without many changes. I understood from the first that it was not to be an official portrait, and I think every one was satisfied that, as it was created among intimate circumstances, its spirit might be the same. The President sometimes came in soon after we 'opened,' and bent a benign and conciliatory eye upon us; never charging the atmosphere with super-dynamic propositions, or inquiries, leaving us sustained and soothed, a unique demonstration, I fondly hoped, of his power as a collaborator. The collaboration of the children was in a special form of entertainment. All the party had the poems of Sir Walter Scott by heart, but 'King Olaf' was a favorite because it was a drama, and rôles might be selected, or rather shouted for. The first in the field, which began far outside the door, being victor for the title rôle. When they all got going, it became a chorus in unison, several preferring to take the same part. Their mother was entirely unruffled by the noise and spirited commotion, which she was, of course, inured to, and in which she took an indefinite part, prompting in all directions, when needed, as she, also, was letter perfect in every drama produced. Generally the vocal torrent flowed around me without lessening or heightening the tempo of the piece on which I was exclusively engaged. Also suddenly, the stampede would be centrifugal, and, in a twinkling, a silence, in which Mrs. Roosevelt neither changed her smile nor her mood, would take place.

I had for some time been much hindered by a kind of neuritis in my right hand and arm, which was not painful, but prohibited me from holding a pen. Fortunately, as one cannot be said to 'hold' a paint-brush, at least not as a pen is used, this did not interfere with my work, and a friendly scribe and a hired typewriter made my letters home possible, though they were very inadequate, and if I transcribe a few extracts, it is because a near view conveys more, if very informally:

Sunday, April 6

'I LOVE MY PRESIDENT. It certainly is a profound human instinct to have a chief, and love him, and I only wish his tribe wasn't too big for him to give each one in it a personal chance. I have made a sketch of him. He sat for two hours, talking most of the time, reciting Kipling, and reading scraps of Browning. Teddy came in, too, and tried to draw him. When I was there at luncheon the other day, we spoke of Leech, and the President said he thought he knew every one of his drawings by heart. I then mentioned the new edition of "Punch," and that my brother-in-law had bought it for his children. They didn't know there was such a thing, and the children all jumped at the idea, etc.'

'Sunday afternoon was very jolly (a small reception, for the portrait). Two Chief Justices came and a stream of

MRS. THEODORE ROOSEVELT AND DAUGHTER

other interesting people. M. Cambon, with whom I spoke French daringly, Mr. Putnam the Librarian, Langdon Mitchell and wife, and others less known.

'At the Reception, the good Procters took hold and saw me through — but anyway, it is all so independent that, if it so happens, one doesn't mind being alone at all. It was for the Army and Navy especially this time, and there was a whole batch of German naval officers — great fun to see, all looking like Axel. Our Chief and Consort stand at the door of the Blue Room, which is a pretty oval drawing-room not very large. The Cabinet Ladies are arranged in a row beside Mrs. R. and, as you pass, you are expected to bow to them, if you can remember. Remembering Grandma's story, I took care not to "fall down before the President's Lady," but I only spoke to the last C. L. Then I went "behind the line," being told to. This is an honor, as it means you don't have to pass on into space. There were no foreign uniforms more remarkable than the red coats of the English — except the little Jap visiting lady, who had been induced to wear a kimono — but couldn't resist a very badly made pink pompon in her hair.

'The most interesting person I met was Archbishop Ireland — of course only an introduction, but I watched him for some time. A most fascinating person, and *seemed* entirely French. I felt as if he were a relation, and must have seen the light first at Avignon. The President gives every one a look of deep sympathy, as if there wasn't time to look it all. Mrs. R. had a big bunch of lilies-of-the-valley, and they resembled her. I met the George Kennans, the Rockhills, and of course Mrs. Cowles. I saw the Wainwrights, and they were delightfully friendly. No one was very beautiful or very wonderful, but the whole thing was easy and agreeable. The R.'s bring their atmosphere into everything. Thanks to the good services of our two "gentlemen in waiting," Peter and Martin, and the advantage of the back way, it was as easy to go, as it had been to come. Mr. Kennan told me it had taken them an hour and a half to get in.'

* * *

Paderewski at the White House

'Sleepy as I am, dear Three, I must send you some record of last night, though I can't hope it will be more interesting than the newspaper account which I enclose. The yellow head of the Lion shone gloriously against the satin of the Blue Room when I entered rather breathlessly, fearing to be late (as I had started with both gloves for one hand). He and Madame were standing alone, as were all the other couples, whispering, and I joined them at once, as I suppose few of the Official people knew them. It is a thrilling moment when the Sovereigns come in, and we all rise, if we have been seated, an act which would turn the head of any ordinary civilian. They went the rounds, and made each of us happy. The President is too delicious when he drops his great square head on one side, with an air of exchanging a confidence with the Country's guest. I was taken in by the Honorable Lucius N. Littauer, and sat between him and the Honorable William H. Moody, and had a very jolly time, as they both seemed ready to be amused. I did not expect to listen to any State Secrets from them, but they both think there is no chance of getting the appropriation for the Improvements.

'Madame P. sat on the President's right hand, and Paderewski took in Mrs. Roosevelt. Have they ever been so honored before? I don't know how they have been treated in the Courts of Europe. There was no general talk, and people heard only their neighbors, but I think the President found more material in Madame P. than in fat Mrs. ——, who sat next to him. One incident amused the President very much. One of my neighbors asked him after dinner who "Miss Beecox" was, and he never forgot to call me by this name when he saw me.

'We all trailed out to the Blue Room again, and all the

people in fine print began to come. The East Room was crowded. Has there ever been a Musical Party there before? — I sat with the St. Gaudenses, the Procters, and Mrs. West Roosevelt, in front, where I could hear and see splendidly. The President was near with Mrs. Lodge.

'Paderewski out-did himself, though he was a little cold at first. I enclose the programme. By the time he got to the Polonaise of all (at least to me), the one with the tragic octaves — well — I think it may have been better than hearing Chopin himself. All of Paderewski's gigantic power was back of it. I don't believe he has ever gone higher, farther, or deeper. I nearly broke under it — which means that I experienced all that I could endure of joy — and was aware that I had tasted the best of its kind that creation can offer.

'St. Gaudens is doing a bas-relief of Mr. and Mrs. Wayne MacVeagh, which I hope to see. The R.'s all go to Charleston on Monday. Mrs. R. is practically done. The President likes it. Don't know how the world at large is going to feel ——Young T. says, "Corking!"...'

I did not stay at the White House while the work was going on, but Mrs. R. invited me to visit them at Oyster Bay in July. A short note says:

Sagamore Hill

'...You will read about us in the papers, but you will not know, perhaps, that the President ate two mutton chops for his luncheon — not much to keep *it* up on. I sat next to him, so I know. I also know that he is a perfect dear. He played tennis a long time this A.M. and I *sat on his coat.*

'Lots of important-looking men are floating around, and some of them are:

'Mr. Secretary Shaw.

'Mr. Secretary Moody.

'The District Attorney.

'At breakfast the President had an ample and well-used

— 231 —

copy of the Oxford Bible by his plate — and between bacon and eggs, etc., he, holding it up in his right hand, examined the family on some of the Hebrew wars. All were familiar with the subject and the ethics of the campaigns, and strategic values were discussed, generally by several speaking at once. Although I had a slight surface knowledge, I thought best not to get into the arena, knowing that I should soon lose my footing.'

* * *

At another time I spent Sunday at the White House. Sunday night supper was a strictly domestic function on this occasion, there being only one guest from without, besides myself — Gifford Pinchot. I had lately been reading a very good translation of the 'Chanson de Roland,' and when the President talked of Jiu-Jitzu at some length, something he said reminded me of an episode toward the end of the final scene of the 'Epopée.' 'Yes!' — cried the President, 'when he throws his glove to God...!' And then followed a rushing résumé of the story, with many details and suggestions. I suppose he had probably neither thought nor spoken of the poem for many years, and that on any other historic or legendary subject that had happened to come up, he would have been equally alive and informed.

* * *

The winters in Boston and Cambridge which followed were full of interesting work. To do Miss Vaughn and little Helen Amory in the cabin studio of Professor Thayer's garden was, in spite of the always to be conquered obstacles, a charming adventure. We had a grand wood fire, but I often had to gather up a dustpan full of icicles from the divan in the other end of the room, and melt down my palette and paint-tubes in the hot ashes, on my arrival.

Miss Irwin, Dean of Radcliffe, allowed me to spend the winter with her. All the best of Cambridge frequented her house, and best of all I could catch constant reflection from her brilliant spirit. Mrs. Gardner I had previously met, and Miss Irwin and I were delighted to be invited together to spend the morning with her at Fenway Court. My friendship with Piatt Andrew, who was then at Harvard, had already begun, and he and my nephew, Henry Drinker, who was a student at the Law School, were also of the party, and Mrs. Gardner gave us her best (did she not always seem to do this?) for several hours. She became later an habituée of Eastern Point, a constant visitor at Red Roof and Little Beauport, and the chief luminary, of course, of every occasion; in fact, we did not consider any party to be worthy of note without her. I am now writing upon a charming table she gave me, and not long before the beginning of her fatal illness, she drove to my door in New York and left a small parcel for me. It proved to be a wonderful bracelet of the finest French workmanship in gold. It had a presence, and might have adorned the arm of the Princess Mathilde, or Queen Hortense, in her mature years.

One day, during a brief visit of Henry James to this country, he came to lunch with me, in company with Mrs. Gardner. It was a day of wet fog which he persisted in admiring, having found everything in America too hard and noisy... unendurable, in fact. Later, in New York, Mrs. Gilder persuaded him to sit for me for a drawing — to be hers. Alas ...what a *supplice* it is to be divided between the interest of such an attempt and the desire to listen to the reminiscences of two such people. But when the drawing was finished, after a fashion, and he came to look at it, his verdict was uttered with more than his usual hesitation:

'Astonishing... a... economy... of... means.'

Okakura, the Japanese scholar and connoisseur, had spent a week-end with me at my first halt at Eastern Point, and later, in Boston, was a frequent visitor at the studio which Joe Smith had let me have for the winter. The delightful harmony of the place, its quiet on winter afternoons, was no doubt sympathetic to his æsthetic sensibilities, and he even brought the materials for formal Japanese tea service one day, and gave me a lesson in the technique of the function. I heard from him also the classic manner of repeating Japanese poetry, in which he changed his whole personality, voice, and especially facial expression. The subject of the poem, which of course was not translated, was 'A mountain landscape in Maine, in winter.' Here also my friend Charles Dyer, sang — and many friends made the winter memorable.

IX

WAR PORTRAITS

IN the spring of 1919, a committee was formed of men and women, prominent in our social and financial world, for the purpose of getting together a series of portraits of the outstanding figures of the War; these portraits to be presented, finally, to the United States Government. A group of artists, five in number, was chosen to do this work. To each artist was assigned three portraits, to be painted, for the most part, abroad, for the chief interest in the undertaking lay in the fact that most of the subjects were to be Europeans of whom only photographs were likely ever to appear in this country, or be owned here, at any rate, by our Government.

The secretary of the committee called on me, and asked me to undertake to go abroad and execute three of these portraits. I accepted with a full sense of the significance and interest of the commission. I was told that the three to be entrusted to me were Cardinal Mercier, Clemenceau, and Admiral Lord Beatty.

I realized the responsibility of this undertaking very keenly, and felt that I must approach it with the knowledge that there should be brought to it much more than my mere equipment as an artist. Great portraits of great people are very rare. Art is a jealous mistress when asked to divide the honors with a great personality, and refuses to wait on the scant times and seasons such persons are willing to spare — hurried half-hours here and there.

Even a vivid likeness, snatched at an artist's strongest moment, and having the convincing power of a few authoritative strokes, always has some of the impermanent quality of an accident when it attempts to show the full weight and character content of one of those rare beings who defy ordinary standards. Each of these is twenty men or more, and to give posterity any idea of their power by an appearance static and material requires in the approacher a conscious and just mind, no less than the gods' gift of subconscious force. I am glad that, as I approached my task, I was aware of this, for at least I had no doubt of what should be accomplished, and so inspired could dare anything, as does a good soldier, not thinking of possible or probable defeat.

This is an apology. Whatever is lacking in the result — which of course fell far behind my hopes — I may lay the story of my adventure, a small wreath among the heaped tributes that lie along the pathway of the great.

* * *

Paris — May — and the War over.

The 'Signing' was about to take place in the Gallerie des Glaces at Versailles. Nothing was very good, but no one knew how much worse it was going to be. The harvest of death and pain still continued; but the Gorgon was prone with limp claws, and no more beautiful youth would go out to the sacrifice. One could not restrain elation, joy even, in the novelty of the 'Concorde' stacked with German guns, and the overflowing presence of 'our boys.' Everywhere they swarmed, looking, waiting, lonely or foolish, as the case might be, but, most of all, touching. Old Paris is a woman, and knows the precious flavor of any kind of youth. The invisible element, in tangible balm, flowed through her streets, and on into her old veins. Our big children were in the way now, but, like all other French mothers, she loved them.

She loved their long waists and broad thin shoulders, the languor of unoccupied youth, ready to spring, tense and able, and with far more force than itself is aware of.

For the attack on the portraits, it seemed natural to begin with Clemenceau, but, as 'Le Tigre' was not particularly in love with America just then, wise counsel feared a complete refusal if he were approached as 'Président du Conseil,' with the last struggle over the treaty going on.

Mr. Henry White, who had consented to open doors for the working performers and arrange with the victims, one day showed me the Treaty. It had just come in, in final form. I had come up to the great rooms *au premier* in the Crillon, the American Headquarters for the Conseil, where one arrived through serried ranks of khaki-clad American lads, never lacking the aura of the home town. The vast crimson-damasked room, its noble windows open on the broad balcony, and the Concorde... France in all her high elegance, was a place I rejoiced to have easy access to.

Mr. White took from a table drawer a great printed volume. As I wrote home, 'I will not tell you what was in it, as it is not yet "out," and the censor might not like it'; but as I only looked into it, and handled it as an object, I could not have divulged much.

What mattered it to wait a month for orders; May and June in Paris in 1919 were months to clasp and hold with the haunting sense of 'never again.' Paris itself, in its array of ordered beauty, was forever the same miracle. Bent old men watched over every leaf and flower in the parks and Champs Élysées. Women and children, with the well-known switch brooms, washed the streets at dawn. The same crystal rivulets ran in the gutters — nothing could hinder these people, the French, in the one right way of doing everything.

Best of all we had a friend — Henry Davis Sleeper — who, after raising fabulous amounts for the support of the Ambulance, had left his creative pursuits in the fine arts and their application to life, for participation in the farthest separation from the same... that is, for the War. When he came to our rescue, on our arrival, the 'Ambulance' at the rue Rayouard was dispersed, and he for a day or two gave us the precious experience of a trip to the devastated region under his guidance.

Thus we were not without a glimpse of the tragedy. We saw Rheims, martyred form, but constant beauty; Noyons, Soissons, and the rest, and passed over the Chemin des Dames: even then a road remade and perfect. Huge piles of rusty barbed wire and empty shells were stacked in serried order, just beyond the road edge. All this was hand work, with stooping back, and in constant danger of unexploded shells from the broken fields. Unemployment in France! Certainly not.

June had thrown a robe over the whole land, the tri-color, in poppies, daisies, and bluets, not mingled, but in great masses as clear as the flag of France. Soft summer sunshine, songs of invisible birds, hope, comradeship were ours, as we moved over the perfect roads in a little French service car.

Why, so near to death and ruin, were we so blessed?

X

CARDINAL MERCIER

WHEN His Eminence Cardinal Mercier, Archevêque de Malines, was asked by our Minister, Mr. Brand Whitlock — by way of my good friend, Mr. White, and the Belgian Ambassador — to allow me, an American artist, to do his portrait for the United States Government, he consented at once; and I found in all our subsequent intercourse that His Eminence was eager, in every possible way, to show his gratitude and appreciation for what we, through the invaluable agency of Mr. Whitlock, had done for Belgium in the War.

We left Paris on July 2d, and as we entered Belgium and approached Brussels, the War came nearer too; but in the fields and farms, all was perfect order and prosperity. Neatly laid ditches, potato fields, all kinds of produce in process of cultivation, seemed to have been that very day trained and tended by hands that knew and cared nought for labor-saving. Even the soil looked as if careful fingers had crumbled and smoothed it. So Belgium was being, and would be, fed. But while we passed through in the waning afternoon, no laborer was in the fields. The order and schedule for the day was as perfect as the result in production.

We arrived at Brussels in a drenching thunderstorm. The vast station was empty, guards and porters nowhere. We spent an hour getting out of the station and into an open fiacre with only the hood to shelter us and our hand luggage from the solid downpour and continuous alarms of thunder and lightning. Miles the poor horse dragged us, but our hotel, when reached, was in a beautiful quarter, near the Palace, and was old-fashioned, and reminiscent, for me, of the time long ago when one expected musty carpets and a *bouillotte* of *eau chaud*.

Brussels was entirely undamaged by the War. 'Why,' the Germans thought, 'destroy a pretty place that will be so nice to live in later on?'

I sent my letter of introduction to Mr. Whitlock and received back, at once, a cordial note in his own handwriting, asking us to come that afternoon — it was July 4th — to the Embassy, where Mrs. Whitlock and he would be receiving.

We had no trouble in recognizing the tall, slim gentleman, who stood receiving, but our names shouted he had somehow missed, and we met the polite smile dealt out to nice-looking American ladies he did not recognize, and knew what it was to join the ranks of the near-superfluous. We took a modest station in the background. The room was full of American officers and soldiers, and I soon felt that we were being observed by a young attaché, who glided to his chief, whispered something, and then approached us, with exquisite tact, assisted by our willingness to be recognized. In a moment Mr. and Mrs. Whitlock had joined us, and with such new faces, and Mr. Whitlock bore us off to other rooms to see his pictures.

He is an enthusiastic patron of art, and while in Belgium, in addition to all his other labors, warmed many a discouraged artist's heart by appreciation and the purchase of pictures. He was eager to talk about painting, and Mrs. Whitlock had to drag him back to his duties as host and his patient smile. It was an interesting side-light on the organizer and philanthropist. Belgium will never forget him, and will honor all Americans for his sake. Unfortunately for us, they were leaving Brussels the next day, and we did not see them again, but Mr. Whitlock left everything in order for my meeting with the Cardinal.

* * *

By train, Malines is only a half-hour from Brussels, and in the broad flat country one sees the Tower from afar. I took an automobile, and a young secretary from the Embassy escorted us.

As all the roads in Belgium are paved with 'Belgian blocks' — square stones not very well fitted — there is little pleasure in a drive, but by car we arrived more directly and had better views of the old town, the *Place*, and, above all, the Cathedral of Saint Rombaud. The apse is badly damaged, but the Tower stands in untouched grandeur and elegance. There was even a gentle warbling of the famous Carillon, as we drew near; the professor was having a half-hour of practice.

A bunch of green trees, in a small square flanking the Cathedral, a narrow, bending street, and we were in a little silent grass-grown *place*, and before the door of the Archevêché.

The A.-V. had the air of being a place one would not think of attempting to enter. A vast green door in a cold eighteenth-century façade gave no sign to encourage visitors, and the loud clang of a bell, when so timidly rung from without, bade pushing Protestants see to their manners and credentials.

Almost instantly the door was opened by a punctilious butler, and immediately behind him a 'frère' in a black soutane, a kindly person whom I afterwards learned to look on as a 'brother,' in plain English. With all the cold and steady politeness of which I am capable, I 'made known' by card and letter, and was suavely told that I was expected. We, the secretary and I, were motioned to follow, and with one furtive glance at the lovely garden and big trees, we passed through long cool spotless corridors, to a *salle* where we could wait...and we did...in a place whose aspect told us that others had previously politely, reverently, not to say patiently, waited in it. As our conductor left us, my murmur of '*trois heures*' made little change in his firm, anonymous smile. No step sounded from the marble corridors. Neither the handsome painted image of the Virgin, nor the suitable and well-thumbed books on the centre table kept our attention long, and after a few muffled whispers, the secretary and I resigned ourselves to admiring the cool grey tones of the walls and the fine, lofty, eighteenth-century windows. Also I was satisfied to have time to feel where I was, and receive even an echo, a sensation strangely familiar and right, to my half Old-World nature. This was a place where hurry was unknown, and I was to learn afterwards, to my great happiness, that when His Eminence gives audience he gives his whole time and attention; no wrist-watch is glanced at; the faltering soul feels that he has 'attained to look upon the beginning of Peace' and goes out, calm and satisfied.

The step in the corridor was heard at last, and we were summoned. Whoever preceded us left at another angle, for we neither met nor saw any one till we reached the foot of a broad carpeted staircase. I looked up and saw the Cardinal waiting to receive us. I had been afraid, but when I saw the tall form against the light, slightly stooping, and with clasped hands, its benignity seemed to reach down, and raise me up.

Perhaps the choicest moments in life are those when an emotion we have heard of, but never quite believed in, becomes ours, and we know all at once the reality of an eternal truth. Never does the soul so expand, or the limits of being open, as to such a revelation. To feel suddenly what humanity can attain to, and the compelling, subduing force of the presence, merely, of the truly great, is one of these experiences. Never before had I found myself a worshipper or at the feet of a mortal. But long hands were unclasped and I was welcomed by the gentlest of voices. I pulled myself together and explained, I now scarcely know how, but he had had time to observe the very sediment of my soul. He knew all about me, and recommendations did not need to be noticed. With an unsuppressable tremble in my voice I told how greatly honored I felt to have been entrusted with the

S. E. CARDINAL MERCIER

portrait of him for my Government, and that I hoped to trouble him as little as possible. I could doubtless find a studio in Malines. He opened a door and we passed into a large bare hall. He pointed to an enormous hole in the high ceiling, roughly patched up with lath where a German shell had come through. The walls were peppered with small holes. A number of armchairs, for Bishops convening, two tables, and a high faded-red throne-canopy at one side, was all the furniture the room contained. There were eight large uncurtained windows on both sides, one side looking into the beautiful garden and court. There was plenty of light and space. He saw my thought and that I trusted this was to be my studio, while still in the first moments of my introduction, but he led on with exquisite cordiality, through smaller rooms encumbered with furniture, which I, of course, politely admired, but secretly could not 'see' as places to paint in. He then said, with his beautiful smile, that I could choose what I wished. It was evident that he had thought it was a matter of *esquisses* that could be taken away and worked from. Here was the moment when I felt that only the straight truth would do. He showed us a portrait of himself and photographs. We spoke of sittings. 'Besnard,' he said, 'had had two.' I made no pretence of being able to work quickly, and explained that if I undertook it in the Archevêché, I would have to finish the portrait there, and would be obliged to spend most of the day there for perhaps a long time. Would it not be troublesome, impossible, in fact? I would do the work by means of studies with as few sittings from him as possible, but I should have to go in and out a good deal.

Certainly, Madame, 'Vous êtes tout-à-fait libre.'

By this time we had returned to the large *salle*, and he turned and said, with a charming gesture,

'Madame, vous êtes chez vous.'

All this, with his tall figure slightly stooping, his hands always clasped. I tried to express my appreciation of his kindness and to give him openings of escape, but the Cardinal had made up his mind. He knew as well as I did that, if in all else lacking, I could be trusted. I spoke of hotels. He said that there were none possible for ladies in Malines; the inns were all '*auberges de soldat*.' But there was a convent where ladies often went *en retraite*. It could be arranged for us to go there.

These details are only interesting as showing a great man's ease and readiness in small matters, to which the Cardinal never stood aloof when they came his way.

By this time I was able to grasp a few details, as in the back of my mind I was seeing the portrait all the time, vaguely. His black soutane was edged with crimson, and fastened by an interminable row of small red buttons, a crimson moiré sash fell at the side of his very long waist, and a flat scarlet cap, the 'Soli Deo,' worn far back, allowed his great forehead its prominence. The Pectoral Cross, on a heavy chain, hung round his neck. Of his face I saw that materially his color was high, cheek-bones broad and nose prominent, his face a long oval, but deeply furrowed as though lying under the threshings of the spirit, in league with an inextinguishable youth.

Of course we spoke of America, and I knew that in gratitude and recognition he would willingly make any personal sacrifice of time and effort in his power. He accompanied us downstairs, and I passed out, dazed by the greatness of my opportunity. Outside, my patient friend had sat out a thunderstorm in the limousine. We had not known that the elements were celebrating a moment of history.

There are eleven convents in Malines, and the Chanoine Francken, the Cardinal's secretary, arranged for us to live with the 'Sœurs de N. D. de la Miséricorde.' The Chanoine Francken spoke I am sure many languages, but his English

was of the purest Oxford, and he expected to use it. He was
the only one of the attachés or staff at the Archevêché who
gave the impression of being thoroughly of this world. His
manners were perfectly in keeping with his English speech.
His immaculate black soutane fitted as no soutane ever did
before, and his whole perfectly groomed person gave
evidence that he did not hold with certain mediæval aspects
of holiness. His intelligent head was full of character, and
we learned afterwards that, as it was impossible for the
Germans to 'entertain' a Cardinal in prison, his secretary
went in his stead and spent two years there.

The convent which he chose for us was in the rue des
Draps, a back street with a long, slight, and interesting
curve; the House, with its white front and high grey roof,
followed the line of this curve, as is the charming way with
eighteenth-century architecture. Its only street door was a
lofty and massive green portal, with a smaller door enclosed, so that modest indigence, and the sisters, could slip
in and out almost unobserved. Beyond comprehension as it
is to the mass-mind of America, there still exist places and
people who actually avoid publicity. Inside, the picturesque
vanished, except the always beautiful, swiftly and softly
moving black-and-white forms of the sisters, and a few old
women in black lace caps, who were wards of the House.

La Sœur Denyse, guardian of the door, let us in when we
arrived, a little anxious about our welcome. But we were
expected, and I think a slight hesitation in Sœur Denyse was
only owing to a perhaps preconceived view of what our appearance would be, and perhaps we were not as obviously
professional as was expected, in ladies who were to have sec-
ular dealings with the Cardinal. However, our modest de-
meanor seemed to satisfy, and very soon La Reverende
Mère advanced to meet us.

I have always respected the wisdom of the Church, and
never more than in its ability to choose personalities for
Places. La Reverende Mère was a lady — small, and not

elderly. A bearing was hers that perfectly combined command with grace. We were guests to whom kindness was to be shown. The Cardinal had spoken. We felt like awkward school-girls. Not ours to think. All was arranged. After greeting us, the small, white compact hands, laid one on the other at her waist, made no gesture or movement. Her voice and smile were one, in suavity, and she left us, charmed, slightly dazed, and with our hearts prepared for obedience.

The picturesque is not sought for in the convent of to-day; I doubt whether it ever was. Once, whatever way seemed best was chosen, and was perhaps the only way. Now, with the same method, an entirely different result appears.

I looked in vain for cloistered walk, ancient garden well-head, or Gothic chapel. There may have been a garden once. Now a small grassed court, partly glazed over, was flanked on the opposite side by a high new building of brick, with narrow windows, and entirely destitute of the art of the one time Flemish masons and carpenters. Under the glazed corridor, however, a stout nun, with endless care and art, produced marvels in begonias, and insignificant flowers, which I dimly recognized as having appeared in the hanging baskets of my childhood, here were developed to a size and richness that only faultless science, love and duty could have achieved. Sœur Denyse, who was to be our constant friend and director, led us up many broad stairs to our chamber, which was in the roof, a long narrow room with two windows on the street facing south. Here at least was antiquity of a kind, whitewashed walls and peaked ceiling. Our beds, placed end for end along the wall, billowed with red duvets and lace. I was happy in the scrubbed boards of the floor, and the meagre furniture. Near the entrance of the room stood two large armoires, and we soon found that furtive old women might be expected to grope through, seeking to examine their belongings therein contained. Also, the large door was partly glazed, and there are no locks in convents.

At the sunny end of the room was another door, where the plump young nun who did scrubbing chores all day might enter when she pleased and pass through. But who would object to this? For my part her sunny face and greeting were always welcome, and she was the one to persuade for an extra towel or can of water. Such was the gently meted out discipline of the house that these intrusions were neither frequent nor annoying. Our privacy was from the world, not from *nos sœurs*.

Our supper that first evening, taken alone in a sort of guests' room on the ground floor, was the evening meal of the establishment. We were told that we might make certain, to us quite important, changes in it if we wished. But food is not eaten for enjoyment in a convent of nuns. Here, pleasure was to appear in other forms, and had nought to do with material things. At recreation in the court, under the one tree, the nuns could be seen gaily chatting, showing embroidery, and carefully discussing it. Laughter of the happiest trilled forth, light forms hastened in and out, and the heavier and older sat comfortably at their mending or knitting.

The Carillon at Malines is said to be the finest in the world, and we were happily near to the great Tower. But I thought that night that I should have to do without sleep at Malines. Every eight minutes the Cathedral clock made some sign; at the quarter and half hour there was real performance; while at the hour, something like a long *Aria* rang out. When we next saw the Chanoine Francken, he assured us that he had had the same experience on arrival, and that in a few nights we would cease to hear it, which proved to be true.

* * *

There exists a very delicate relation between a great individual and the limner who undertakes to grasp, or divine, and pass on to posterity the external signs of a large and complex personality. The artist is, indeed,. fortunate who has been honored by the confidence of his great subject. Not only confidence, but sympathy in the undertaking. For with confidence on both sides comes freedom, a large space in which to place the ethics of the matter in true relation to the material, the purely plastic and irreducible element of painting.

I felt at once that the work would never be hindered by the slightest misunderstanding between the Cardinal and myself. What a small matter it was compared to those he daily had in hand! But it was for America, who had given bountifully to Belgium during the War, and he accepted me, and my paraphernalia, as constant occupants of the Salle des Évêques, for two months (or as much time as I wanted), with perfect liberality and graciousness, before I had been in his presence five minutes. Of course, I never abused this trust, and of course he knew I would not. I have no doubt he knew more of me in those five minutes than I have ever known of myself, and if I had to sum up his character in a word, which would be impossible, I should say, 'With him nothing is too small, nothing too great.' He had the grandeur, the universality, and the unconsciousness of Nature: the highest peak, the deepest river, and the way of the butterfly in the air. I should be sorry for any one, however, who went to him on a false pretense, however well authenticated. After the confidence of the Cardinal, my supreme advantage lay in the distance of the noisy world from Malines, the convent, and the Archevêché. Here there was no hurry, none of the sterile drain on nerve force, that cannot be escaped in America. Here there would be time to think, and to turn over and reject most of the infinite possibilities that at first would present plans and schemes.

The Cardinal knew that it would take several days to settle in, in my vast studio, and arrange necessary details. An ample table was found for me somewhere *en bas*. I hired a large and comfortable easel from a photographer, but chiefly I sat in the silent great room among the shell-holes, with its view from high windows on the Cardinal's lovely garden. Many times before coming to Malines, I was congratulated on the great opportunity for color that would be mine with a Cardinal for subject. I have never loved the strident values of red and black, as such, and had secretly hoped that in the splendid robes there might be some combination of red and violet. But after I had seen the Cardinal, all ideas of color for its own sake diminished in importance, as did the majesty of his official costume. It always seemed to be somewhere behind him, as if he had been dressed by some one, as was no doubt the case; and although he wore and managed the encumbering moirés so gracefully, he seemed as little aware of them as is a princely infant of the satins and laces of its christening attire.

To paint a red picture, I pondered, with all the bounty of crimson and scarlet silks — the purpling half tones on the forms of rich textures. No doubt blue could be found somewhere on the edge of shadow, as well as lines of orange. A seated figure, of course, for this, where a model could be easily substituted, and long mornings spent in turning a single fold, and finding a precise value in color.

All this might have been, but was not, tempting, and was soon put aside. I thought of Cardinal Mercier's will to defy Germany, and protect his country, his flock... the shepherd towering over the wolf, a father fearless before savages who are seeking the lives of his children. Moral grandeur in action. Impossible to reach this height, but the Cardinal must be standing, the head slightly bent, and, somehow to be attained, the semblance of a forward movement.

In frequent contact with such gentleness and suavity, it would be difficult to remember these things, for the attributes of a great fighter had been dropped deep into the abyss, not to be brought forth again until needed. But nobility would never be absent even in the most friendly moments, and humor, too, would be always ready. Life must be attained without leaning upon accident or occasion... vivid from within only, and this in spite of scarlet and black; and if one sought the root and spring of his strength, of course one must find it in a character great enough to be the exponent of the highest religious faith and sanctity.

Servant of God he was first of all. This, later, I was to feel more and more, and that his heart was always so near the altar, and so at home there, that all his acts were performed, as it were, from the steps of the Temple, and his intimate and human touch on those he blessed was warmed and annealed by the humility that was never unconscious of God, Eternity, and the great Sacrifice.

It cost me nothing to throw over all my usual habits and predilections as a painter. The pursuit was in a new field. The delights of the eye and the enchanting glamour it was used to throw around the chosen and visible must be held in abeyance; I must not depend on correct or even much posing. I must construct through knowledge gained little by little. Also I must be sparing in demands on him. Although I knew that he was accustomed to stand for hours at great ceremonies, weighed down by heavy robes, posing would be a different matter, and I dreaded to put any strain on a physique like his, abnormally tall and lean, 'crevé,' in fact, whether by temperament or abstinence. The idea of building up, rather than seizing, grew on me, and I began, after settling on the composition, to construct a head from memory.

Many sentimentalists would like to believe that form and the material dimension have little importance where spirit is preëminent. 'Show me the soul!' they cry; 'I am not interested in the body.' But his identity is in the whole nature of the man, and seek as one may to discover the essential in personality, one can never fully estimate the whole mechanism of union between body and spirit. The body fits the spirit better and in more ways than can ever be perceived by the most able searcher. Of course this is because they are identical, but this fact only increases the difficulty where life must be visibly seen, shining through the material semblance of the body, on canvas. The power of the spirit must be offered for view, and the artist who would deal with this problem has solid matter, only, at his disposal: the outer man, the flesh and blood of the subject, and the pigments and panel and other materials of his craft, the latter bringing with them the most obstinate sequences of resistance that matter has in reserve. I knew only too well that almost all the evidence in favor of certain faculties lies in the ear position, and the distances above and below it. Equally important is the space between the eyes, and the length from brow to nostril, the depth from brow to ear. Garble any of these facts, or misunderstand them, and you make an image that can never contain the man. For these truths memory is a guide not to be too much trusted; therefore at each new view of the subject, one must secure, not so much an impression as some one pregnant actuality in its relation to others.

I had made a small color composition and fully decided on the pose before I asked for the first sitting. I had also started a color study of the head, upon which I could work with as little resistance and ground-breaking as possible. I never at any time worked on the big canvas from the Cardinal, but always from drawings and a color study: a very well-known and ancient method, but one not yielding very strong results when dealing with minor personalities. I could make no attempt at modelling any part, much less attach the whole at the first *séance*, to which the Cardinal came with the gracious manner of having nothing else to do, and in which his efforts to be in any position were touching.

Impossible to give directions or to pull him about, as I must confess has been my custom. I abandoned all ground except his presence near a window, and tried to persuade him that this was all that was needed. But his mind would not rest in *being* there only. With that perfect belief in the abnormal faculties of an artist, which supposes him able, out of all other men, to make his most concentrated effort, and at the same time follow the workings and questionings of another mind, the Cardinal, always looking outside of himself, began inquiring of me concerning my *carrière*. Had I always painted portraits? To amuse him and make a little story, I told him how, when I was a girl at home and far from being an artist with a studio, I drew and lithographed fossils for scientific books. At this he threw up his hands and bowed over, laughing like a schoolboy:

'Et vous continuez encore!' —

* * *

As I never allowed the Cardinal to be wearied, or kept him more than a short time, I think he found in his visits to the Salle des Évêques a momentary release from care and was always ready to be amused: indeed, the Salle must have been a very different place when the Bishops were in session there. How seldom I saw the Prince of the Church, or he who had carried Belgium in his arms!

On that first day, going on with my stories, I spoke of teaching; of how I had often found, especially among women, those conscientious workers who continue feverishly many hours, with exhausted nerves, producing studies more and more inanimate, to whom I had often said: 'You are thoroughly tired out. No use going on with this. A half-hour flat on your back or a cup of tea alone can help you.'

He was much interested in the idea that production in Art depended so much on anything that might be called physical, and soon after crossed the room and rang a bell. Whereupon appeared one whom I learned to know as 'Jacques le valet.' A quiet order was given, and soon Jacques entered with a tray and a modest service of tea. It was placed on my painting-table, and the Cardinal smiled his invitation. We sat down, and he questioned my preferences as to cream and sugar, pouring out and offering my cup of tea, like any hostess. I tried to give some expression to my sense of what was happening, and under and within my historic memory was registering, 'Tea poured by Cardinal Mercier,' over and over, clasping the fact, sealing it as the choicest of all episodes. Asquith had been calling on him that morning, and he seemed pleased to tell me of the visit, though he did not communicate the result, and it was probably only a polite call, of which he receives hundreds. He is so modest that he even seemed pleased with my perfectly banal speech of appreciation, about being permitted to paint his portrait, and said that never before had he so quickly felt a friendship for any people as he had for America, a friendship *vraiment intime*,' and that it was because they had the same ideals of liberty and truth which made them turn with such sympathy to Belgium in her struggle for freedom.

Speaking of another nation, he said they were very different from us. They admired material force — '*La force du taureau*' — while we were sympathetic toward Belgium, because it was feeble but valiant.

Thereafter, every day at four, came Jacques with the tray, and I, wishing to assure myself of the best, once asked a question. 'Oui, Mademoiselle,' he said, smiling. 'C'est son Éminence qui l'a commandé.'

I soon had another *séance* after spending the morning in preparation. All was ready at two-thirty, a new window chosen with better light, assistance from little but obsequious butler, and female attendant. My friend Lucy Taggart was also there, and was to be presented. But no 'Eminence.' We waited until nearly four, then descended to private regions below, and after ringing an immense bell, which resounded through echoing corridors, the concierge appeared and hastened off to find His Eminence. Returning to the Salle, I saw from the window, walking serenely, the Cardinal far away in his garden, easy to discern, though only a small spot of black and scarlet. I saw him throw up his hands and hasten to follow the concierge, and in a few minutes he entered, breathless and apologetic. He had forgotten. We did a great deal of incoherent talking, for, for me really to accomplish something, speak French, and endure the darkness of a thunderstorm was beyond the limit of my powers.

The Cardinal almost habitually wore the mantelletta, a crimson moiré cape, very full but not heavy. The long red mantle, which has an immense train, is to be worn when he rides on state occasions, and then the train covers the horse also. The flat scarlet cap is his constant head covering. It is the 'Soli Deo,' for God only, and is not removed in the presence of kings or potentates of any rank. At first it seemed as if this should be worn in the portrait, but His Eminence being so tall, and, as he was facing out, it retired behind his broad forehead and became only a thin scarlet line, hardly visible, though, seen from the back or in profile, it was very effective. On a console and under a glass case, in one of the rooms I daily passed through *en route* to the Salle des Évêques, I had observed a scarlet buretta, the high three-cornered hat somewhat resembling a crown. I asked His Eminence whether it would be entirely fitting for him to wear this hat in the portrait, and on his assuring me that it was just as fitting as the other, it was decided on. The gold chain and Pectoral Cross he took off for me to see and hold in my hand. He always wore the broad ceinture of crimson ribbon, and the black soutane, with its short cape, and all edges bound with crimson cord.

The Carillon at the Cathedral not having been heard for a week, I inquired of the Cardinal concerning it. He told me it was being regulated for new tunes. The President of France, Poincaré, and the King were coming to Malines for a ceremony, which would be at the Cathedral.

His Eminence invited me and promised me a good seat near the chancel. In the mean time my friend and I went to Brussels for the great Thanksgiving Mass at Saint Gudule, to which the King and Queen, all the royal family, the Staff, and other magnates were to come in full regalia. We stood on chairs in the street and watched the procession sweep into the church glittering in morning sunshine, a superb spectacle. L. T. stayed over and saw great things the next day, but I being, as the Cardinal says, a *femme du devoir*, posted back to work and accomplished several important things, among them a good talk with the secretary, which straightened out various matters. He entered to arrange for my going to the ceremony here in the Cathedral, the next day. It is the presentation of the Croix de Guerre to the Cardinal. The King and Crown Prince, Poincaré, Foch, and Pichon were to be there.

The church was packed, but I had a good place beside a Belgian lady who seemed glad to speak with an American. She had suffered everything and had lost a son in the War. She was firm and patient, and gave me the impression of great strength and endurance, at which I was not surprised. I was constantly struck with the energy and endurance of the Belgians. Besides other manifestations of this, they can stand or kneel indefinitely.

The Cardinal, entering in full canonicals from a side entrance, went down among the people to the great front door, and welcomed the guests, while the *Marseillaise* thundered from the organ. Then he escorted them back to the choir and altar and made a speech in French, that I could not hear, and to which Poincaré responded. His Eminence gave me the paper the next day with the full account. Poincaré then decorated the Cardinal, and I could not help thinking that there was a lack of proportion between the great man and the decoration, important as it is. The finest moment came just at the close, when a young chanoine in purple and lace, a great, noble-looking, dark-eyed being, stood up in the end stall and led the whole congregation in the Barbaçonne, the Belgian National Hymn. Never have I seen such a face or such enthusiasm. He nearly went up all the way, and I know now how the saints looked when they died singing.

The next day I had a great *séance* from the Cardinal, and he told me what he and Foch said to each other. It was terrible to have to paint when he was talking and describing, with splendid gesture and flashing eyes. I only made notes, which I transferred to the big canvas. I often thought that I would rather have put the *words* down with a pencil in a notebook. I know, however, how dangerous this is, and how garbled the language of eloquent spontaneity always is, by report: particularly when it is not a clear-cut epigram that one hears. Also I felt very strongly the sanctity of the permission to enter and be at home, as an *artist*, and the Cardinal, trusting me, felt perfectly free to speak when and as he wished.

The picture progressed, but as the light was plenty, but broken, I never felt that I perfectly saw the canvas or knew exactly what I was getting in the way of '*ensemble*.' The head, and the expression and pose, I always knew, were going to be superior to the composition.

The secretary got me a young abbé, a tall beautiful person, to pose for the mantle. He turned out to be interested in painting, stayed on afterwards talking, and seemed fascinated by the picture, or rather by points in the head, which was a hopeful sign for me. He was to come again, but, alas, did not...and I never saw him again.

Soon after this there was a convention of Bishops in the big room and I put all my things out of sight and took off the strain a day or two.

At this time also there was a fête in Malines. It was a day for the surrounding towns to meet there. There was a grand choral service in the Cathedral with the Cardinal officiating. When I saw him at a distance leading a great assemblage at High Mass, surrounded by the sanctity and grandeur of his office, and towering above every one in his splendid robes, I was glad to bend humbly in my corner, and realize that I was, actually, often near him, in free intercourse and association.

In the congregation there were literally hundreds of Boy Scouts, dressed just as ours, and with the same dash, only that the neck-handkerchief was yellow for Belgium. I knelt among them, and it was good. No matter how small and unaccompanied, Belgian children, like the French, are always reverent and devout in church.

After the convent dinner, which was always finished at twelve, I went with a nice *vieille demoiselle* of the *pensionnaires* to see the Cardinal review the Boy Scouts in front of the Archevêché. We stood long in the crowd, and finally the big door opened and His Eminence came out in the mantelletta, and followed by a lot of priests and high hats. He stood on a raised platform, the grandest and most benign of figures. There was a band from Antwerp, and the boys came down the curving street and filed past in perfect order. All the saluting and head-turning was diligently done by even the littlest, the Cardinal bowing and smiling, and loving them — one could see that. There are six thousand Boy Scouts in Brussels, and all eager and happy in it. They little know that the original of their costume is that of the American cowboy of the West in America.

* * *

It stopped raining about this time and the sun was as hot as it is in Philadelphia, in July. L. T. did a good deal of sketching in the streets, and one hot morning started out in a gingham dress, cut square in the neck. As she was going out, Sœur Denyse called her back, very sweetly smiling, and made her pin a handkerchief across the space, which was a very modest one, saying that it was not *convenable* for a '*pensionnaire* at a convent.'

By this time we had discovered that we were *pensionnaires* in common with the old ladies mentioned before. There were a number of them, in black lace caps, many bent double. They were permanent; that is, they had come or been brought by their families, with all they had of property and belongings, to reside and be cared for at the convent as long as they lived. They always sat in a large room near the door with windows on the street, a kindly arrangement, for they could not only be entertained by the life of the street, but could see all the coming and going at the big door, though they never stood about in the hall or encumbered the entrance. My friend and I had our meals alone, waited on by Sœur Denyse, to whom this service had every appearance of being a pleasure. Some of the *pensionnaires* were ladies, and we were introduced and invited to visit them in their rooms, which were comfortably and even luxuriously furnished, with *meubles* inherited from better days. It was one of these *pensionnaires*, a more youthful and very agreeable and intelligent person, who had escorted me to the service for Boy Scouts, and this lady also did us another very great kindness. When we first arrived, we had been given the butter of the convent, which was indeed of a very low grade, and as we depended very much on the bread-and-butter end of our diet, we told Sœur Denyse that we would be glad to pay extra for a higher grade. Thereafter the butter very greatly improved, but one day soared to such a pitch of perfection that it far exceeded any butter we had ever tasted before or ever dreamed of. We were voluble in our ecstasies, and Sœur Denyse told us with radiant smiles, that Mdlle. —— had '*cherché partout*' and found and carried home in her own hands, the most delicious of all products, one which America is incapable of

MRS. ALEXANDER SEDGWICK AND CHRISTINA

producing in such excellence, and which we revelled in during the rest of our stay.

We found that the convent had an annex in the rear, across a narrow street, and one day Sœur Denyse took us over to visit the drawing class for *jeunes filles*. They were making drawings like samplers, with hard lead pencils. Once we would have called it old-fashioned. Now it is '*haute nouveauté*,' though they don't know it. I gave them '*petit conseils*,' having been very humbly asked to do so by a sister, and they were very reverent and grateful. One of them had a hideous photograph of President Wilson which she was inserting in the page, among wreaths of flowers. Think of his being embalmed in the heart of this remote convent! One of the sisters, when she heard that I was an American, said, 'You have saved us. Without you we would have starved'; and many know and realize it. Many of them fled to England and like to talk about it and show off their little English.

As I came out, I noticed a framed photograph of His Eminence hanging in the hall. I was told that it was one taken just before he was made Cardinal. I was stricken between discouragement and enthusiasm. The face was younger than the one I knew, but worn with the strivings of the spirit, lined with sufferings, and even joys, the rest of us knew little of. I longed to possess the photograph or a copy, and my appreciation of it seemed to give pleasure. How often I have found that joyous ready response of these unspoiled hearts, to whom little pleasures come like morning breezes. The next day there was a parcel for me in Sœur Denyse's keeping. It was the photograph in its frame, with a little note from the 'Directeur' of the convent, asking that I would accept it.

Malines is not a large place. The new part is sober and respectable and not very modern. The streets are quiet. Our quarter was near the Cathedral and the *Place*, and the river, a narrow stream, much like the canals of Bruges, and as picturesque. Sketches, and especially water-colors, were waiting to be made at every turn. Our walks were taken chiefly after our early supper. We had to be in at eight, or else would have kept Sœur Denyse from her narrow bed, from which she had risen at four A. M. We always went to bed by daylight, as there was nothing else to do. This was our time for reading, and the regularity of our days was the greatest of my blessings. I had neither time, inclination, nor strength for working in the streets. In the precious early twilight hours I could look and wonder and brood over the beauty, without the worry and fatigue of performance and the chagrin of carrying home a fiasco, in which the secret I had adored had somehow escaped and left only a little bungled 'self-expression' instead of the enchantment I had *seen*.

Military automobiles sometimes rushed through the principal thoroughfare, and there was often a car, and touring Americans, in front of the Cathedral. We always managed to slip by unperceived, as we had no wish to recognize friends. There appeared to be very few well-to-do or 'city' people in Malines, and, as there were no hotels, visitors were for hours only, and we were doubtless often wondered at for our continued presence. As we were constantly seen going in and out of the convent, our respectability was fully understood, and we always felt a friendly atmosphere about us which was extremely gratifying. Mothers carrying babies would smile at us in passing, and would show the child, saying, 'English baby, born in England, speak English,' delighted to talk (as every one spoke French as well as Flemish) and to recount their experiences. The population of Belgium is not diminishing *now*. I have never seen so many children, or with such life and energy, or such a look of *promise*. There were many widows with a horde of small children to feed and bring up. Big sisters of six had charge of several younger ones, some of them obviously belonging to neighbors; and babies of four sat on the edge of the pavement holding babies of one year, patiently controlling and comforting them. We got to know some of them, and were especially interested in a tiny and very engaging little chap who was obviously a leader of a group, who lifted up his queer little face and explained that he was a 'Wolf cub.' This seemed to be an association of English origin, and we frequently saw him and the other 'members' convening on the pavement. They wore paper caps, and the club seemed to have a partially military character.

One day I came across a group of small boys and girls playing 'hospital' on the narrow pavement, quite unhindered by the busy neighbors who were going their way swiftly as usual, and nearly walking over them. The 'staff' had rigged up an old piece of some indescribable material against the wall, for a tent, inside of which the wounded lay. Two Red-Cross nurses wearing the uniform which had somehow been achieved by means of a towel for the veil, bound about by the band marked with the usual cross. There were several doctors, solemnly bending over the patients. Something white pinned on for an apron, and a white paper cap, distinguished these from the interested friends, of whom there were many, and the whole performance was being conducted with the energy and zeal which marked every act and movement of these vital and unsubdued people, big or little. We have all heard of the wit and ingenuity which they steadily showed to the Germans, even in their moments of greatest trial, and I never went out without seeing an instance of their indomitable energy.

No time seemed to be wasted in Malines, and no one was afraid of work. One day I watched from our upper window the delivery of a hand-cart, full of bags of potatoes, at a small provision shop, on the other side of the street. The cart was in charge of a girl who might have been fifteen. She was barefooted and barelegged, had no hat, and wore a sort of potato bag for a dress. She had no assistant, and had obviously pushed the cart and its load in from the country,

probably several miles. She 'drew up' at the door and
sprang from the cart, unloading the heavy bags without
help, and carrying them into the shop, back in an instant
for more. It was straining work. The 'goods' delivered,
she started off without a moment's delay, pushing the cart
with all her strength, and bent over double, as cart-pushers
always are. She was no slavey, and had nothing in mind
but her good Belgian *will to do*. (Marvellous that there were
no Germans to steal the precious hoard.) Potatoes are above
all valuable to Belgians and their chief staple of diet. During the War the Germans took all the potatoes and brass
they were clever enough to find, for the Belgians were in-
genious in hiding these two articles, which they joyfully dug
up later. Now one could get them to town without danger.
She had the money in her pocket. What to her was it to
sweat under the load for hours on the stones of the road and
trudge back to more labor until night?

One night, early in August, the town celebrated the refusal of Belgium to admit Germany, and the beginning of
the War. Everybody was in Sunday garb and walking in
the streets, and in the *Grande Place*, a dense crowd. The
Carillon, which, when very light compositions are played,
is a musical box on Cathedral scale, rippled out all sorts of
tunes: 'Tipperary' and Scotch airs. Every one looked
happy when the chimes played; there were happier faces
perhaps than one can find at the 'movies,' of which there
were none, then, in Malines. There was no other music in
Malines, but things were getting back astonishingly to the
normal. The little shops improved daily, and in the devastated area of the town, incessant work went on. The apse
of the Cathedral had been much damaged by shell-fire, and
was already repaired, but not finished. The Tower was
fortunately untouched; also the region in its neighborhood.
Its supreme beauty and grandeur never ceased to move me,
and I never saw it without that rush of joy upon the heart
that only the noblest reaches of Art can give. How I

blessed the fate that permitted me to approach, and pass under, its lovely shadow on my morning 'way to work'! How far this was from sight-seeing, from the weary tourist, trying to 'get it' on a scratched and tarnished page, filled with a scumble of yesterday's impression! There was no light of day or evening that I did not know it by; pale against dark clouds, or shimmering and mysterious upon the morning light. What joy to choose my distance, and then stand and note some new member that a change of hour had developed, some subtle variant in the mounting periods of its height, and, above all, to get the full sweep of the long upward lines, richly broken, but unhindered! I wondered at its creator's power to adjust perspective to the eye's demand for perfect satisfaction, in the upward slope from the broad base to the summit which diminished its square mysteriously in union with its foundation and one's desires.

I always felt that the Tower was the architectural type of the Cardinal, a supreme example of simplicity in richness, height and depth, full of holy joy, like the carolling of the upper bells, and with the profound resonance and majesty of the greatest bell of all, and the most moving, which I one day heard tolling with its deep voice the years of a life.

Every few weeks a special performance was given on the Carillon, and on these occasions people came for miles around to listen in the streets. It seemed that not far from the rue des Draps there was a well-known locality, where, it being a retired street, and doubtless for acoustical reasons, the 'hearing' was especially good. Hearing, after our supper, the concert beginning (the great instrument was to be played by a distinguished performer), we started forth, I am glad to say, noiselessly, on our rubber soles, and suddenly came upon a street packed with people, all standing listening intensely, and of course in absolute silence; not a whisper was exchanged, not a movement made. We joined the throng in the same spirit, and I gave inward thanks that we had not been chattering when we turned the corner.

I could have wished for more choral and less operatic music, but measuring my needs against those, at this time, of *any* Belgian, I was forced to admit that joyous *roulades* and youthful sentiment and the good old variations might be more grateful to 'survivors' — for that they all were.

* * *

Henry James once wrote a lecture on 'The Lesson of Balzac.' It was intended, of course, for writers of fiction, but its substance is applicable to any form of art production. Oddly enough, he uses the term 'painter' very frequently in speaking of novelists, meaning perhaps 'portrayers' of life. It is difficult to cull fragments from the solid and complete amalgam of the essay, but I cannot refrain from transcribing a few passages, so ably do they express the indispensable value of the elements, of every description, from which a subject is, as it were, to be mined.

Speaking of the really cosmic depths and widths in which Balzac 'found' his characters, Henry James says, with a splendid burst of conviction: 'Where, with so strenuous a conception of the use of material, was material itself so strenuously quarried? Out of what mines, by what endless procession of laden chariots, and tugging teams, and marching elephants, did the immense consignments required for his work reach him?' 'I hold,' he goes on to say, 'several of his [Balzac's] faults to be grave, but they never come back to that fault in the artist that amounts most to a failure of dignity, the absence of saturation with his idea. When saturation fails, no other presence really avails, as when on the other hand it operates, no failure of method fatally interferes.... There never is in Balzac that damning interference which consists in the painter's not seeing, not possessing his image, not having fixed his creature and his creature's *conditions.*' These creatures being 'interesting as subjects of fate, the figures around which a situation closes, in proportion as sharing their existence, we feel where fate comes in and just how it gets at them.'

I knew there was far more to be learned, and observed, and felt, in the sphere and placement of Cardinal Mercier, than could ever be put into any painting; in fact, that such material should not occupy visible and static or recognizable place in the portrait. Truly to discover the Cardinal would mean to get something, even very small, into the painting which was not to be found in the biographies. This alone was of value, and in raising and solidifying the foundations, doing one's best to apprehend and relate the many forces perception might discover on the ground, the upper levels of conception might eventually shimmer out nearer the sky.

No place could have been more favorable for observation and reflection on the great subject than was found in Malines. The frame was exactly right, and had the ripest consistence and maturity. I could see the grand figure from without even, at exactly the right distance.

Malines is small, and the church and outlying seminaries and convents predominated above every other interest in the town. Nevertheless, the business of the place was carried on by the inhabitants with lively energy. They were a strangely homogeneous *bloc* of which the forming medium was the Faith. Observing them it seemed that the quality of their reaction upon the Cardinal might have one large simple characteristic, derived fundamentally from the teachings of religion. I doubt whether anywhere in Cardinal Mercier's great flock, at Malines or elsewhere, could have been found that teasing struggle to present individuality that is so prevalent, now, with us. No one seemed to be specifically 'looking for notice.' I suppose the inflation of personal small currencies could never have escaped rebuke or dismissal. *Any* one could see His Eminence, and this fact was the strongest proof that the *petit bourgeois*, and small shopkeepers and farmers, that formed the population of

Malines, never trespassed upon the generosity and 'open-ness' of their Cardinal. This sense of proportion would have been in their humble minds no more than decent reverence, and proper conduct '*envers son Éminence.*' No one in his high position ever felt more the care of his people. He was acquainted with their sorrows and carried them on his heart. But what rich fertile sustenance, what support on both sides, lay in such confidence; and where the impact of this great group touched their beloved chief and shepherd, it became a channel for inexhaustible love, not a drain upon overdrawn nervous energy. The Cardinal's benignity might be viewed against such a part of his background, a soft light reflected from millions of faithful and reverent hearts, all over Belgium.

We saw something of another group also, a much smaller one. I had letters to the Comtesse d'U, and she and her daughter showed us constant and warm hospitality. Their château was a few miles from Malines, a small but charming eighteenth-century house standing in its woods, and the only one of their homes in which since the War they could afford to live, though it was not roomy for their large household. Their great house, which was at a distance, they had given to be a sanitarium and home for War Orphans, and in it three hundred of these found protection and shelter. Comtesse Louise, the oldest daughter, devoted her time and strength to this work.

One day Mdlle. d'U. came for us in their car, and took us to call on friends of hers, the Baron and Baronne L., at their mediæval castle and beautiful park. The house was full of fine Flemish furniture. There were many chimney-pieces similar in style to those in the Musée Plantin in Antwerp, and one room high up in a tower could have been the retreat where any legendary princess might have sat all day long among her ladies, bending a delicate head over the embroidery frame. The rich faded hues of tapestry and hangings and the high carved bed bore no trace of intervening centuries. Our host and hostess were delightful people, and lacked none of the high, indomitable, and even gay spirit we had so often admired in Belgians of a different social order. They did not go away at all during the War; were really in No-Man's Land, between the lines. By a miracle, nothing was destroyed. Finally, when the Germans passed over, the house was filled continuously with German officers and soldiers, hundreds of them sleeping in their rooms, drinking their choice wines, and making themselves at home in every uncleanly fashion. The L.'s had buried all the brasses, so the Boches carried off *only all the mattresses*. What luck it was that the Germans should have had such faith in their ultimate success as to wish to preserve Belgium's finest objects! They seemed to have had, in their devastations, chiefly in view the intimidation and demoralization of their victims, who always, in their irritating way, refused to be either intimidated or demoralized.

The d'U.'s also took us to see the château where Rubens lived and worked, a lovely place, now enlarged, denatured, and revamped by its present owner, an able and sporting industrial. We visited one small château, standing towered and high, in its moat, which Maxfield Parrish might have used for a model. It had guardians, but no inhabiting master, and all but one of its rooms, a small dining-hall hung with tapestries, were drearily dismantled, yet bearing traces of joyous living, not so very long ago. It was one of our greatest pleasures to be so cordially admitted to such homes as those of the d'U.'s and L.'s, and to feel in them the same universal devotion to the Cardinal. They all loved and reverenced him and brought him the same confidence as did the towns-people, only under a higher form of culture.

* * *

The Cardinal never received in the morning, which was sacred to his daily work. He rose from his narrow bed and straw mattress at five, and went to his private chapel for prayer and meditation. Mass was at seven.

Of course, upon the administrative side I could see nothing. I sometimes caught a glimpse of him walking in the garden with bent head, seriously listening to the appeal of a visitor, never a layman, in that retreat. After carrying Belgium in his arms and upon his heart for five years, he was, I believe, profoundly weary, but this he never showed unless taken unawares. Late one afternoon as I was walking in the *Place*, the Cardinal's automobile passed, and for an instant I saw him, leaning far back in a corner, utterly discouraged, spent, and grey. He was returning, no doubt, from some errand in his diocese which had bitterly taxed his faith and patience. Or his physical strength had collapsed under heavy pressure, for probably even then the seeds of a mortal malady were undermining his natural forces.

* * *

Thus it seemed that one of the deep sources of the Cardinal's strength, or rather a powerful conservator of it, was the relation of his whole flock to him. He was, first of all, the Shepherd. Organizer, ruler, defender, were all included in this, and I often felt that the strong faith of his entire people was one of the mainsprings of what I can call no less than the fresh and youthful joy that frequently seemed to inspire his whole being.

He must have rested upon their faith as well as his own; and this gave a broad untrammelled field for his power and imagination to rise from. Also he and his people were one in courage, and in the humor that naturally lifts itself from the courageous heart.

It was these evidences of a relieved spirit that made selection a long pursuit for me, as an humble investigator, for I was determined never to lose sight of initial purpose and conduct, no matter what might appear intimate and smiling in a reaction.

In 1919, the Cardinal was visited by many delegations from other countries. These were always, of course, persons of importance, and he often accompanied them to the Salle des Évêques, always — marvellous courtesy — sending to know if this would be convenient for me. At these times I saw the suave and welcoming Prelate and host. Gay, exchanging sallies, and pointing to the great scar in the ceiling. An Italian, looking up, said, 'Voilà le fresco Tedesco!' If my letter, relating the story of this gibe, had been opened by the German censor during the occupation, I would have been sought by the police and dragged to the Kommandatur to answer for my uncomplimentary repetition of the Italian's little joke.

A curious fact in relation to the great shell-hole probably saved the wing of the building from destruction, to say nothing of the lives of those who were still under its roof. It happened that a huge consignment of mattresses for the hospital, or barracks, had been piled temporarily in the Salle, and the shell, plunging through the roof, had buried itself in these and spared the basement and occupants.

One day, as my work was beginning to take shape, a party of English and Scotch officers came for audience with the Cardinal. When I arrived in the afternoon, I found the British flag hung out, and English and Scotch airs were being played on the Carillon, and the servants were all in formal attire and posted about. The Cardinal himself was waiting in a corner of one of the reception rooms, and I had a word with him as I passed. He asked, as he always did, so politely, if he could bring the visitors to the Salle, and soon they all came trailing in, exquisite beings, as usual. English people are always interested in portraits, and soon they flocked in my direction to 'have a look.' I tried to hide behind the canvas, as I was in painting garb, crownless hat, and not very tidy apron, and I was torn between wanting the 'fresh eye' and possible encouragement and being unready to show my offspring. However, I had a nice little talk with the General, and felt that wonderful sensation of having struck fire, which is the chiefest of rewards. There was a Belgian among them, an accompanying official, who expressed himself very emphatically. Laymen, all of them, but it was the first lift that I had had from without. But the reflection I received from the Cardinal and his *entourage* had been helpful and inspiring from the first. One day, as he passed through, I asked if he could give me a few moments on the following morning, and told him how the sun hindered in the afternoon. When he came back, a few minutes later, he clasped his hands and said, 'Oh, Madame, j'ai pitie de vous, j'ai pitie de vous.' Like all busy people, the Cardinal's mornings were precious; he could have given me more time in the afternoon, but the sun was busy, too, and had definite hours. He also had to find out that I would not tire him. He admitted it one day, saying that he had found artists rather cruel. I said, 'You did not know I would not be,' and he smiled and said, 'No.' As for putting a strain upon him, I cannot conceive how any such undertaking could be estimated as having the value of one ounce of his strength. He begged me to stay on as long as I wished to work there, and looked rather sad when I told him it would be better to finish the picture in a real studio, on account of the sun, and my staying would only be for what he could give me. There was, I knew, a definite limit to this, as he was to sail for America in September.

All sorts of people came to the Archevêché, and some were given freedom to wander by themselves. One day the door opened quietly, and two friars, in brown frieze with rope girdle, barefoot and bareheaded, tanned and weather-worn, peeped in. I spoke up in French, and begged them to enter. They came forward as naturally as if it was an every-day occurrence to find a lady in a crownless hat and soiled apron painting in the Salle des Évêques, and their good manners, good sense, and *savoir-faire* made nothing of the distance from the Middle Ages that lay between us. They stood for a long time with me examining and talking about the picture, and being Flemish-French, they did not need to have passed 'Fine Arts 2' in order to have a knowledge of Art.

Le Frère Florent, a felt-soled, but not light-footed attaché, just above the servant class, and a constant and 'tout dévoué' attendant on His Eminence, began to look at the picture with surprised admiration. One day I asked him if he saw 'Son Éminence' in it, and he almost shouted, with grand gestures, 'Mais oui, Madame,' as if that went without saying.

The Cardinal, also, was happy to dramatize a little incident. His nephew, a young priest, had passed through the Salle, and had started, seeing the picture, thinking 'que c'était moi!' He thought this an eloquent tribute to the portrait. He also wished to tell me how interested the whole household had been, and that when he asked any of them if they had seen its advancement, he found that they all went early in the morning to look at it. All the same, the result I hoped for seemed far from realization, and a letter before me to my sister, expresses this only too well:

'I never fought anything as I have this whole experience. It has been like trying to swim the harbor, and at times that faint blue line between the waves seems never to get nearer. Strange illustration for one who cannot swim a stroke. But I know.'

One of my greatest difficulties was to reconcile what I daily saw in the Cardinal with what I *knew*. Mrs. Kellogg has called him the 'fighting Cardinal.' A portrait for America must show moral force and resistance, and yet have static dignity. It should have *weight*, and bear the furrows of the great conflict upon it.

But the Cardinal had taken off his armor when the War ended, and was now busy in the establishment of Peace. He was now to administer healing and encouragement as well as point out the way of duty. As I have said before, I saw him often with his guests; welcoming, gracious, benignant always, often humorous, and with that astonishing fountain of youth always ready to spring forth. Not to fatigue him, I made the 'sittings,' so called, extremely short. They were really investigations, new facts accumulated, impressions corroborated or discarded. So when he came to the Salle — and he never excused himself — it was, I suppose, a little change from the toil and doubtless worry of the day. He often entered looking grey and old, and with sunken eyes, and in a moment the change of scene, the work of the studio, so different from that of his study or reception room, would alter his mood, youth would spring up and glow in his eyes and bring color to his face, and he would drop off, not ten, but twenty-five years.

Being well aware that I was ignorant of Catholic speech and manners toward great dignitaries of the Church, I made a general apology for my awkwardness in this respect, by telling the Cardinal that I was a Protestant, which, of course, he had guessed already. With a deep and kindly look, he said, 'Mademoiselle, nous sommes tous Chrétiens.' And I never felt anything but perfect harmony and understanding in his presence.

Once at the convent I met the Reverende Mère as I was going in after seeing the Cardinal. I was full of hope, and she said, with her serene grace, 'Every one comes away happy from Son Éminence.'

The Cardinal sometimes spoke of America and of his sympathy for and appreciation of American traits. He liked what he called our '*franchise*' and the '*sans façon*' of our manners. He saw chiefly our soldiers and officers, who, having heard of his greatness, were probably completely disarmed by his simplicity and warmth.

* * *

It was nearly the end of August and the Cardinal was to sail for America from Brest in a few days. He was to travel on a troopship, carrying five thousand of our boys. This was a great delight to him. More time would not have availed much for me, as the most important parts of the portrait were now advanced as far as I could hope to carry them.

One afternoon two secretaries from the Legation came to call, and possibly to see the portrait. Mr. A., the secretary-in-chief, was one of these. Mr. Whitlock was in America. Mr. A.'s impression was very gratifying, as he represented the sort of opinion I was anxious to have before the Cardinal left, and it was a glowing moment, for His Excellency was saying all over again what a pleasure it was to have the work going on there, and many other things good to hear. I told him that I wanted him to be pleased with it, and that that alone would satisfy me. He had told me before that he intended to write on the photograph that he had for me, 'À la grande, et *patiente* artiste.'

The next morning he brought three volumes of his works to the Salle, inscribed, and also the photograph as above, in his small, fine, and immensely powerful handwriting.

The next moment was one of the supreme moments of my experience, and I am glad to say that, even at the time, I knew this. The Cardinal looked at me very seriously and said:

'Mademoiselle, il y a beaucoup de portraits, de bel peinture, de beaux tableaux, mais vous êtes la seule qui a fait l'Âme, vous êtes la *seule*, qui a fait *l'Âme*.'

To me came the words of Simeon, 'Lord, now lettest thou thy servant depart in peace.'

So that, although the hands were chaos, the background a mess, and there was very little really good painting on the whole canvas, I was glad to leave it to be taken up again in *ensemble* in Paris, where I had the promise of a fine studio. The Cardinal would leave first; that would make it easier, and after that break was over, I should have time to deal with all lesser ones. He was going to America, and was happy and satisfied that this would mean to him new knowledge of the United States and strengthen the bond between the countries. In this he was not disappointed, for nothing could have been more glowing than the warmth of his reception here. My brother and sister were given a private interview and were made happy by his reference to me.

I saw him once again at this time. He came down the long room to see us, looking wan and weary back of his smile, but he gave so much that no one could leave him with a sense of *loss*. That must come later, and I felt it when the next day, hidden behind the blind of one of the big windows of the Salle, I watched him get into his automobile and disappear, well attended by his devoted servants and secretary.

It was hard to say good-bye to the Archevêché, even after its soul had departed, and to look for the last time, for although I might and did go there again to see the Cardinal, I very well knew that I should never be *chez moi* in that place again, nor indeed in any other Arch-Episcopal Palace.

Malines

Malines is easily a place of pilgrimage in itself and in its treasures, and I might supplement the guide-books wearyingly, but after the Tower, and the obvious charm of a partly mediæval town, what most dwells in memory are the two pictures by Rubens in the Église Saint-Jean and the Église Notre Dame. One is an immense 'Adoration,' and the other a triptych, of which the central panel is, I consider, the supreme work of the Master, 'The Miraculous Draught of Fishes,' although it would be hard to choose between it and 'The Elevation of the Serpents' at the Prado. The first of these had been taken down for safety during the bombardment, and had not been rehung. It was leaning casually against the wall of the choir, and could not be well seen, only guessed at, in *ensemble*, but the figures, more than life-size, in the *premier plan*, were laid in with a synthetic power joined to realism, unknown to any other hand, and which

CECILIA BEAUX
Self-portrait

perhaps only a painter could fully enjoy; and there was a keen relish in examining it at close hand, and exactly where one would choose to be if actually in the act of execution, at arm's length and eye's height. The scale of Rubens had never been so forcibly brought home to me. A picture to be placed high above an altar, not very well lighted, and perhaps to be seen at a distance of fifty feet and farther, must have carrying power of an emotional order, in spite of all these diminishing forces. Color must project, from such obscurity and distance, the full moving power of color seen close at hand. Line and relief must demand without question the following eye, and literally bear up the beholder and quicken his pulses.

Rubens's religious pictures were painted for waiting multitudes in churches, not for strollers in art galleries...and although his prodigious *volonté* was its own unanswerable reason for all he did, his ideas of what was necessary for the success of his impression were practical and efficacious.

Seen over cathedral altars and doorways, I had never thought of *size* in his great compositions. I had received their overwhelming stimulation with a bounding heart, and, I must confess it, through tears of joy. Now there was a chance to get closer to method and design. Evidently Rubens held that the subject must be the centre of a sphere; it must be in the middle plane; other figures must come between it and the spectator. Must it then be diminished, faded? Shall the mother and child not have their undiluted flavor in color and forms? She must be enthroned among humble worshippers, but must wear the glamour that his eyes beheld, as the young mother with her baby, posed near him, surrounded by light, and those near beauties of cream and roses, ivory and pearl, pungent red and blue, sweeps of velvet brown, and dark liquid green and gold on the garment of an attendant warrior. Shall these not have their full revelation, and offering? Without a doubt, or compromise! Therefore, into the foreground went giant shoulders, heavy rugged heads, huge tanned and bending backs, and, in the picture at Malines, actually a child's head...a child's head as big as a man's. An abortion, it would have been, by any other hand, but this brown-eyed boy turned a serious, intimate, and perfectly charming face, from where he knelt, and made his appeal as a 'little fellow,' in spite of undeniable measurements.

'The Miraculous Draught of Fishes,' with its companion panels, figures of saints, hangs in the *ambulatoire* of the small church of Notre Dame au-de-la-Dyle, just behind the *maître autel*.

It is not a large picture, and would appear to have been painted under an impulse of concentration, rather than expansion. Rubens does not often deal with *moments*, or times of day. But he seems here to have been profoundly touched by the sleepless toil of fishermen whom he beholds in the twilight of dawn. Day is coming, and they have 'labored all night and taken nothing.' It is not dark. Any one who knows the hour of daybreak knows how well-lighted objects are under the sky, when day is coming. The stooping figure in the foreground, the net and the fish, are a spectacle of beauty, seen, and conveyed, with an enthusiasm which only Rubens knew how to join with the material of pigment. He excels himself, here. Here he would not be satisfied with less than the ultimate rendering; and so by this, the painters' own right of mastery and bounteous procreation, does he tie to earth and human cognizance his sense of morning around figures, men of toil who have known the night, a mystery that he has not seemed at any other time to have been desirous to approach.

And there is great mystery in this performance, for none of the usual time-of-day-and-atmosphere methods are used. Why, even without the story, would one know it to be that weary hour! Rubens is no sentimentalist, and with him, story is always stated in general terms, but he is a poet here; he commands a feeling his 'readers' cannot account for. It is without artifice, an act of the germinal impulsion of Art, creating an almost cosmic revelation of astral forces, joined naturally and without strain, with the weariness of men who have labored and have not slept.

XI

CLEMENCEAU

MERCIER... Clemenceau... It would be easy to find that nothing could be more diverse than the two immense personalities that must appear in close sequence in this slight survey. But, strangely enough, in passing from one to the other, one feels no jar, and not even mental readjustment is necessary. In the presence of the mightiest of saints and the most convinced of sceptics, the same emotion shakes the heart and bows the head.

All except a few irremediably perverse minds cease to argue when humanity reaches beyond the normal heights. In the few authoritative indications inscribed high up upon the cliffs of History, these two diverse thinkers appear under the same signs; signs beyond our vision, only heard of by us, for they do not indicate the germs and shoots of qualities it is to be hoped we all possess, but the supreme development of those qualities. How well we know their titles! — Patriotism, Faith, Courage, and Endurance.

And over the names of these men is written an even rarer sign, Incorruptible.

Well it was for Belgium and France, and for the rest of us, that with Cardinal Mercier and Georges Clemenceau, integral, dynamic force was the servant of will that swept before it the threats of armies and lesser men.

Between their country and the enemy within and without each 'withstood.' One of them had denounced Saint Paul openly, but he was really of the same mind. 'Having done all, to stand.' Both these heroes did so. They stood to receive death or worse, if need be, for Belgium, for France, and, as we now know, for the World. They withstood the Nation's despair, and made way for hope and new effort, and such was their strength and destiny that neither fell under the weight they upheld alone, for it was the soul of their countrymen that they bore up, inspired, and equipped for victory.

Here all comparison must end, and we must approach Clemenceau as one man to another. *He* is not superhuman.

Among all Frenchmen, no man is more typical, in broad lines, than Georges Clemenceau. Uncompromising materialist, accepting, even revelling in its most drastic findings, he is able to observe, as a literary impressionist with a heart of pity, the lives and deaths of the poorest peasants in his village in La Vendée. The man who wrote 'De la Génération des Éléments Anatomique,' with authority, as well as originality, also wrote 'Jacques Fagot'; and when I asked him one day if that story was not one of the best, he nodded gently with an artist's momentary satisfaction in the perception of another.

In constant attendance as Municipal Councillor for Clignancourt, after the Commune, he devoted himself for five years to his doctor's work, giving gratuitous advice to the poor around him. Have there been many Municipal Councillors who used their spare time to help infants into the world, and with a strong hand support the aged and other wrecks of poverty and misery 'across the Bar'?

No doubt his patients rebelled against his prescriptions of hygiene and cleanliness, but also, one may be sure that he was indulgent to comforting superstitions, and old wives' mixtures, when they were harmless.

And these are the slightest elements of his versatility. Those who are in any way familiar with French character are aware that in the equilibrium of opposite qualities is its main strength.

In Clemenceau's long career of service to the French people, the dramatic contrasts in his thought, word, and action were indissoluble bonds between him and his fellow Frenchmen. It was not strange to them that the first man in France, which at numerous crises he was found to be, should not only use freely the dynamite of his fierce irony, but in a moment descend to the roguery of the Paris *gamin*.

Few men have ever united without friction the passionate boldness of a fanatic with the cool sagacity of an experienced statesman. Like his own perfect mental equilibrium, his estimates were never lopsided. Although all his life he was an ardent republican and destroyer of oligarchies of all sorts, he would never join the ranks of the Socialists as such. He saw too well that Socialism would never succeed as an armed force, and, although he was with it in principle, he knew that it must arrive, if ever, by the way of a broader understanding of real values by individuals. Contrast again, the so-called Tiger deciding in silent purpose, on the wisdom, in this case, of lengthy process.

His own generous estimates were all that he would accept as moral code, but to this freedom he was a stern master. It would have seemed to him that any purpose worthy of a man left no room for self-indulgences, such as luxury or money-lust. But Clemenceau, on purely human lines, has never preached anything but honest thinking and respect for Natural Law; and he has never denounced anything but bigotry, oppression, and traitors, especially when the first of these ventured into the domain of Art for purposes of destruction.

Science was his first love. Art; he could have written volumes on it of learned and fascinating criticism. Editor, journalist, political leader, story-writer, his versatility was anything but shallow, and the outstanding feature of it is that any one of his gifts would alone have furnished out the career of a lesser man. But this rich material makes up one man, with one purpose. He is Frenchman and Patriot.

Arriving in Paris in the spring of 1919, the artist upon whom had been placed the responsibility of producing an interpretation of this personality, in a painted portrait, had long to wait.

The Président du Conseil, it seemed, had had (outside of 'our boys' and their officers) *plein le dos* of Americans. He was in no mood to resign himself to any polite suggestion from us. Moreover, any one could see that there was no time. The preparation of the Treaty was going on. The great event of the Signing was near. The elections were imminent. The gracious member of the Council who had charge of our rather inopportune affair decided that it would be useless to approach our victim at such a time. In fact Clemenceau was the last of the group assigned to me to be actually reached, and it was nearly a year after this that I had my first meeting with him.

There was nothing, therefore, for the solicitor to do at this time but follow the example of Kipling's mongoose, 'Run and find out.' The field was clear; there was no time limit; no report of progress expected. There was that precious sense of space ahead and margin all around, so dear to the seeker and which many Americans go abroad to find.

For many years everybody has been familiar with the physiognomy of Georges Clemenceau. There is a sprinkling everywhere of gossip about his vehemence, his duels, and his success in making enemies. Many were the newspaper prints of his bold, ironic head as he sat at the council table with Wilson and Lloyd George. In many of these there was not even a thin veil over the exposure of his boredom. With the exception of the representative from Great Britain, how slow they were, the Council, how little *documenté!* But one could not be too widely informed about even the merely superficial aspect of the man, and all that pursuit could furnish in print, photograph, bust, and painting at all ages and in all surroundings, I made my own.

But while I was quietly, as one might say, nibbling at the great subject, there came at last one of those swift openings into the next 'Square' so enjoyed by Alice. The shining spear flashed overhead, as when Pallas Athene used to swoop down for the deliverance of her adherents.

I had a message from Mr. White that there would be a seat for me in the 'Loge Diplomatique' at the Chamber on the Monday after the Signing, when Clemenceau was to present the 'Peace' to the Senate.

With only the power and protection of my ticket, which was irrefutable, I went alone to the remote Temple I had so often passed on foot and bus, at only a few yards' distance. Crowds and confusion hung about the outskirts, and there were many narrow, grudging defiles to pass, where uniforms were on guard. When the last suspicious functionary showed me up the last dark stair and shoved open a door, I entered the Historic Theatre. There were other occupants of the Loge, which faced the Tribune, and all were grudging but one, who made a place for me in the front row of seats.

I was more glad than sorry that I knew no one, and had, as it were, the place to myself; that the Président du Conseil had not yet come in, and that I was to have my impressions in the ascendant.

There were no artificial lights, and dusky daylight filtered down from somewhere high up, marking in strong simplicity only the salient forms of heads and figures. There was a low hum of many restrained voices, and serious Frenchmen stood about the entrances and the Tribune, in close and intense colloquy. There were many women in the loges and a few magnificent old men, who looked as if they had seen '71, the Commune, and the rest of it, had perhaps listened, as young men, to Gambetta, and might have taken part for or against the release of Blanqui.

Right and Left, the seats were full. No member was absent, and soon there would not be standing-room at the packed entrance.

But suddenly on the left of the Tribune, the crowd gave way and there entered a small old man in a dark grey suit. A great shout went up, and turned into a continuous roar, but the small man with the great head seemed not to know it was for him, and moved unsmiling among his friends to one of the front rows of benches, on the Left, of course, and took his seat, resting his grey gloved hands on his stick.

I hardly know what happened next. I suppose the proceedings began. The elegant Duchanel, in faultless *redingôte*, used the hammer incessantly. French Deputies are not always either polite or patient.

But what the President said or the next man, I did not even try to get. The back of the old man's head was turned my way, but even then it diminished every other in view. His face was slightly turned upward to the Speaker, and he listened, as a good disciple might, to his Professor in class.

I had felt the shock of a great presence, and could not, at once, get over it. All I asked was to deepen and hold the impression.

But it soon was evident that Clemenceau had not elected to appear in any of the rôles usually assigned to him. He was not there to hurl biting sarcasm or to upbraid and denounce, or even to inspire. It was not a time, it seemed, for eloquence nor intimidation, nor even to convince of the truth. He at last slowly mounted the Tribune, spread out some papers before him, and standing, as I had always imagined him, head thrown slightly back, his arms straightened to the finger-tips, and seeming to hold down the desk in front of him, he began, gravely, to read the Treaty to the Chamber. And he gravely continued for nearly two hours. Very frequently from the Left, and particularly from one man of rather revolting appearance, Renaudel the Socialist, came violent interruption, contrary opinions or opposition shouted with fierce or insolent insistence. Pandemonium it was, indeed, where the voice of the hammer was drowned. But the Tiger was chained up somewhere; he could not be drawn. The great fighter paused, waited until the noise was suppressed, and then continued to read the Treaty to the Chamber.

Coming from such a man this presentment was extraordinarily impressive, and is, like all strong impressions, even more powerful in retrospect. His was the hand that as Président du Conseil des Alliés, must give the result of its deliberations to France. No doubt there was much in the document that he deemed compromise, and he hated compromise. Although dissatisfaction in the amount of indemnity to be demanded of Germany was to be expected, he doubtless, with his long vision, saw that even what the Treaty required would never be obtained from the conquered invader. He had given his best to it, for France, and it is pitiable to think of what the Treaty would have been under a lesser man.

But Clemenceau was a man to act and lead alone, and the Treaty was composite. That he presented it as a Document of Destiny, not as a salutation to Victorious France, is another evidence, if any were needed, of the profundity of his vision and courage. With him, the deeper the mine, the richer the ore.

But my *lorgnon* was not bent upon the Treaty, nor what it might contain. When the Président du Conseil began to read, which he seemed to do without much consultation with the sheets before him, but with no sign of extemporaneous speech, I saw that the old man was young. He had had no dealings with age, an enemy who would have to wait.

The top-light brought out only the large masses, the superb construction of his head and his rich healthy color. How thankful I was for the simple lighting, and even for the distance! — and I learned that the great should always be seen first, if possible, *from a distance*, and without contradictory detail, by those who wished to study them. In this way the big forms and gestures become and remain predominant.

I then and there determined that, though Clemenceau was student, writer, and above all Leader and Governor in Council, it was from the Tribune that he had had the strongest and most continuous influence, and that a study from memory of what I saw then, though probably incomplete, would be truer than if I attempted to 'do' him directly from sittings, if I ever got them. In fact, at our first interview, when I explained that I was not going to do 'un Monsieur dans un fauteuil,' he seemed relieved.

Strangely enough, memory does not provide me with the final phase of the dramatic *séance* of September 25, 1919. The impression of Clemenceau in the Tribune, facing a partly hostile audience (hostile, at least, to the Treaty, for all France now knew and either feared or adored his strength), took all one's capacity for absorption. More could not be carried away.

In considering the drama of a portrait of this man, there could be no question now as to the form the composition should take in order to give future wanderers in an American museum some idea of Clemenceau's personality in visible action.

The Tiger was not to be seen this time, if ever, and the chosen prototype, however comparable in the swiftness and devastation of its attack, did not contain the real secret of Clemenceau's physiognomy. In the horizontal setting of his eyes, without the slightest sideward slant, and the great overhang of the brow and backward placing of his head on the short neck, one could trace primitive man to an endlessly remote root. Some one of those great climbers and treaders of the wilderness had thought to break a sapling and demolish his enemy with one blow; or had thought to lead his family away from the forest he knew as home, where food was scarce, to other unknown forests, and by his descendants, through the drifts of the ages, the place that was to be called France had halted the seeker and a cave facing south had satisfied him. He went no farther.

The strongest traits are the most enduring, and Clemenceau's birthright has been the primal, essential will to decide, and the physical form that could contain and execute developing projects.

Down through the Periods there had been no deterioration, no weakening, no unnatural use of the sources he derives from. His inheritance was as fresh, as inexhausted, and as ready in action as ever, and of the same quality of strength. All the refinements and developments of the last billion or two of generations had not changed or complicated the main lines of the pattern. Clemenceau was a natural phenomenon, like Vesuvius or Niagara, and as young as they. He, himself, would find it no insult to resemble the first leaders in an unbroken line that became what we call humanity.

No, Clemenceau was not a Tiger.

The *voice* of Clemenceau has prevailed during his entire career. Sometimes it has roared like the old *Soixante-Quinze*. Sometimes it is as quiet as lightning seems to be, and as effective. To enumerate his speeches is to name the chapters of his life. Events and crises followed each other swiftly in France, between 1860 and 1918, and Clemenceau has been identified with them all. In times of stress his speeches were tornadoes that upset and rolled about Assemblies and Premierships. In the Tunis affair, for example, when the policy of expansion pushed on by financial intrigue was becoming popular, and like all Colonial enterprise at this time was violently opposed by Clemenceau, he declared:

'To build up vanquished France again [after 1870–71] we must not waste her blood and treasure on useless enterprises. But there are much higher reasons even than these for abstaining from such wars of depredation,' etc.

He always saw France as an individual whose character and honor must be maintained, not by blindly following the policy of other countries, but by carving out her destiny according to her form and especial potentialities, and in clearing the way for her deepest currents and originalities.

Then there is the speech after the Panama affair, which,

though primarily in his own defence, tore away the defences of the forgers and turned the cold reception of a hostile audience into a tempest of cheers.

Greatest of all, perhaps, was his speech in the Senate on the 12th of February, 1912, in opposition to the Treaty with Germany, about Morocco. Clemenceau was always perfectly informed, and after arranging in detail the policy of Germany toward France since 1875, in Tangier, in Morocco, and Casablanca, he said:

Germany believes that the natural consequence of our defeat is vassalage. We do not countersign the decree of abdication and downfall issued by our neighbors. We come of a great History and we mean to continue to be faithful to it. The dead have created the living, the living will remain faithful to the dead.

Clemenceau knew even then what were the real intentions of Germany and continued to warn against and expose them. This was, indeed, the first chapter in the Caillaux affair, when Clemenceau was summoned to appear before the Committee of the Senate as a witness in the serious indictment of this man, who had not only been Prime Minister of France, but had previously been Clemenceau's intimate colleague. But Caillaux's old associate was in possession of documents which could not be gainsaid and which showed Caillaux's recent proceedings in a very ugly light. Clemenceau did not hesitate. Nothing ever stood between him and the welfare of France. He had just taken office. The country was crying out for the truth in this affair, and a month later Clemenceau declared:

The Government has taken responsibilities. The Chamber must also shoulder responsibilities. If the Chamber refuses to sanction the prosecution of Caillaux, the Government will not remain in office.

Probably the greatest speech Clemenceau ever made was in 1917 at the age of seventy-six, as newly appointed Prime Minister. The veteran of the Radical Party, the *Tigre* of the old days, rose to deliver his Declaration to the House. It is mutilation to quote from it, but I cannot refrain from citing a few sentences toward its close:

One simple duty is imposed upon us, to stand by the soldier, to live, suffer, and fight with him, and to throw everything aside that is not for our country.

The rights on our front, the duties on our rear, must be merged in one. Every zone must be the army zone. The silent soldier in the factory, the old peasants working, bent over their soil, the vigorous women who toil, the children who help in their weakness — these likewise are our '*poilus*,' who in times to come will be able to say to the men in the trenches, 'I, too, was there.'

But, alas, there have been crimes, crimes against France which demand prompt punishment. We solemnly pledge ourselves before you and before the country that justice shall be done with the full rigor of the Law. Personal considerations or political passion shall neither divert us from fulfilling this duty nor induce us to go beyond it. Too many such crimes have cost us the blood of our soldiers. Weakness would mean complicity. There shall be no weakness, as there shall be no violence. Accused persons shall all be brought before courts-martial. The soldier of justice shall make common cause with the soldier in the field. No more pacifist plots, no more German intrigues. Neither treason nor semi-treason. Our country shall not be placed between two fires. Our country shall learn that she is really defended.

These are our unshakable resolves, gentlemen. We ask you to give them the sanction of your approval.

The summary from which I make this short quotation is by H. M. Hyndman, an English Socialist, a friend of Clemenceau and a generous and clear-sighted observer, whose book, 'Georges Clemenceau, the Man and his Time,' should be read by all those who wish to remember fairly and honestly the records of their own time, of the greatest war in history. Mr. Hyndman was never able to persuade Clemenceau to join the Socialist Party, but bore him no grudge on this account. Clemenceau saw bigger than any group with a single-track theory, but he could inspire the full confidence and regard of a thinker of another race and fully committed to opinions which the great Patriot could not adopt as a creed. When I asked him which of the biographies then printed he preferred, he replied at once, 'H. M. Hyndman's.'

It, Clemenceau's declaration, swept the Chamber away as the recital marched on. But organized attacks at once followed. Now came the supreme test of the mental and physical efficiency of this wonderful old man whose youth was so amazing. He could read a manifesto with vigor and effect. Would he be able to reply with equal power to a series of interrogations in an atmosphere to which he had been a stranger for so many years? Questions, by no means all of them friendly, poured in upon Clemenceau from every part of the Chamber; no point was missed that might embarrass or irritate the statesman who had undertaken to stand in the gap. He showed immediately that he was fully capable of taking his own part. The fervor of a new France was heard in every phrase of his crushing reply.

* * *

The events and deeds which followed should be too well known and remembered, even by Americans (though, alas, it may be feared they are not), to be rehearsed by an amateur historian. Clemenceau won the complete confidence of his country. Frenchmen of all creeds, political and otherwise, knew that it was the old man they called 'Le Tigre' who put iron into their failing endurance, and made them strong to believe in and follow their great generals. Clemenceau and Foch shared equally in the resolution unanimously voted by the Senate and which was placed in a conspicuous position in every Town Hall and in the Council Chamber of every Commune in France:

Georges Clemenceau, President of the Council and Minister of War, and Marshal Foch, General-in-Chief of the Allied Armies, have well deserved the gratitude of their country.

Clemenceau made other great speeches; none greater than his address to the Senate after this resolution had been voted in his absence. 'When he entered,' to quote again from Hyndman's account, 'he received astounding welcome. Every one present rose to greet him. Men, who but yesterday were his enemies and are still his opponents, rushed forward with the rest to applaud him, to shake hands with him, to thank him, to embrace him. The excitement was so overwhelming that Clemenceau for the first time in his life broke down. Tears coursed down his cheeks and for some moments he was unable to speak.'

Clemenceau at this time and in the Chamber, where he received, with only a few exceptions, the same enthusiasm that had greeted him in the Senate, sought to turn the glory and credit for the overthrow of the Germans and their confederates from himself. This he has always done, and here more than ever. 'The spirit of France, the citizens of France, the soldiers and sailors of France' — these were they who, in comradeship with the Allies, had 'achieved the great victory over the last convulsion of savagery.' And as he no doubt was able to REMEMBER what perhaps no other man present but himself had witnessed — that is, the events of 1870–71 — he spoke of those who had upheld the Republic at that time.

'I wish to speak of Gambetta' — and the whole house rose with prolonged cheering — 'of him who, defending the territory under circumstances which rendered victory impossible, never despaired... to these men let us say, *pass in first, you have shown us the way.*'

Among the most prized photographs that I was able to collect was the series taken when the Président du Conseil made his visits to the front. Unfailing as a young man in prime condition, he left Paris at least three or four times a week, at four or five in the morning, and went to the front, keeping in touch with the generals, officers, and soldiers all along the lines. On one of these occasions, he walked about under fire as if he had come out for the pleasure of risking his life with the *poilus*. Nothing could have united him as this did to the soldier's heart of France. He wished to be one with them, and he succeeded.

Then, having saluted and talked with the Maréchal and officers, and chatted with the rank and file of the soldiery, he rushed back to Paris, arriving at the Ministry of War at ten or eleven o'clock at night, ready to attend to such business as needed his personal care.

Again I wish to quote *verbatim* from Mr. Hyndman what even Clemenceau's opponents would not dispute:

No man of his time of life, perhaps no man of any age, ever carried on continuously, such exhausting toil, physical and mental, as that which this marvellous old statesman of seventy-seven undertook and carried through from November, 1917, to November, 1918. And all the time cheerful, alert, confident, showing, when things looked dark as when the great advance began, the Prime Minister of the Republic never for one moment doubted the Germans would be hurled back to the frontier and France would again take her rightful place in the world.

And that is not all. Clemenceau's influence in the Council Chamber of the Allies was supreme. The old gayety of heart remained, but the soundness of judgment and determination to accept no compromise of principle are more marked than ever. Many dangerous intrigues during the last few months, of which the world has heard little, were snuffed clean out by Clemenceau's force of character and overwhelming personality. The French Prime Minister wanted complete victory for France and her Allies. Nothing short of this would satisfy him. There was no personal party he wished to build up, no political object he desired to attain, no section or party that he felt himself bound to propitiate. Therefore, the other ministers of the Allies found themselves at a table with a statesman who was something more than an individual representative of his nation. He was the human embodiment of a cause. Read aright, his actions do all hang together and constitute one complete whole. Having forgotten himself in his work, the man Clemenceau will never be forgotten. He will stand out in History as the greatest statesman of the greatest War.

I did not see Clemenceau again until the following spring, the experiences of Malines and London having intervened; but I had had the great *séance*, and, although it might never be carried out, the project for a portrait was formed in its minutest detail, and when I finally, as one might say, met the illusive subject on level ground, I had made a sketch that I could not much more than fill out on the large canvas.

When I returned from London in January, 1920, Clemenceau was in Egypt, and no one knew for certain where he might be next. Mr. White, my kind friend of the spring of '19, had gone home. The Embassy had but a feeble interest in matters held over. I got to know the refined voices of the young secretaries at the 'Chancery' very well, on the telephone, and in the Salon there, where a few other compatriots and I eyed each other jealously.

But at last I found myself again in the Ambassador's private office, and, after a short reminiscent interview, our wise representative thought that Colonel M. would be the one to intervene for me with the rather dreaded Président du Conseil, who had just returned to Paris.

Colonel M., who was then summoned by his chief, was a tall, well-set-up officer in the full military uniform of our Nation, with (to quote my letter to my sister) 'miles of color on his chest.'

As briefly as possible, I explained the situation. Colonel M.'s face was grave, and he then spoke for the first time with a deep and pleasant drawl.

'Why don't Miss Beaux and I go to see Clemenceau this afternoon?'

What an advocate I had! It was as simple as Lindbergh's, 'Is this Paris?'

GEORGES CLEMENCEAU
Preliminary study for portrait

Such are the methods of the gods. But I must take the West Wind and not be borne away by it.

'No,' I said, 'that will not do. I cannot go. This is not a personal matter, and I cannot, personally, solicit anything.'

Somehow I trusted, in the less than instant occupied, that Colonel M. would see the matter as I did, and big as disaster would have been for me if I had been wrong, and wide open as I had thrown the door for any escape toward the facility of failure, I could see no other way.

Revision was accepted, and, to use that phrase so worn but not worn out, the end justified the means, means rendered so much more unpalatable to the Colonel in that he must now, instead of merely gallantly introducing the solicitor, become the solicitor himself, and meet the unpleasant result of a possible refusal, or at least reluctant consent, of one with whom every one wished to be acceptable. There was not the least doubt of Clemenceau's unwillingness to give even a little time to an American portrait-painter of whom he had never heard, no matter by whom accredited.

The interview between Le Président du Conseil and Colonel M. was not recorded, and this scanty narrative must suffer. Clemenceau always favors the bold and direct, and I am sure the big soldier, who was the Embassy's messenger, wasted no words, and that Fate, for the moment kind, had prepared the great man's mood. At all events, in an incredibly short time a note from Colonel M., left at my hotel, informed me that M. Clemenceau would be glad to see me the next day at two-thirty.

I never saw the Colonel again, and was never able to get him to come to see either me or the portrait, so our account is unsettled and my note of thanks remains the only and meagre evidence, to him, of my eternal gratitude.

'The day began as other days begin.'
Richard Watson Gilder's line, so potent in expression for

all who have not had the misfortune to overlook it, came to my mind the next morning, knowing that the day was for me to be big with destiny, good or otherwise. Mr. Gilder's day was to hold his first sight, in the Morgan Library, of the Keats manuscript of 'Endymion':

'Now all the wrong Fate did thee rose; through Memory's draped portal
Trooped in wan figures all thy tragic story.'

I felt sure that the turn in the road that I was to take was to contain an encounter, rather than a meeting. I could not add to my equipment for it. I had to go without sling or stone to meet the giant; and even now, in spite of my brave precursor, my head might be carried out in a basket if I were not nimble; and my vast respect for the giant would not serve me.

Opportunely enough, Mr. Gilder's daughter Rosamond accompanied me to the appointment, and we went right gaily, savoring mutually, after all, the adventure.

Number 8 rue Franklin is not very welcoming in appearance. A grim court first, and one faced an ordinary house; front door at the side, with two large windows with yellow silk curtains. It might have been the home of moderate means in one of the New York cross-streets.

Not an ancient servitor, but a good-looking young valet, answered our ring, and looked a little incredulous when I asked for M. Clemenceau; but I told him that I had an appointment with M. Clemenceau and was a little *avant l'heure*. Taking my card, he immediately returned smiling and said that Monsieur le Président du Conseil was engaged, but would see me *dans un moment*. He showed us into the room with the yellow curtains, large, high-studded, and rather dark, in spite of its high windows. It was undoubtedly the dining-room, and the long table, with its modest *décor* of a plate of fruit, peopled itself at once for me with the master and his guests, never very formal, but there would be high, resounding talk, with asides by the head of the table, followed by shouts of laughter. Or Clemenceau would be taking a solitary *déjeuner*, or a cup of hot bouillon and a bit of cold chicken at 2 A.M. On the sombre walls hung many pictures and objects, obviously gifts and mementoes. The same well-known type of tribute filled the obscure mantel at the other end of the room — a man's room, and perfectly destitute of any thought of renewal or other attention on the part of its owner. Strange that such rooms — and I have seen others like it — should mysteriously bear the stamp of life, mind, and personality upon their dingy furnishings, and, without offering anything, have the power to satisfy and detain the visitor.

I had almost forgotten what we had come for when the door opened behind me and a great head wearing a black silk skull cap literally popped in. I believe I made some sort of noise — Rosamond said, I whooped — and in another moment I was crossing the hall with him to his study.

Sans façon, certainly. Why send for me when it was easier to stop for me, after seeing the other man out, and this small incident showed me how little waste there had been in the giant's life.

When the door of the study was closed behind us, the little old man — for he seemed this now — turned on me and shouted, almost savagely, 'Vous parlez Français?'

'Oui, Monsieur,' I said; 'but you know English so well that, if you please, we will speak English.'

'Very well,' he said, rather gently, and then, turning on me again, 'Well, to begin with, we hate each other.'

'No, Monsieur,' I said; 'that's only half true.'

Whereupon he threw up his hands and laughed aloud, and I felt that the assault was over and the breach opened. I had an instant to observe the scene. There was the great horseshoe table, with books and papers surging up at either end, so familiar in the photographs. The room was small and full of books. On the large chimney-piece were Greek fragments, very likely to be original, and over the mantel hung a beautiful drawing of an interesting woman. The main feature of the room was the broad window. The horseshoe stood in front of it, so that, when the master sat at his work, light poured in on his right, from a little green garden and an ivy-covered wall. Nought could be seen from this window but a tapestry of green leaves, which even in winter must have sustained and comforted the writer's tension. Queer to feel at home in this place; perhaps it was because green branches have always been my choice for a window view in a working place.

I was invited to sit at the outside of the horseshoe. Clemenceau took his chair within its protecting extension, and we at once became quite gay.

Strangely enough, I have no recollection of this part of our interview. I suppose because all but my automatic faculties were engaged in SEEING. The eyes of my *vis-à-vis* took my whole attention. The big modelling of the head had been conspicuous from a distance, at the Chamber, but the eyes there were only caverns. Now I got their full dynamic power, though the general form of the head, seen so near, became, paradoxically, somewhat diminished. In a moment practical matters surged up.

'What do you want from me?' he said.

I replied with the usual formula, 'As much as I can have.'

He said: 'I have just come back from Egypt. I have had pneumonia. My doctors prescribe a few days' inaction. I will give you a half-hour to-morrow, and the same on the two following days.'

'That would be no use to me,' I said, desperately clinging to the exact truth; and then went on to explain, he listening with a sort of curiously amused interest.

'I have seen you in the Chamber, Monsieur,' I said. 'I watched you for two hours through a glass when you read the Treaty last September. I decided on the composition then, and have not changed my mind. I have already made a sketch, and laid in the composition, life-size. I have spent much time examining every bust and photograph of you to be found. I do not count on regular sittings from you which you would not have time for.

'It would do me no good to come to-morrow, as I must work to-morrow on what I have seen to-day. I am not going to make a "Monsieur dans un fauteuil." '

Clemenceau seemed to approve entirely of this method, not offering any objection to it, and another appointment was made. My mind was fully assured that he would be generous, and that I must be short; that he would not endure an instant of boredom in such a cause. I at once got up to go, he escorted me to the door, and I had a chance to introduce my friend as the daughter of R. W. Gilder of the 'Century,' who was perfectly well known to him by reputation.

I was glad that at this meeting I had not been rapt away to the extent of being unaware of what was going on. I could now remember the voice of consciousness, whispering as I sat at the outer arc of the horseshoe: 'You are alone with Georges Clemenceau in his study. You are talking like old acquaintances, across a narrow table. That small hand in a worn grey glove resting on some sheets of paper covered with black handwriting — his — is the same that defied Germany and hoisted France out of the pit. That bit of a quill pen, worn and jagged, which he has just thrown down, is the very instrument which has been called mightier than the sword. You, thinking that it is all a dream; could that small black tie a little on one side be fictitious? Or the individual bristles of those grisled eyebrows and mustache? The eyes are, indeed, unreal, in what is meant commonly by reality, because of what one must look through to see them even from so near. You must perceive and remember what they have looked on and into. Take this moment Fate permits you, and be thankful.'

* * *

The next day in my exquisite retreat at 15 rue de Cherche Midi, there was much to be considered and not a little to baffle and dismay.

Fortunately for my 'morale,' which could look for no support from him who had supported France, I had not an instant's doubt as to the choice of the design and drama of the *donné*, the main lines of which were even now before me on an easel.

True, Clemenceau, who was of all men absolute and 'there,' it would seem should be seized in all his reality. Reality? But what reality? The reality achieved by values seen under equally real and constant lighting? And where? The studio, with its big charming windows and delicate grey walls, had no resources to fit my plan, even if the Président du Conseil could be persuaded to come there for a couple of tempestuous half-hour sittings. I had no illusions. Sargent was the only artist in the world strong enough to wrest an *œuvre* from such a meagre opportunity, and a rapid summary, however suggestive, was far from my view of my obligation to the chance Fate had offered me.

No strong lighting could be found in the little salon, and Clemenceau's study was worse. There was no room for me there with canvas, easel, and paints for the direct attack, and the mere sight of these things would have done for me with my subject. Never again would I have been allowed entrance. Nevertheless, if the room had been lighted from above, I might have tempted my fate.

But that soft side-light from the window, so intimate, so near, so momentary, would have been the death of synthesis and simplicity, and, indeed, would have veiled, rather than revealed, the force of Clemenceau. One must remember, too, the destiny of the portrait. It was to be an attempt to give the public of another country some idea of the Frenchman, the Patriot, the Leader, the Denouncer, the Supporter. The design was just. I must do what I could, lacking the zest of momentary revelation.

Clemenceau must be seen in the Tribune, lighted from far above. Color was of little consequence; the great head and the action alone important. By seeing him as often as he would permit, I might continually refresh my knowledge of forms, correct mistakes of measurement and proportion, and above all get a repeated first-hand view of his positive, yet so intricate, personality.

* * *

On my second visit to the rue Franklin, I took a board with a piece of paper to make notes. I knew I could not draw.

He came in, saying, 'Well, I would like to kill you, but our laws do not permit it.'

But he took hold of me by both arms, a good-natured shake, not terrifying at all. I climbed over some armchairs and got my back to the light, and Clemenceau got into his horseshoe, facing me. I had brought a photograph of my portrait of Lord Beatty, which he examined with approval.

'Why, that is good — that is very good.'

His obvious surprise that it should be was a comment on his concession to the request of the committee, but it gave me a chance to amuse him with some Beatty *histoires* while he sat opposite me, leaning his head on his hand and fixing me with those wonderful eyes. If I had been a little dog, I would either have run away or adopted him as my master.

His eyes are clear, dark depths with yellow lights across them, not a sign of age there; and in spite of those gleams, under all, when one sees deep enough, there is disillusion and more of pain than of bitterness.

His eyebrows bristle out, grey, with terrific energy.

I did not stay long — that is, I got up to go — and then he began showing me things. He had a great little picture by Daumier, a gift he had just received, and, although it was framed, he insisted on holding it out at arm's length, for me to see, and was full of understanding and enthusiasm.

He helped me on with my coat, and it was then that *he proposed my writing to him when I wished to come again.*

* * *

This sign of confidence touched me deeply and I confess to feeling a pride in it far out of proportion to its intention. In fact, all dread of his irony or irritation was past. He was a great piece of Nature, a mountain, a river, or a whole landscape and the sun over it. Why should a lesser parcel of the same feel anything but harmony in relation to him? I felt like a brook that, blessed by a spring freshet, was tumbling along on the mountain-side on a day in early summer.

When I arrived one morning for an appointment, made as he had proposed, he entered holding up both hands in dismay.

'Alas, I have made three engagements for this hour. Can you come to-morrow?'

'Certainly, but there is no need. I am seeing *now* what I came for.' And then, as he stood ready to be measured and examined, and I remarked that it didn't take long to see something when one knew what one wished to find, he shouted, '*C'est vrai! c'est vrai!*'

And when I was going out, he said very kindly, 'You do not need to make an appointment. Come any morning at nine-thirty.'

And I was gone before the other man arrived.

* * *

One day, as I was leaving, I told the *Président* that I had bought, and been reading, some of his works. He shook both hands in the air and groaned ironically. '*Désastreux!*'

But not long afterwards he went to the bookcase, saying that he would give me the latest, and of course I asked him to sign it, which he did with the same worn-out but very efficient quill — '*Souvenir Amical.*'

* * *

Besides learning a great deal about the veritable Clemenceau in my visits to the rue Franklin, I learned how simple are the accoutrements of real greatness, especially in France. Most of all, how few if any of their compatriots have thought of them as meat for daily and devouring appetite, for individual increase. Small editors or great, or their secretaries, or the literary free lance, did not seem to be pestering Clemenceau for an interview or reminiscences, something to bolster up the just started and unsupported periodical. The visitors I sometimes passed in the hall were plain, serious, middle-aged men, who did not look like either fools or angels. They knew the rights, I might almost say, the decencies, of their approach. Perhaps with the steady increase of the 'American idea' in France, the French may acquire our habit of thinking that the great are people who may be used for anybody's small advantage.

* * *

If to feel, to know, and to imagine were all that is necessary for an artist's equipment, his happiness would be far beyond that allowed by Heaven to any man. But the artist suffers agonies known only to women in the perils of childbirth, and, like this very large class, he suffers least when most powerfully aided by Nature. His conception can have no recognized existence until it passes, by way of his entire being, into material shape and body. In fact, this process and this deliverance are the only proof of his having had a feeling, a conception, an imagination.

One often hears it said of some one that he has 'the *soul*

of an artist.' To which the answer is, 'How do you know?'

The struggle then is, the effort to bring forth the idea, and to give it a body acceptable. Sometimes in the artist's performance there is the almost savage joy of gladiatorial combat, the 'throwing of the beast'; but it is more often a birth, and then the question is, What of the result? 'By their fruits ye shall know them,' a Scriptural utterance never more applicable than in the case of the artist. Indeed, an artist is a fruit-bearer. 'I sat down under his shadow with great delight, and his fruit was sweet unto my taste.'

Often when I returned from one of my inspiring visits to the rue Franklin, to my sanctum in the Cherche Midi, when I had climbed Mimi's stair, and dared to look upon the canvas that contained the shadowy indication of my hopes, I wondered what would most stimulate my imagination for the carrying on? What of all my knowledge gained and my enthusiasm for the subject? Could I make a channel through which this would flow and find itself at last embodied, I might almost say entrapped in pigment, manipulated to contain it? I knew that everything depended on the vision absolute; a vision much more definite than what I had seen afar of Clemenceau in the Tribune; mental vision of tones I had only seen from a distance, for there were no color values, such as would have appeared in the Tribune at the Chamber, to be seen at the study in the rue Franklin. Mental vision — for it could not be called memory — must show me the color of the half tone next the shadow on the forehead and the nondescript modelling of the mighty chin, partly in shadow. Unless these tones had in them the elements of truth and relation, they would be without substance, and Clemenceau without substance was out of the question.

Never for an instant was an abstract view of Clemenceau to be considered; that is, any intentionally abstract view. After the drama had been chosen, any personal or limited view of Clemenceau was unimportant. Unimportant was any conception of the man that I might put forth as subsisting on that ground — that is, the ground of my individual conception.

The only value the work could have would be in showing HIM, the man, body and spirit, irrespective of theory, or of the tendency in Art, any artist might have. The portrait of a very great man should be as far as possible a true story. The artist is important in that his language and style should attract and convince readers. Above all should be shown the form which could contain what the subject summed up to, his scale in relation to lesser men, the signs of a foremost member of the species.

Begone all personal conceits! There was no room here for any one but Clemenceau.

This, at all events, should be an artist's feeling in approaching such a subject. His own greatness, if he have any, will take care of itself. The powers of an artist are never in any danger of being crowded out by his unconsciousness of them. The true artist never perfectly materializes his vision. How can he but be humble?

* * *

So, day after day, without the joy of seizure and the moment's victory, the search went on. Bit by bit, changing, refreshing, chiselling, adding new evidence, and above all maintaining obstinately the prime conception. In this, strongest support was in the sketch, which had, however, the lightness of a sketch and must be developed to something more elemental.

The series of photographs taken at the front were very illuminating from the intelligence with which they had been taken. No one had asked the President and the officers accompanying him to turn about, and show their faces, and particularly their teeth. In consequence the photographs were vital and revealing.

One of these groups — 'Visite de M. Clemenceau sur le front de la Somme: M. Clemenceau, Capitaine Delorme, et Lt. Guynemer' — shows the whole party from the rear, some, notably Guynemer, seen in profile, and all palpably unconscious of the camera. This view of Clemenceau in silhouette, *profile perdue*, was especially useful to me, as showing his massive shoulders and back, the angle of the jaw, and placing of the head.

Another, equally revealing, is a group taken at the front at Maurepas, an officer earnestly describing to Clemenceau some movement in the battle, as they halt for a moment in the devastated *forêt*.

Unconscious of the camera as these groups are, the results show the spirit and mood of each individual, as in a picture where Clemenceau is having speech with a *poilu* by the path. This really contains a volume on the French spirit. Acute absorption in the drama of the moment; humor; sympathy; and on the part of a *poilu* in the rear whose gaze is fixed on *le Tigre's* back, adoring affection, obscure, unconscious, but perfectly caught by the camera. It is a real deprivation that we cannot be told, much less guess, what words of sympathy, spiced with Gallic wit, have illuminated the shy face of the soldier with whom Clemenceau is having a word.

But constantly I felt, in Clemenceau himself and in all the views of him that I looked over, the element of tragedy. He literally suffered with the army. He endured with them and for them, and he suffered that in the world there was no other better way than this; and if gleams played about the Gallic steel of his will for France, they were sharpened by the reality of the sufferings he was powerless to assuage. Steady cheerfulness he had by nature, and would have showed no other face, but knowing all, by heart as well as by head, the bitterness of it ground lines upon his mask, more even than did age.

* * *

Clemenceau left Paris rather suddenly, but not before the fibre of my visual receptivity had taken up all it was capable of. I could not make any more discoveries of an important nature, I could only enforce and simplify. *Plus accusé* was the word I heard often from my friend and critic, André Dezarrois. Of course, I was not satisfied, but to work done by the method I had used, there is no end. One's model, being a vision, is always at hand.

I improved the portrait quite a good deal, after I set it up in my New York studio, with greater distance; but anything done away from the magic of the rue Franklin, and the charmed seclusion of the Cherche Midi, was hard going.

I saw Clemenceau once again in Vichy, where my friend and I went for the month of July. His hotel was not far from ours, and a stir in the always-moving and unctuous crowd (most of the women were there for flesh-reduction) often warned us that he was near. There were husky whispers, 'C'est lui — c'est lui!' — and he would pass briskly in neat morning suit, a Panama jauntily placed, swinging his cane.

If he came for a cure, he had no look of needing one.

We never allowed ourselves to cross his path, and he never saw us, but his doctor proved to be the same as mine, and he laughed at my scruples.

'I shall tell him. He will want to see you. I will leave a note at your hotel,' he said.

And when we came in from our morning in the beautiful park, there was the bit of folded paper among our letters.

The appointment was for that very afternoon.

This time I was fearful. All was personal now. There was no definite purpose in our visit, except our very eager wish for it.

We were led along a dim corridor, down which le Président advanced to meet us, holding out both hands, a kind welcome. He led us into a room where he had been writing at a table, beside a window — the constant arrangement, I dare say, wherever he happened to be.

We were very gay, sitting beside it. When I asked him how he liked his cure, he held up all ten fingers:

'Le Président Wilson avait quatorze points. Moi, je n'ai que dix.'

He did not tell us what his ten maladies were, but none of them could have been very vital. We had a joyous visit, and when we were leaving, he put his hand on my shoulder and said a few words to me that I shall always be happy in remembering.

He left the next day, and we did not meet again, but a gleam of life and reality had passed our way, and we could endure more patiently the hot, eventless days of water-drinking and the *douche* at the huge Bath Palace. And there were quiet hours under the majestic trees of the park, in near view of a certain magnolia, where a few great, creamy, half-opened blossoms hid under dark, shining leaves; a place fit for the renewal and memory of profound experience.

* * *

But the near and surface visions of the great Patriot always faded quickly. The permanent and real presence was that of the Tribune — the voice of France.

And more constant than all is Clemenceau's own summing-up of what was his life effort.

'I have combated ideas, not persons.'

XII

QUINZE RUE DE CHERCHE MIDI

I HAVE once or twice alluded to the apartment in the rue de Cherche Midi, and it must be admitted that to place and set this jewel as fond admiration desires is an act of pure self-indulgence.

It cannot be hoped that contrast may be accepted as an excuse. A rude modern attempt to show the old twentieth-century hero, taking form in a dream chamber of the *dix-huitième*, adds little to the force of the one or the grace of the other. But it is a fact that in this account the two are inseparable. The gracious reader, if such there ever may be, is only invited to leave the episode of a portrait of Clemenceau, by way of a room and a garden in a charming other world.

Not only had the possibility of securing an opportunity of any sort from Clemenceau seemed doubtful, but what appeared at first quite simple to achieve became more and more uncertain; the finding of a studio to work in.

Inquiry on all sides opened up what seemed to be good prospects.

Many were the stairs I climbed, and the hidden *ateliers* I visited, always hoping that the artist incumbent would be tempted to fly from Paris on the proceeds of rental. Few seemed busy, but to their credit be it known, no one succumbed.

I became desperate. But desperation is often the state nearest to relief. My really poignant anxiety was soon absorbed into a group of one of the happiest series of benefits that ever came my way.

In my distress I turned to my friends, the Paul Bartletts.

Our friendship had long been one of my most valued priv-
ileges. I had the greatest sympathy and esteem for the force,
and above all the integrity, of Bartlett's work; his deeply
rooted belief in life and nature as the source of inspiration;
his bold and noble grasp of the profoundly understood and
desired form; his solid building upon the fastness that lies
between abstraction and reality and the rich sensuousness,
that with him went hand in hand with strong and earnest
purpose. Alas, that these gifts and in the vigorous and
fruitful years of middle life should have been doomed to
sudden destruction. I knew the studio in the rue du Com-
mandeur well, the racy give-and-take of the sculptor's
idle moments, and the teasing irony that played over his
ready kindness and genuine loyalty. Paul deserved well,
and life had been lavish to him of the best gifts. After the
rich endowment of his own nature and talent, surely his
brightest good fortune lay in the devotion of his wife Suzanne, his brilliant auxiliary and support. Paul's work was
the only burden he had to carry, a big one, but well matched
by his forces. No care of any sort in relation to his work or
outside it was allowed to touch him, and what the artist
desires most, freedom for thought and creation, were his.

Number 15 rue de Cherche Midi is the old Hôtel Montmorency. Its serious façade joins the humbler ones that
flank it without obvious difference; but when it has really
been perceived, it gives at once the sensation of majesty in
reserve. This soon explains itself. By the great height and
proportion of the windows *au premier*, one divines the state-
liness of the interior.

The entrance is the ordinary massive portal, which opens
with a heavy click at the will of an invisible concierge. Inside, the usual shallow tunnel leads into a long court, with
an intensely green central parterre, decorated with repli-
quas of the Louis XV Sphinx of the Louvre. The hôtel

proper occupies three sides of the court, the other being a high wall nearly covered with ivy. Within the court, at the right, true elegance begins. A spacious doorway, a broad, low rising marble stair rounds in the mild curve that is the hall-mark of the *ancien régime* in France, its accent of design in the rich iron ramp. Mounting, one passes a perfectly placed niche with a charming bust of an eighteenth-century *Grande Dame*, just where the living one, now dust, would have turned to bend a mocking smile upon her cavalier, closely following. The same piquant profile would be hers that the marble shows us from its warm *patine*, a little stained, and chipped at the base, only resting now in safety on its somewhat longer way to earth.

The formal salons of the early proprietors are, of course, *au premier*. The *étage*, the apartment, has conquered, but has fallen luckily into the best hands. Nothing is lost to the high, noble rooms, rich with all the graces of France in the seventeenth and eighteenth centuries. Suzanne Bartlett has known how to live here without once slipping away from the charm of the past, or chilling the senses and the soul with either a too precious formality or some reminder of what, in such a place, one most desires to forget, the too much light, noise, and contrivances of our recent living.

One may sink into a nest of comfort, old silk and down, near a small lingering wood fire. A mild light enters by majestic windows and there is no sound from the court. When Suzanne approached, I heard her tiny heels on the marquetry by succeeding doors, and she brought a soft glamour, a warmth, in her very person, exactly in harmony with the color and surface of her *décor* and with the astute brilliance of its spirit. Just such a woman — and they are rare in any age — must, in those leisurely old centuries, have held out a soft little hand to the favored visitor, just so have smiled away his jealousy or his ennui, and now, although only a woman and a distraught one at that, it was my turn.

Suzanne made little of the woes of her petitioner. No unoccupied studio was known to her, but in the rear of her apartment and by another stair was a salon with accessories. It opened upon a little garden, also *au premier*. She did not use this place; had taken it to protect herself. This description seemed big with prophecy. Something vitally gracious was approaching.

* * *

The entrance at the other end of the court was in a dark corner of the *rez-de-chaussée*. All lovers of Paris and of its history, will agree that no detail is more significant than those old stairs, worn, polished, so that the knots are luminous. The narrow, austere, iron hand-rail, with its slender posts, has been smoothed by innumerable hands, going up and down, to love, life, or death. Of course, it is a circular stair, lighted not at all at first, and after the first turn, dimly, from a window above. It was Mimi's staircase, and one might have passed Rodolphe running down on some errand of love's necessity.

Our interest was in the grey door, *au premier*. The key did not work very well, though from appearance it was the original instrument.

What folly to try to convey the personality of a place!— and when it has both obvious and obscure fascination in itself, it is as illusive as a person so gifted.

When it became my privilege to spend most of my days in this place, many visitors came there, but always singly (the whole charm would have vanished with a crowd); no one ever entered without pausing, astonished and charmed. Most people began by asking for it. It was what they had always dreamed of. They would not be refused, and always inquired at once for how long I had taken it.

The room we entered was empty of everything but its own beauty. Over the doors were those inserted paintings in curved mouldings, so dear, so indispensable, to the taste of the *dix-huitième*, so enriching to the desired pearl-grey of the walls and panelling. We faced the small plain *cheminèe* and tall mirror, and on the left were the two high windows, with *croissée* and inside shutters, open and turned to receive the light, exquisitely, on their panels. These windows and a second door and vestibule opened on a little garden, gravelled, with high ilex bushes and a low parapet above the court. There was no door of communication with the hôtel proper, only on each side of the mantel were three or four steps leading up to two offices, one large enough to be used as a bedroom, and having a window on the garden; the other had been converted into a bathroom *quelconque*. Both had panelled doors decorated above, and these double-leaved doors a short distance above the floor, and the large windows upon the garden, gave a sense of continuation and expansion to a place which seemed complete in being only one large room, where a feeling of secrecy and *éloignement* and delightful privacy accompanied its stately reserve.

In spite of its enticing accommodations, I never came to sleep in this place. The cares and paraphernalia of living would have been a rough intrusion on what I found there.

Suzanne put down an antique rug of perfect size and color, before the mantel, and a huge easy-chair, unparalleled in line and simplicity, and broad enough to accommodate any sort of luxurious reclining upon its thick cushion. My kind friend also brought tables all seasoned for our use, a couch for my post-prandial siesta, and which the long wall called for, and some lesser chairs. I would have no *objets* of any description, for space would be the only reconciler between the character of the place and our presence and that of the easel and canvas, which came near to being forgotten altogether.

It was early June when the spell was cast, and although we did not sleep in what we humbly called my studio, our *déjeuner* there was one of our best periods of happiness in it.

What joy to find and provide our small *batterie* for this meal; also for modest service of tea! Sweet to command a few pieces of wood and the bundle of selected fagots for kindling, at the tiny black triangle stocked with fuel, its bags of charcoal at the door. Just within it, the cobbler occupied a foot of space and hammered all day at the worn *chaussures* of the *quartier*. The shoe-mender's child of four played about on the *pavé*, and I envied the careful workman's social opportunities.

We came to have habits, and a delightful, uninterrupted routine. At twelve-thirty exactly, I left work and made the fire. At twelve-forty-five, when it was just right for broiling, I heard Rosamond's step on the stair and she entered with her bulging netted bag. It would contain two fresh, perfect *côtelettes; petits pains;* butter of the most expensive, strawberries of the same mark, and cream in a white paper parcel. Our bottle of wine, which stayed with us, was brought from its cool corner and the round table drawn in front of one of the great open windows. Rosamond might *réchauffer* the peas, but no one might touch the chops but myself. She took a photograph of me, in my painting apron and eyeshade, stooping at this task, and when the chops were *juste à la pointe*, we sat down to a feast Olympus never knew.

How fine was the bottle upstanding beside the strawberries, and rich russet of the *petits pains*, in the cool light from the garden! There were flowers, too, on the low window-sill.

The place was obviously, to me at least, an appanage of the main apartment of the *hôtel*, though not directly communicating with it. In spite of its air of secrecy and *éloignement*, it never seemed to me a place for intrigue, for love, or family policy.

I saw no pretty powdered phantoms in the hour of rest when I lay half dreaming on the long couch. I surprised no officer's cloak and sword upon the chair by the door. No brace of small portly schemers in brocade and lace entered for private council; but I had one constant and recurring vision. I saw a slight, delicate old gentleman, in black satin. He wore powder and the filmiest of ruffles hung about his thin, white, idle hands.

Sometimes I saw his fine profile, as he sat at a table before a great sheet of paper, writing with a tall quill, laboriously, slowly, leaning back to ponder with a sort of proud anxiety. Then suddenly, with long, jerking strokes, and hard service of the pen, the signature, and the petulant shaking of sand over the paper.

With him I never saw but one other person, a tall, good-looking valet. Dead, this man was, to a certainty, but his jovial vitality filled the room and no doubt warmed and comforted his lonely old master, who was lingering too long in the opinion of those frivolous, neglectful relatives below. Sometimes a couple of stout fellows in livery appeared in the door, and I could see Antoine lay a fine cloak about the elegant old shoulders, handing Monsieur his hat with fond and pitying respect.

Monsieur's 'chair' waited below, but for no pleasing *rendezvous*. I never saw him smile.

Had Monsieur escaped the guillotine, or was he to be led to it in proud non-resistance? Horror, murder, injustice, were rampant in his day. When has a nation been so drenched in blood, so racked by torture, while a golden stream, warm and self-sustained, flowed on in her veins, native and undisturbed, through all the bitter years before the final cataclysm. Brutally dismembered in politics, religion, and thought, in taste she was as one, and the desired form, texture, color, was desired by every one in all things.

From the smallest, humblest detail of life to the King's garden, furniture, dress, coiffure, wall decoration, the same delicate proportion, the same rich texture, was as present as the atmosphere. Do I forget the *chaumières* of the peasants,

— 313 —

the wine-shop? Are we not ransacking France for their chairs and tables, and are they not always charming? There is no breach here. All have felt the hand of the careful, instinctive designer, and if the old aristocrat who seemed to haunt the apartment in the Cherche Midi ever stood on a cottage hearth, he saw nothing to shock or offend his taste, even in the *pot au feu*.

The great old radical, whose face was to appear roughly on the canvas more than a hundred years later, would have had a heart tender to a vision of the sad old phantom and the beauty that was his inseparable aura.

Tout comprendre, c'est tout pardonner.

During the winter and spring of 1919–20, while I waited in Paris, and, indeed, in later visits, when I returned to the living spring always longed for in absence, there were charming friendly homes where I was always welcome. From the Léonce Benedites' stored and mellow apartment on the rue Dougay-Truin, and Florence Este's fascinating nest on the Avenue de l'Observatoire, emanated a very special and very individual allure. One had to climb to both of these apartments by many flights of silent carpeted stairs ... past many doors whose privacy seemed more than closed, and where one met no one. At the door of my dear friend Florence, one pulled a long green cord and tassel and a little bell jangled gently within. What afternoons I spent with that brilliant artist and glowing spirit!... She gave me, in her water-colors, her own view of Brittany, where she spent all her summers, and was much appreciated by her *confrères* among the artists of Paris. Our friendship had begun far back in the Concarneau days... but I shall find her no more when I return.

Léonce Benedite was for many years Directeur of the Luxembourg Gallery and later of the Rodin Museum in the Hôtel Biron, in whose great old tangled garden I was permitted to wander when I pleased. At their table and informal receptions, I met Cottier, Lucien Simon, and others of their world, and André Dezarrois, Directeur of the 'Revue de l'Art Ancien et Moderne,' and for years Benedite's right hand at the Luxembourg. Dezarrois gave me valiant aid and counsel during all my sojourn in Paris for the War portraits, and I am happy in the continuance of his friendship. He greatly distinguished himself in the War, being one of the twenty-three members of the Guynemer squadron, of which only seven survived. Dezarrois was severely wounded, and still suffers from the result, but his indomitable spirit continues to carry him through his crowded life of responsibility and labor. He is now Conservateur des Musées Nationaux. M. Benedite visited America a few years ago in order to give a series of lectures, and at the time saw my picture 'Sita and Sarita.' Of course, I was much gratified when he asked for it, for the Luxembourg.

At the Bartletts' I met one evening at dinner Besnard and Madame Besnard — a superb pair, reflecting the rich, calm life in their *milieu* where the art and literature of Paris were at home also; and Paul Pichon, the owner of the Hôtel de Lauzun, on the Ile de France, where I dined later in company with the Bartletts, a small party, but memorable in that magnificent relic of the *dix-septième*.

Here also I must speak of my friend Lieutenant J. J. Lemordant: artist, hero, martyr — too well known for eulogy. Totally blind, crippled, and always suffering, his energy and will to labor in the cause of Art and idealism remain for service. He was just forty when struck down — an artist already welcomed and rewarded, a Breton with all the unspent force of his race, one of the big coming men lost to France... for whom France has no substitutes.

A last visit to Paris in 1924 was fraught with dire consequences, and put me *hors de combat* for much of the kind of activity that preceded it. But one may be hindered without being defeated, and on my return to America, Fate threw me a liberal *douceur*. In my sofa corner I was obliged to go through a large box of the kind of mail-matter which enjoys a temporary-reprieve from the waste-basket, under the head of 'To be disposed-of-on-return-do-not-forward.' Faithful examination revealed only one item for salvage; a long envelope bearing the wrong address, and a scribble by the Post-Office, 'Try,' etc. But it showed large in the upper left-hand corner, 'Royal Italian Embassy. Washington.'... Worth opening... It proved to be so. It contained a note from Prince Caetani accompanying a very polite letter from the 'Ministero della Pubblica Istruzione' at Rome, and was from 'His Excellency the Ministro Gentile: Direzione Generale della Antichita e bella Arte.' The letter described the origin and nature of the Medici Gallery, at the Uffizi, in Florence, named a number of the artists represented, from Rubens to Holman Hunt, by way of Reynolds, Romney, Delacroix, and others, and invited 'La Gentile Signora' to present her 'Autoritratto' to the Gallery. I had seen the collection, and although the Delacroix had been the outstanding impression in rather a hasty passage through the group, my astonishment and satisfaction were witness to my deep appreciation of such an honor, and, although I had not tried to paint since my accident, I at once began dragging myself about, settling on the composition, etc. The result accomplished under great disadvantages, and the utmost that I could produce, will always be a source of regret to me.

XIII

BARON BEATTY OF THE NORTH SEA

IT is a formidable characteristic of the British mind that complete difference of opinion, in matters of national interest, may exist between persons whose information is equally complete, and who are equally desirous to maintain an impeccable honesty of judgment.

The American Committee on War Portraits, setting about to choose representative figures from England's Army and Navy, rested their decision upon a general view, rather than on any one of the fixed centres of opinion in England. Field Marshal Haig and Admiral Lord Beatty were approached through our Ambassador, Mr. Davis. Both kindly consented and kept their engagement with the readiness and 'sense of duty' that is part of their code.

In 1919, the part Lord Beatty had taken in the War and his Government's recognition of it were still fresh, although a mystery hung over the Battle of Jutland that was not resolved into its absolute and irreducible elements until several years later, at least so as to satisfy serious inquirers, outside the circle of those who had in their office and responsibility watched and waked with the British Navy.

Even then, however, in 1919, England could rejoice in a naval hero after her own heart. Beatty's part in the opening actions of the North Sea Fleet, and his later participation, gave evidence of what might have been expected of him if the cataclysmal meeting for which both navies were prepared had taken place.

Beatty was young, in the early forties, a gallant man; and in his spirit and conduct had fully measured up to the stern tradition of the British Navy.

The British are called a commercial people. The average Englishman will do his best to make himself pocket-comfortable, and in the higher regions of Government and diplomacy will be cunning to find the advantage in values, but his idol, his worship, his high reward, is what he calls by the grand old name of 'Valor.'

Nothing moves the universal British heart as do those two words 'For Valor,' which suffice for the supreme tribute bestowed by the Victoria Cross, and this quality should not be confounded with the ordinary, decent currency of courage that is spent to get us through the trials and crises of life and accident, even attack by thieves, and disease. Valor is born of War. This peerless virtue is the first fruit of carnage, blood, and agony. In countless instances it springs into being in deeds never seen or heard of and is never conceived by private enterprise or ambition. It is a pure white flame suddenly illuminating even the most rudimentary nature, humbly serving in the line of duty. The act is performed in response to an impulse which has had no time to think of notice or reward; often by one who is entirely unconscious of the grandeur of the act, that is the instinct to save or strengthen the State, to protect home and family, or to offer one's life for a comrade in peril.

And this virtue owes its highest and purest existence to War, because in War the individual is in the main body only a tag and number, and from this obscurity, this tag and number, War demands that the crowning eminence of the human heart shall arise and shine.

Even in the deadening routine of the soldier's life, where the mother country offers little comfort beyond the chance to shave and his tea, even under the dull multitudinous minutiæ of obedience and always obedience, War may at any moment call for the divine impulse in the soldier's or seaman's heart and brain, for Valor has more than moral strength.

Also Valor should not be confounded with the kind of courage that accompanies adventure or sport, all of which are more or less sullied by some form of ambition or desire.

Vice-Admiral Beatty came home from the Battle of Jutland double starred by an approving Nation. Behind all that the Englishman means by Valor, as it may and does appear in humble adherence to duty, was the Commander, swift, ready, and resourceful, using to the utmost his portion of authority over a squadron of battle-cruisers, formidable as the first to advance in search of an engagement which, as a whole, involved power and magnitude never before set forth by conflicting peoples at sea. A resolute man. It was he who drew the enemy to meet the British Grand Fleet, and his commanding officer Jellicoe. What developed from this opening was in the hands of Jellicoe, but Beatty was to urge and to strike twice again. The Lion and her consorts were alone in the last, as in the first, encounter of great ships at Jutland and in the War.

As all that his portrayer ever knew of Lord Beatty was far from touching the experiences or temper of his real life, it seems fitting, for those who are not likely to have attacked the formidable volumes that have appeared since the War, to transcribe two scenes from Winston Churchill's account of the Battle of Jutland, in his book, 'The World Crisis.' One relates to the Vice-Admiral on the Lion, and the other describes the conduct and death of Major Hervey at his post on the same ship.

Meanwhile the Vice-Admiral [that is, Lord Beatty], pacing the deck among the shell fragments rebounding from the water, and like Nelson of old in the brunt of the enemy's fire, has learned that the Indefatigable and the Queen Mary have been destroyed, and that his own magazines are menaced by fire.

It is difficult to compare sea and land war. But each battle-cruiser was a unit comparable at least to a complete infantry division. Two of his divisions have been annihilated in the twinkling of an eye. The enemy whom he could not defeat with six ships to five are now five ships to four. Far away all five German battle-cruisers — grey smudges changing momentarily into 'rippling sheets of flame' — are still intact and seemingly invulnerable. 'Nevertheless,' proceeds the official narrative, 'the squadron continued its course, undismayed.' But the movement of these blind, inanimate castles of steel was governed at this moment entirely by the spirit of a single man. Had he faltered, had he taken less than a conqueror's view of the British fighting chances, all these great engines of sea-power and war-power would have wobbled off in meaningless disarray. This is a moment on which British naval historians will be glad to dwell; and the actual facts deserve to be recorded.

The Indefatigable had disappeared beneath the waves. The Queen Mary had towered up to heaven in a pillar of fire. The Lion was in flames. A tremendous salvo struck upon or about her following ship, the Princess Royal, which vanished in a cloud of spray and smoke. A signalman sprang upon the Lion's bridge with the words, 'Princess Royal blown up, sir.' On this the Vice-Admiral said to his Flag-Captain, 'Chatfield, there seems to be something wrong with our...ships to-day. Turn two points to port' — [i.e., two points nearer the enemy.]

Thus the crisis of the battle was surmounted. All the German damage was done in the first half-hour. As the action proceeded, the British battle-cruisers, although reduced to an inferiority in numbers, began to assert an ascendancy over the enemy. Their guns became increasingly effective, and they themselves received no further serious injury. The deterioration in the accuracy and rate of the German fire during the next hour and a half was obvious.

This extract accounts for only a section of the battle, and is cited as a dramatic instance of Admiral Beatty's character in action.

Mr. Churchill, in his detailed account of the battle (the main facts of which are taken from the official narrative of Jutland), concludes with these words:

The ponderous, poignant responsibilities borne successfully, if not triumphantly by Sir John Jellicoe, during two years of faithful command, constitute unanswerable claims to the lasting respect of the Nation. But the Royal Navy must find in other personalities and other episodes the golden links which carried forward through the Great War the audacious and conquering traditions of the past; and it is to Beatty and the battle-cruisers, to Keyes at Zeebrugge, to

Tyrwhitt and his Harwich striking force, to the destroyer and submarine flotillas out in all weathers and against all foes, to the wild adventures of the Q-ships, to the steadfast resolution of the British Merchant Service, that the eyes of rising generations will turn.

Of Major Hervey he says:

All the crew of the turret except its commanding officer, Major Hervey (Royal Marine Artillery), and his sergeant were instantly killed and Major Hervey had both his legs shattered or torn off. Each turret in a capital ship is a self-contained organism. It is seated in the hull of the vessel like a fort; it reaches from the armoured gun-house, visible to all, fifty feet downwards to the very keel. Its intricate hydraulic machinery, its ammunition trunk communicating with the shell-room and magazines, all turn together in whatever direction its twin guns may point. The shell of the Lutzow wrecked the turret and set the wreckage on fire. The shock flung and jammed one of the guns upwards, and twenty minutes later the cartridge which was in its breech slid out. It caught fire and ignited the other charges in the gun-cages. The flash from these passed down the trunk to the charges at the bottom. None but dead and dying remained in the turret. All had been finished by the original shell-burst. The men in the switchboard department and the handling parties of the shell-room were instantly killed by the flash of the cordite fire. The blast passed through and through the turret in all its passages and foundations, and rose two hundred feet above its gaping roof. But the doors of the magazines were closed. Major Hervey, shattered, weltering, stifled, seared, had found it possible to give the order down the voice tube, 'Close magazine doors and flood magazines.' So the Lion drove on her course unconscious of her peril or by what expiring breath it had been effectively averted. In the long, rough, glorious history of the Royal Marines there is no name and no deed which in its character and consequences ranks above this.

The War being over, Baron Beatty of the North Sea found himself a very busy man, no more, no less. The British Admiralty in its London office was far from bearing any but the remotest resemblance to the deck of a flagship, still less to the bridge of the same, or the armored cell from which issue the laconic decrees on which the fate of Great Britain rests. Although Romance is now bound in armor plate, and there is little searching for the enemy with field-glasses over wave-tossed horizons, but only listening in the dense atmosphere of turrets to radio messages from aeroplanes, still, beneath the many stories of the warship's iron keel, there is the same unconquered ocean that the sailor has had to reckon with, and die in, for the last two thousand years and more, and the Admiral is always a sailor first and last.

When I came to know Lord Beatty, he told me that when he first met Clemenceau, the old man looked him over and said,

'Well... You're a British sailor.'

The Admiral did not seem at all displeased by this terse greeting and might have answered, 'Yes, I am just that.' It would have been enough. I have sometimes thought that his mornings at the Admiralty Office in time of peace, with their prolonged debates and interminable detail, may have slightly helped the cause of those who desired a portrait of its Head, for America. At all events, he readily consented when the request came to him from our Ambassador Mr. Davis, to give the necessary sittings for it. (Lord Beatty confessed that two other people were 'after him,' but he had refused to give them a moment.) And I soon had a note from his secretary saying that His Lordship would see me at his house in Regent's Park.

Of course, it was a simple matter for any one to have a general idea of the appearance of any and all of the heroes of the day; shop windows, newspapers, and magazines displayed photographs and reproductions liberally. The well-known figure of Admiral Beatty in cap or Panama, slightly tipped, I had often wondered over, feeling that more than that must be found in the real man, and when I called at Hanover Lodge on an October morning, the soft English quiet of Regent's Park, the lawn, big trees, and pretty yellow house seemed a strange introduction and contrast to the personality I was in search of.

But it is nearly always from such tender English scenes that England's heroes have emerged. Also it must be remembered that fair little English boys of all ranks had early found something in their existence, very unlike the mild temper of their climate. Few of them, in at least one generation past, could remember anything in life that was not mixed with discipline, and much that would be severe hardship to the boy of the present day in America. Chilly classrooms, early rising in the dark, cold-water washing, corporal punishment, fagging, borne without a whimper by very little boys — a state of things that made home and holidays the heaven of the schoolboys of England, and their great reserve of comfort and pleasure. The full meaning of the word 'Home,' so rich to English ears, is coming to mean not much more than 'house' to us. We are throwing away most of the old methods, in many cases wisely, but without glancing into the scrap-heap to see if they really are quite worn out, and without seeking to know why it was that they succeeded so well as makers of men. Certainly they produced a resistant and tenacious fibre in character. Above all, one that would be expected to adhere and perform without counting on personal recognition or publicity.

In the quiet hall of Hanover Lodge, as I passed through, I heard quiet voices, probably the family still at breakfast, and it was doubtless from his morning newspaper that the Head of the House came to his appointment with the unknown American woman, said to be an artist.

I had been shown into a pretty drawing-room with Jacobean furniture, modern antique, where I thought I saw the energetic hand of the American wife (Lady Beatty was a Marshall-Field of Chicago), and in a moment Lord Beatty entered. I had to be careful to conceal the fact that I was an observer of detail. A middle-sized, unsmiling man in a blue serge suit shook hands with me, and I had time to see not much more than was necessary in view of the 'engagement' about to take place. Good-looking, of course, and very business-like. As his eyes were upon the landscape out-side the window, I had an opportunity to see that his hair was thick and brown with a wave that had been suppressed to clinging smoothness over a strong cranium, and an in-tense, lined face, although he was then only forty-odd. I was standing when he came in and he shook hands, hardly smiling, and did not ask me to sit down. How did he know I might not linger or attempt an 'interview,' or that if en-couraged it might not be awkward to get rid of me?

But I, too, could be business-like, prompt and short, and he soon relaxed a good deal as we paced the deck.

I explained exactly what my object was, which he did not really know, being only concerned to accommodate the American Ambassador. I told him that I had been asked to do three portraits, Cardinal Mercier, Clemenceau, and himself and he exclaimed, 'Cardinal Mercier is in America now!'

'Yes,' I said, 'I have finished it.'

'Oh.'

And we all know what the English can put into that vo-cable, which we others find it necessary actually to say.

He then invited me to come into his study, a tiny place where no secretary was tapping. A pastel portrait of himself hung upon the wall, and he pointed to it asking how I liked it.

It was a sentimentalized rendering of a handsome fellow in a light blue shirt open at the neck. I said I thought he had a stronger face, and he replied, 'Well, that was done eight years ago, and there's been a war since then.'

Early in our interview he had said that he would give me one or two sittings, on which I did not comment. He now took out a small notebook and asked me when I wished to begin.

Of course, I said whenever it suited him, I had no other engagements.

'How about to-morrow?' said he, adding politely: 'It's just

ADMIRAL LORD BEATTY
London, 1919

as well to get disagreeable things over, eh?' With this appeared his first smile and a nice one.

I had my studio and needful furniture, but nothing else, no other of the very important preparations made; but of course I agreed; eleven A.M. was entered, and I left at once.

I was greatly struck by the simple methods at 'the top'; the absence of underlings to be consulted as to engagements, etc.

Also, as he wrote, I had a chance to watch his small, fine hands, and smooth and tapering fingers, exquisitely groomed. Later I came to know his handwriting, even more astonishing in such a man; for the English are not grudging in the use of pen and paper, and even the most occupied think it not derogatory to write a few lines by hand, even about a business engagement. So one by one small facts of character could be noted.

The impossibility of finding a studio in London was even more marked than in Paris, and it seemed all the more hopeless, for my artist friend, an inhabitant, declared that there were none (with proofs).

Everything seemed to show that she was right. Was she not lodging us, when not a room could be found in any hotel?

London was packed with Colonials, people from New Zealand and Australia who did not want to go home! All kinds of things were 'short,' and there was very little coal. In my friend's tiny house there were only small grates, and of course no furnace. But what a refuge! What hospitality, on which, literally, my fate depended!

In pursuit of a studio, we ran up many blind trails, but at last, as we were leaving a picture show at the Grosvenor Gallery, my friend recognized the lady at the desk, a forlorn hope often tested before, with the result that some one was thought of who knew some one, who knew an artist who was known to have been persuaded to let her studio by the month at slack seasons.

This was a moment when the stars were on my side, and fortunate was the hour that led me to Miss Berkeley-Johnson, kind friend, able and enthusiastic champion.

Number 3A, Claireville Grove, access to which is by great thoroughfares, is a shady side lane opening from Kensington Road. A little garden gate leads into a narrow court and Miss B.-J.'s studio was at the top of a flight of outside, but covered, steps. The place was modest in size, but somehow good, and a large square window at the north looked into yards and gardens. I at once noted what to me was of vast importance, another window opposite this by the stairs, which gave a veiled but cross-light. This, in its relation to my 'model,' came to mean to me the low light from leagues of ocean — the North Sea, in fact. I could not have imagined from the quality of light that was bestowed anything more suggestive.

It mattered little, however, whether the windows faced north or south. One did not have to fear patches of sunlight in London, in November. In a sort of alcove opposite the large window was the chimney-piece and coal grate; of course, the only means of heating. But I would like to write the following in letters of gold. When I arrived every morning at ten, I found my landlady superintending a charwoman whose work was just done; a glowing fire shone in the grate, lighted since early morning, and Miss B.-J. was ready to leave the moment she had learned any possible desires I might have. Also, I was instructed and assisted in providing myself with all the many materials I needed, even to the poor actor out of a job, who later posed by the hour, for the cloak and accessories. True, when the door closed on Miss B.-J. I lost all possibility of communication with the outside world. There was neither bell nor telephone nor neighbor. I had to learn to rest upon the quiet of my desert island, and to put aside all material anxieties when I actually got to work. The stillness was intense, and I could have spent hours of idleness in the low chair by the fire, feeling it.

Turning my head ever so little toward the soft veils of London atmosphere between the trees and walls outside the high window, all the surfaces, long used to the dry friction and strain of American life, relaxed and expanded, became in fact normal, and knew their native air.

Quietness became, as it were, strength. Nerve effort to supply the waste of useless friction was done away with. Reserves accumulated. Subconscious energy deepened, and sustained the urge of performance, when it took place; and if at any point of the difficult job I had undertaken, I surprised myself in ease of performance, I owe it to England's climate in the much-maligned months of November and December.

Such was the lure of the studio that I often went there on Sunday mornings, and not to paint: to consider the picture as critic, to read, but most of all to rest and recover from the pressure and waste of years; to let sense and spirit receive to the full what waited there of restoration, so close to the old heart of stupendous, illimitable London.

Here I seemed to feel cause for the greatness of England's poetry, the humanity of her imagination, and her deep reasonableness. In just such obscurity as I was experiencing had her virile intellect given increase. Has it not been in such retreats that were developed and polished the best of English lines? For London has solitudes as deep as can be found in the remote counties, the upper chambers of tiny Inns, or the shadowy rooms of Oxford.

Lord Beatty was prompt for his appointment, as might have been expected, and I asked for only time enough to make a few decisions in regard to position and lighting. The direct light of the studio brought out bold forms that were not so striking in the confused surroundings of the drawing-room at Hanover Lodge. I saw that it was a falcon face; the nose broad at the base, unbelievably fine at the end, the brows bending toward it, eyelids heavy and full, over-large, far-seeing grey eyes. A falcon ready for the chase.

'Well,' he said, when the very short *séance* was over. 'What is America going to do for *me?*'

'What would you like to have her do, Lord Beatty?'

'Ratify the Treaty.'

No appointment was made for the next sitting; as I proposed that he should let me know when it would suit him to come. I would be ready, and this plan, with a man of his regularity, answered very well.

* * *

The theory set forth in the well-known phrase 'Art for Art's sake' contains an eternal verity of a very grand and irrefutable nature. But there are times when it must be accepted with reservations, such as when it comes into conjunction with other cosmic verities in relation to which its importance is at least disputable.

Doubtless there are some who would contend that Art does not exist because of, or for, humanity. Perhaps no one stream of Nature's energy is superior to another; but at least Art, as distinguished from Nature's marvellous proceedings, Art, the kind that is for Art's sake, certainly proceeds directly from the mind of man and from nowhere else.

Thus, logically, man — that is, humanity in full content — outranks it, a question too big and too diverse to be pursued here. Suffice it to say that, in portraiture, this conjunction has frequently to be reckoned with, of course especially when the personality in question stands out, for one reason or many, above the average, or far above it. Frequently this threatens, and often succeeds, in dividing an artist's purpose, thereby lowering the value of the result inestimably. Here, the artist's breadth of view—that is, the honesty of his conception of life, himself included — must intervene.

On — on — my soul! To grasp both of these supreme

elements, to fuse and harmonize them, is the work of a god.

Here I awoke.

* * *

After I had seen Lord Beatty, I never had any doubt as to the type of painting that, if successful, would best present him. I saw no room for synthesis or idealism in treatment. This was no time for eccentricity. Tradition being the mainspring of his life, it must be the starting-point of his portrait, but this once accepted, the treatment might be free as thought. It must be something seized, not thoughtfully accumulated and built up. Full power of rendered observation must accompany every passage. In the head, at least, there must be no going back in search of improvements; all should be addition, one direct revealment after another and in the right, that is, in the strong, regular order of Nature's building. A programme, indeed, requiring, above all, perfect preparation, no strength leakage in exigencies that should have been provided for. And there should be no staleness either, no loss of momentary heat; one must make room for the divine moment, and then forget, in the completeness of one's absorption, that it might, or should be, approaching.

All this should apply chiefly to the head, and to sustaining the idea of the action. Of course, there was to be no action, so called, the only movement being in the permeating vitality of the whole, a stream, a unity of expression never crossed or contradicted by any accident, or misplacement of detail, conception not likely to be realized, given the minimum of opportunity.

Admiral Beatty's personality was, in the main, a strong current that would bear before it all opposition. The strength of a current is in the unbroken continuity of its passage, and whatever of force might be put into the design, or, if it may be so called, the architecture of the portrait, the *manner* of the painting must supply the convincing and conclusive element. *It* must contribute the elements of youth and stimulation and, dare I say it, beauty. The supple medium in untortured freshness must move over the forms with easy power in the act of creation.

Alone in the studio, with a dark cloak hung over a chair and touched by the two opposing lights, all sorts of dreams of distant sea horizons and grim smoke screen might float about that resolute head in a rich harmony of blue and gold.

* * *

The aftermath of these musings was very practical. Suppose that there should be only one more visit to the studio. The Admiral had *promised* no more and might 'find it impossible,' after the next appointment, to continue. There seemed only one way to persevere and that a very direct one — by preparation.

Before the next sitting, which was really the first, I had made the composition, *in parvo*, on a small panel of the exactly desired shape, which had already served Miss B.-J. for a study begun and painted out.

With her aid the stretcher was made and the canvas mounted. The background was rubbed in. A blank space was left for the head and a few other indications gave the canvas that look of promise which has caused such thousands of artists (and subjects) to cherish false hopes.

I thought it would be wise to begin without disturbing the canvas, and so prepared a board and paper on another easel for a charcoal drawing, to be transferred. A drawing must be made which must contain all the elements of the head and which would be my only material, if I should never have another sitting. This must be done within the hour, for no more time had been promised for any sitting. For in this case I felt that a drawing, character and pose, would contain all the fundamental support of the portrait.

To his second appointment Lord Beatty came with a valet

bearing his sword, which I had asked for, his naval cloak, and dark-blue jacket with gold-laced cuffs, and all eighteen of the decorations attached. It was amusing, when the Admiral put on the cape, which hung unfastened upon his shoulders, that the only one of the decorations that was ever visible was the 'Croix de Guerre.'

The valet was dismissed at once, and Lord Beatty at the close of the hour took off cape and coat, folded them thoughtfully in, of course, the only way, and laid them on a chair, placing the sword beside them, a seaman's simple habit of order, automatically followed.

When I came to the studio the next morning, Miss B.-J. was standing beside them and said, leaning forward and strengthily whispering, 'We won't tell anybody we've got *Beatty's sword!*'

There, indeed, lay the dark blue-and-gold accoutrements in all their huge significance. England's emblems — 'Britannia rules the waves.'

Concerning the fateful hour that the next visit filled, I have little to report. Lord Beatty looked at the two easels, the blank paper and partly covered canvas, and made no comment. I said: 'I have to draw the head first,' and we began. Little was said, at least that I can remember. Neither of us was obliged to rest, although I stopped long enough to offer mercy to the model. I did not actually forget the Lion nor the North Sea nor the German Fleet, but I found the forms of the very original face before me intensely absorbing.

The drawing turned out to be, for its purpose, the most comprehensive as well as the most direct drawing I ever made, just less than life-size, and easily transferable. The clarity and simplicity of the sitter seemed to take possession and pervade everything. If this had been Lord Beatty's only visit, a painting could have been made from it, and he did not say, as I feared he might, 'Two sittings, and no painting yet.'

Remembering that strategy is the most successful tool of limited power, I continued to attack the portrait in reverse order, and to endeavor to make all possible misconceptions and blunders before the next appointment — indeed, before really beginning the attack.

To one accustomed to innumerable sittings of three hours each, the enterprise was strenuous hunting, and could not have been carried out on continuous days. How thankful I was for the quiet studio, for the absence of calls or engagements. Except during Lord Beatty's visits, I could be as slow and reflective as an owl appears to be. I was literally alone the entire day, lunching at a decent, and to me very characteristic and amusing, restaurant near by on Kensington Road.

* * *

The bus ride from the Hans Crescent Hotel (where we finally found shelter) to Claireville Grove was an admirable beginning for my day. To be alone, in the new adventure of bus travel, yet not uneasy. To become familiar with the route and 'sights.' To be entirely unnoticed and unsuspected, though American, by the kindly other travellers. To hear frequent expressions of sorrow, from the most considerate race on earth, addressed to me and each other in view of the slightest inconvenience that might have been caused by social travellers. To try to guess by the words he uttered what the conductor was saying; to rejoice that I was not obliged to question him; to feel pride in knowing the exact fare and in having the coppers ready. I had only to be calm, decent, and considerate, like the rest of them, and as a result of all these influences, I could enter the garden gate unruffled, contained, and unburdened by extraneous thoughts.

I have spoken of the atmosphere of the studio. London out-of-doors was equally satisfactory. Not that we had what would be called 'fine weather' — no one expected that. There were occasional drifts of pearly and suggestive light through the mists, and my journey to Claireville Grove was full of the morning. The scene was an effect of superimposed veils, behind which loomed the masses of the body of London, a warm mauve where the sun seemed just appearing. Even in the real rain, when morning, noon, and evening were the same, the smooth, colorful complexions one passed on the sidewalk, and the cheerful sense that the weather was after all unimportant, supported one's common-sense view of it, without in the least interfering with the deep romance and glamour to the stranger, that is even in the place's name — London. Then, of course, being of the foot, and bus, and all-kinds-of-weather class, I was dressed in wool and rubber, like the others, and knew that the good studio and the good fire were ahead of me.

After the sun had been taken and the course laid — that is, after the drawing was made — I felt probably a little like the small spider which I once watched entrap a huge and struggling wasp, trussing it up with a million invisible web windings, then retiring to another corner to stretch its six legs and await the dinner hour.

* * *

When Lord Beatty came to his third appointment, which he was kind enough to do without protest, the drawing still stood beside the canvas, on which the head was now drawn and lightly massed in, in monochrome upon a background which was likely to 'fit' with very slight adjustment. In this instance, it seemed best to prepare the palette beforehand, ignoring a superstition which prohibited doing this until after the arrival of the subject. The sluice was open and at least every obstacle removed.

When the hour was over, the Admiral came behind to look.

'Oh; you've done the hair and the forehead...'

— 333 —

'Yes,' I said, indicating the three main divisions of the head. 'Next time it will be the middle space, eyes, etc., to the base of the nose, and the time after that, the lower division.'

The Admiral made no objection, although he might have said, 'That will be five sittings.' And perhaps it had been wise to make the most of the idea of sequences, complete in themselves, to allure one accustomed to constant and logical regularity. But when he was gone, I awoke from my trance and looked to see what had been done in the hour and whether the *bloc* would take its place as a living part of the whole, without one sneaking return, one degree of lowered temperature.

* * *

The little Cockney actor was an essential support. Always ready, cheerful, glad of the fire, where he might even dry his soaked shoes, build up the greying coals, and fill the kettle. With his help I could proceed upon certain spaces in the canvas requiring careful adjustment, without strain. What was important in gold braid and buttons could never have been found with any zest between two lights, if Lord Beatty had been wearing them. Even the hands could be done (for the first and only time in the experience of the artist) from the model, from the queer bony hands that mended the fire. They held the sword by means of the same mechanism and action and, in some way, Lord Beatty's smooth fine fingers appeared in the end.

One day the Admiral had a very pleasant suggestion to make. Why not bring the portrait down to Brooksby, their place in the country, and finish it there?

This opened a charming vista, and I could have pretended it would help and have taken the picture down there. But at the moment, I was thinking 'straight only.' How little could he imagine that this plan would be good for everything but the portrait? How could he understand that *it* would be sacrificed, or at least weakened? I had to fall back on the finality that some artists might be able to do it, but that I was not good enough to go on with the picture in another place and lighting; I would have to begin all over again and a second 'go' would suffer from diminished energy. It was new to the Admiral that such tests would be applied to painting, but a quick look showed me that he understood that nothing for the moment was of any importance to me but the portrait, and its final value, as such, and perhaps what he would have called my 'attention to duty' made him quite ready to go on with the sittings, which became seven in all, and would have been more, if more had been needed.

It happened that Clemenceau came over at about this time, for three days' conference with Lloyd George, days secluded and momentous.

Lord Beatty said, 'I thought maybe you'd be having a shot at him.' — painting being considered to be something like hunting (which it is somewhat) or War Correspondent's work. But I was not concerned with Clemenceau then, and would not have found much fruit in peeping at him under the elbows of a crowd.

In the opportunity given me to 'engage' Lord Beatty, I fully realized that I was not there·in the rôle of a reporter, and of course never took advantage of the chance I had to draw him out, even if he had permitted it. Also, he did not wish to talk, but to be amused, so that during the hour I was pretty well occupied. When I told him my best two first-hand Lincoln stories, he listened so strengthily that it was almost upsetting. Once the background had to be moved and we could not reach it, so he lifted and arranged it with his sword-hilt.

In regard to the Treaty, which was then under the fists of the Republican Senate, it seemed as if the new offer of the Allies to accept reservations must have some effect. When I said that Lodge was punishing Wilson, Lord Beatty said, 'Well, he's punishing the world'; and then he added, in a gruff undertone, 'And I'd have done the same.'

He wanted to know all sorts of things about America.

'Why do they hate us? Why do they want the biggest Navy? *They* don't need it. Germany is taking heart, now. They see disruption and are hopeful. They have begun laughing at us already.'

* * *

The more I saw of the Admiral, the more I was aware of that childlike, earnest quality that all great performers have —along with all the conscious ones, which must be reckoned with. Absurd as it sounds, it is the quality which can only be called 'innocence' as a child is innocent. I have recognized it in such men as Roosevelt and Cleveland. Undoubtedly Lincoln possessed it, and I believe it can be found in all outstanding characters and is one of their most winning assets. Napoleon had it; Anatole France called him 'un enfant, mais un enfant grand comme le monde.'

* * *

Another time the Admiral said, 'Lady Beatty is very anxious to see this portrait.' The polite response was made to this with the reservation that the picture might be a little further advanced first.

'Yes, that is what I told her,' he said, adding aside, as he would have to a crony at the club, 'You know what women are.'

* * *

After two months of uninterrupted work, and having reached my furthest limit in it, it was perhaps well that my separation from the picture should be brusque. I was summoned to Paris, and, as kind friends looked after it and all affairs concerning it, I did not see it again for some time.

What I remember as the final episode took place on the next to the last of Lord Beatty's visits to the studio.

He had been standing before the drawing, and said something that manifested his appreciation of it. I expressed a desire to give it to him — he had been so kind about posing. A slight shade of doubt crossed his face, and I at once went on to explain that the drawing was not mine, as Mr. Pratt, the chairman of the committee, had stipulated that all studies and sketches made for the portraits were to be his. There could be no doubt that he would be delighted to present the drawing to Lord Beatty, if he cared to have it.

The Admiral turned quickly and said like a true Briton, 'Tell him to come over and fight me for it.'

Then we laughed, and the drawing was his.

XIV

GREEN ALLEY

CLOSELY woven from scene to scene, as most records of living may be, there is generally one — and sometimes maybe two — clearly marked and outlined spaces separate from all the rest, as an isle from the mainland. Although I had anchored myself at Gloucester, long before my visit to France in 1919, since that is ended, and Green Alley and life there still exist, it is not exactly a chronological error to place some account of it, as part of the *cadre* of more personal record at the end of this informal story.

I am glad that the seeds of what grew for me in Gloucester were sown by the members of my family, who, now that my father and grandmother were gone, continued to be the centre to which I was attached, no matter what my wanderings, as long as they lived.

I began to dream of a change, of a *pied-à-terre* even then — of a shift of the year's divisions — for work, and rest. Why not, I thought, have the summer for my working time, and take my rest in a short winter period? I had never looked on painting as toil, but I had sometimes felt that the city-winter contained too much of everything, and that the summer, if considered as a holiday, was boring in being *désœuvré*. Why not have long, unhurried bouts of painting, when off hours would be spent in delicious air — morning and evenings of thrilling loveliness — a long, long summer.

In what came of this change, and its development, in its life and associations, it is to the friends, so indissolubly bound up with it, that I owe a large part of its interest. But the scene is large; many of the figures worthy of close scrutiny. But they are living and moving...the *cadre* will not

MORNING AT GREEN ALLEY

hold them. 'Another story' is needed. I have neighbors whose biographies will be History, in widely differing fields. One of these has only recently performed a high public service with a courage, sincerity, and ability that we must look backward in our History to find the like of: I am glad that this neighbor, Piatt Andrew, blazed the trail for me at Eastern Point by finding me my first and temporary halting-place, the survey from which showed me where I would finally find...not rest...but a new life.

* * *

Part-way between the lighthouse and the town of Gloucester, I began to notice a thickly wooded space on the harbor side of the road. So solid was the tangle of catbriar, primeval blueberry, ilex, bay, and sassafras that entrance upon it was impossible. Over all rose tall wild-cherry trees. Two great maples stood with only a gate's-width between them on what was then the narrow gravelled road to the Point. There were many high, flat-branched trees showing above also, and which I found later to be tupelo, and to be to the number of forty on the triangle of rock and twining, branching shrubs, whose stems were thick and gnarled with age, and as if drawn and composed by a master artist. It was a 'bosquet.' No other name quite describes it so well. When, sometime afterwards, a connoisseur walked in the, literally, sculptured paths, he said it was Wistman's Wood, in the Doone Valley. And when, before this, I literally carved my way through it, George Herbert's 'Then to Care's Copse I came, and there got through, with much ado,' used often to be in mind: and it was this thick, inviolate wood that caught me unescapably in its branches. People said that there was no place on it for a house — it was the 'stone that the builders rejected.' It did not become mine for a year or more, but the intervening winters I spent in Boston and Cambridge, having commissions there, so it was not difficult to be in close touch with the mysterious early stages of growth, in which my chief part lay in trying to keep the urgencies of reality from spoiling a dream and a vision.

On the evening of August 7, 1906, the first fire was kindled on the hearth at Green Alley, and I made a feint of sleeping there that night.

* * *

It would be difficult for a robin to describe her nest — or a tortoise its shell. The latter would have certainly to depend on hearsay in regard to the exterior, although very well conscious of the *fit*. I had very special vision in regard to certain points in my nest-building, and these, like the above-mentioned species, had much more bearing on meanings interior than on the outside; also to the exigencies of economy and the ready-made I was forced to give way, lamentably. This, however, did not interfere with vistas, nor the shape and sentiment of windows, as seen from within. Here I would resign nothing. Of course, the Wood favored every move in these matters.

* * *

In spite of my New England ancestry, I could not see my building as following the strictly Early American of my forbears in this country, and, although deeply conscious of its pristine, mystic quality, I could not see myself complicating this for the demands of modern life, neither could I in any way have afforded it. I also knew that I must not attempt to imitate a small French manor house, or farm, here. The idea 'Tropical Colonial' kept recurring, and the nondescript little house answers best, perhaps, to this tendency. After living had begun in it, I passed in an ocean liner close to the shore of one of the Azores Islands, and was somewhat re-enforced in my choice by the sight of small white stucco houses with peaked grey roofs, embedded in emerald verdure, strong and encompassing, like ours, here. I built the studio as large almost as the house — separate, on a somewhat lower level, for seclusion. The whole pretty much achieving what it was intended for — work — and friendship — the two main divisions of its owner's interest.

* * *

I had managed — starting between the great maples on the road — to cut a way in through the thicket, without levelling a tree or even the old giant blueberry, and ilex. The bay was always sacred. For some of the paths I penetrated alone, with a small pair of scissors, clipping my way — fascinating pioneering. I never planted anything in the wood save the mountain rhododendron, and then only beside a pool at the innermost point of seclusion. I contrived, with the aid of my incomparable Italian servant, Natale Gavagnin, to give the pool the appearance of a spring, or well, confined by an oval of mossy stones. Tall tupelos arched above it, and a great fern now hangs over and sometimes dips its fronds into the dark water where the rhododendron reflects its long heavy leaves and shy, pink-tinged flowers.

The place had integral romance which had no need of emphasis — only to be persuaded, as I once did a brook at Tyringham, making it more a brook with better opportunity for its soft rustle around stones, and limpid passage in shadow and sun. Green Alley was an unsafe place for lovers on the verge of yielding, and some who, as in 'Cupid's Alley,'

> 'Danced an age or so,
> Who came for half a minute,'

return to live over again the precious hours.

Natale... without whom I could never have persisted nor carried out my wishes for the development and maintenance of the slight but very special character of Green Alley. Also without the peace of mind and support that his faithful efficiency brought me for so many years, I could not have given myself so entirely to the demands of my work. I could never enumerate the forms of his service, nor overpraise his fidelity. This... alas... is 'In Memoriam.' His loss meets me at every turn, his figure and beautiful carriage, so identified with the paths and terraces, are still here in my vision, and will remain so.

Among many memories his dry humor often returns... and especially in one of those small and intimate episodes that fill the byways of country life. One morning in July, when I was breakfasting in the leafy shadow of the east loggia, having noted with regret the color of the first cleft in the opening buds of the hollyhocks which we had been waiting for, Natale, in his broad hat, came round the corner.

'The hollyhocks are PINK!' I wailed.

'Madame,' said Natale, with his Latin gesture of both hands, 'it is the same as when one says, "It is a girl..."'

* * *

Work. I never exhausted the resources of the studio. Many half-conceived designs are waiting under its dark rafters, and in the mote-full shafts of light from its high east window. My niece, Ernesta Drinker, was my choice, and chief reliance, as a model. Three times on three different years she gave me long periods of opportunity; but in these I was feeling my way, and never satisfied (if ever I was). The summers as I had planned them were long, from April to December — each month, but especially the early and late, were enough in themselves to satisfy a long hunger for what the city does not give. The late summer and autumn of 1914, strangely enough, was the period when the best that was to come of our combined effort took place. Perhaps, although at that time, to read the papers was the limit of our part in the crisis, something of Portent acting on our unconsciousness, which would not grasp the idea of what would come, roused dormant currents, fed the energy that was moving in comfortable action, and keyed it to its farthest

IN THE LOGGIA

NATALE

projection. But in any case, after the idea of the composition was born, and this was before her arrival, the sight of Ernesta, even among the queer surroundings from which I got the needful accessories, was enough to obliterate every other possible scene.

It was during this summer that the then Italian Ambassador, Marquis Cusani, was established in the neighborhood and often came to the studio. I did a drawing of him and it was from him, on that splendid summer afternoon when the fatal news came, that we heard it. His view, in his clear and perfect English, would have been interesting to remember — but how little we guessed that we — *we* — were just entering the most awful moment of History.

* * *

A large part in the contribution to life that Green Alley has offered me has been the opportunity to achieve the rounding-out of friendships that had not had place or time for full satisfaction: happy days, with one, wandering in the pine woods of Annisquam — evenings by the fire in late October, with another, listening to a rich voice reading our favorites from a volume of Emily Dickinson, and discovering to me precious findings I did not know. Counsel as well as companionship, there was time for, what hospitality there was room for, and, happily, some music.

* * *

But the little house in the wood had its own way of being memorable, of making a lover of its inhabiting servant. How I rejoiced in submission, in the morning, awakening near my big eastern window, to which I could creep in the early mornings of late June and see Venus flashing in a primrose sky, among the moving fringes of the tree-tops. And the nights when great patches of moonlight lay on the living-room floor, and, mounting to the upper terrace, one could find long rays upon the little columns and glittering vine leaves of the terrace house; the even rhythm of small waves crashing upon the pebbles of the harbor beach, and to seaward the sense of the Ocean's presence and distant organ tones.

This beauty — in its constancy — accompanied the griefs that were inevitable when Death came near, as it did to all of us — and left sacred wounds.

And in absence, too — what longing!——

'I have not had enough; O give me more:
More of the Autumn morning's coming, after dawn:
More of the dew-dimmed clover's tiny jewelling,
Where spreads the cedars' shadow on the lawn;
More of the mild mist on the distant shore.'

And do not forget, O Recorder, the midday meal on the terrace, in the shade of the great birch, looking down by the cedars to the harbor. Do not forget what it was, after a morning of fierce effort, to sink, silent and exhausted, at the little table, and be restored in every sense. Perhaps it was an echo from the remote 'Provençal way' that gave such zest to these *déjeuners* under the boughs, lightened by the birds who partook with us: the catbird's plea, sweet and raucous, the silent and timid little redstart, the song-sparrow trilling at safe distance; the robin going her own way, not needing our assistance in her housekeeping.

Do not forget the pine's perfume in the sun, the deep caves of shadow, and in the season's later days the orange and scarlet tupelo leaves afloat upon the dark pool in the wood. Do not forget....

THE END

Appendix

APPENDIX

THE stimulating power of the following extract from M. Paul Bion's letter to St. Gaudens, upon my own outlook at the time, and in view of what French criticism seems to have been then looking for in the New World, will, I hope, have sufficient significance to beginners in Art in this country, should they happen upon it, to warrant its being included in this record.

Mon cher St. Gaudens,

Nous arrivons au bout de notre excursion. Je n'ai plus à me creuser la tête pour tourner en langage familier des explications ardues et spéciales, dont la spécialité ne t'est pas d'un intérêt ni d'un utilité bien immédiate. Je puis laisser courir ma plume. Nous en aurons meilleur temps l'un et l'autre. Il se fait tard, mais nous n'irons pas plus loin que le Champs de Mars; mais le Champs de Mars suffit aux considérations que je voulais sur l'originalité en Art, et pour finir achever le coup d'œil donné en passant. Il ne vous reste plus qu'un nom à tirer de pair — (plus de théorie) et autour de cet aimable nom les lauriers seront facile à tresser.

Madame Cecilia Beaux.

A peine aurai-je une petite restriction à lui faire (est-ce bien une restriction?) il faut bien qu'une île ait son rivage et la mer qui la borde; même enchanteresse, elle ne saurait accaparer la mer; à Madame C. B. posons cette seule limite qu'elle n'est pas toute l'Amerique... et tâchons de balancer proprement l'encensoir.

Elle en est un coin de l'Amerique, retiré, discret, ombragé; disons un bosquet, et nous resterons dans l'atmosphère douce et recueillie où s'épanouit son admirable talent.

La brosse s'exerce tout à l'aise, intimement Américaine, et nous montre de simple aspects, mais vrais, mais disant le dessin paisible de vos mœurs de famille, justement ce que de loin nous ne distinguions pas, et c'est un plaisir inattendu, avec le petit frémissement de la découverte, le charme de voir apparaître cela soudain, comme au détour d'un rocher, quand on penche un peu la yole pour attérir sur une plage nouvelle, avec un beau sable sous le pied. Parmi le grand déballage de peinture Américaine, dont nous ne songeons d'ailleurs pas à nous plaindre, il y a bien un peu beaucoup de banalités dedans, mais…c'est la plus jolie surprise de découvrir les portraits de Madame Cecilia Beaux.

Voici donc la nouvelle qu'elle nous apporte: — que toute les jeunes filles Américaines n'ont point l'assurance, — je n'ose pas dire le toupet, — de courir au devant du monde pour lui rire au nez … non, elles ne babillent pas toutes comme des perruches en troupe; …Madame C. B. nous démontre qu'elles ont chez elles des airs reveurs les plus naturels et les plus gracieux, presque de la timidité, sans même être devant le monde, et avec cela, gaîté autour, fraicheur et rire, comme rayon de soleil entrant par la fenêtre. Jolies comme prunes sur l'arbre, Madame C. B. nous les présente comme 'fruits du jardin,' n'est pas? bien Américaines;

…qu'il y a aussi, dans le Connecticut, de respectable grand'-mères dont la tenue retarde de trente à quarante ans sur celle du jour. La vénération qu'elles inspirent veut faire bon ménage avec l'affection qu'on leur apporte. On sent bien, à regarder cette digne dame, qu'elle saurait placer juste une réprimande, et ceux qu'elle atteindrait en ont une peur qui donnerait l'air de ne plus pouvoir les aimer autant…autant qu'on aime ces grand'mères là.

Mais le plus beau de tous, le chef, en vieux français le vieux chef qui veut dire la tête, le keeper du home, celui qui le garde sur, inviolé, dans la paix, la liberté, la franchise, l'urbanité et la discrétion, de ses usages domestique, le voici aussi, au naturel, dans le fauteuil du bon Docteur Grier peint en plein lumière par Madame C. B. Figure intelligente d'homme distingué, sans doute un savant, nous disons un homme capable, n'importe sa spécialité, mais arrondissant aux angles sa science pour l'aimable laisser-aller des siens, le regard clair, comme sa probité, comme l'eau des lacs de montagne.

Ce ne sont que des portraits. Quelques-uns ne sont que des études, des morceaux coupés pour tenir dans le cadre, et on ne voit pas le haut de la bonne qui mène promener cet enfant — ce n'en a que plus d'attrait pour nous…

Cela vient d'un atelier, pas d'une fabrique, ni d'une pension d'élèves. Cela vient d'une atelier où l'artiste s'étudie lui-même, quand le modèle a passé.

Madame C. B. possède son mètier, et une facture extraordinaire — c'est plus habile que du —— pour ne parler pas que de l'habileté, et c'est moins inquiet, moins en danger de malverser, la recherche est plus souple, avec une naïveté de maître peintre qui s'amuse de si bien réussir.

Si elle avait un grain de vanité personelle, une petite pointe permise à se complaire en admirant sa main peindre, Madame C. B. paraît de celles qui se pourraient permettre de gentils tours de forces pour agréablement stupéfier les personnes de la société... houpe, mes amis!... pas plus malin que ça...! Mais je me défie que Madame C. B. doit être modeste.

On ne portraiture pas dans 'le home' de ce genre, sans qu'il en traîne quelque chose en sa propre âme.

Seulement ce n'est q'un coin, et je me plains, que les autres coins d'Amérique n'aient pas leur C. B. Voilà tout.

Je salue. Si tu trouves que mon hommage a été propret, salue aussi, et passons. Prenons le ton grave, — mais pas de théorie.

Vous êtes un grand peuple, qui va grandir encore, dans des proportions qui défient la pensée. Mets cela à part dans ta cervelle, pour y revenir... etc... etc.

INDEX

Adams, Prof. and Mrs., of Cambridge, England, 187
Adams Monument, work of St. Gaudens, 199, 200
'Alice in Wonderland,' 61
'American idea,' the, 301
Amory, Helen, 232
Andrew, Piatt, 233, 339
'Angelus,' 37
Annisquam, Mass., 343
Anschutz, of the Academy of Fine Arts, 95, 98
Antwerp, 110, 111
Arles, 167–69
Arnold, Matthew, 183
Art, reform in, 82; of Belgium and Holland, 110–15; and Nature, 151; Italian, 166; silent treatment in, 173; Faith necessary in, 173; the student and the master, 173, 174; for Art's sake, 328
Artist, influence of environment upon, 202; his equipment, 301, 302; and his vision, 303
Asquith, Herbert Henry, calls on Cardinal Mercier, 253
'At Home,' painting by Miss Beaux, 220, 222
Aus der Ohe, Fräulein, 210
Avignon, 167, 169

'Bab Ballads,' 61, 101
Barbaçonne, Belgian National Hymn, 256
Barclay Street, New York City, 5, 6
Bartlett, Paul, 307, 308, 315
Bartlett, Suzanne, 307–11, 315
Barton, Mrs. Fred, 220
Basle, 159
Beatty, Mr., 212
Beatty, Adm. Lord David, 299; in the War, 317–21; in time of peace, 321, 322; the painting of his picture, 322–37
Beatty, Lady, 323, 336
Beaux, Aimée Ernesta, 13; marries Henry S. Drinker, 86. See also Drinker, Mrs. Henry S.
Beaux, Cecilia ('Leilie'), parentage, 3–12; childhood and first impressions, 13–28; her early reading, 22, 26; her interest in dolls, 23, 24, 27; her education, 29–63; her musical instruction, 30–35; her instruction in art, 35–40; her schooling,

44–56; in Miss Drinker's studio, 58–60; at Art School, 64–71; as teacher of drawing, 71, 72; takes private pupils, 72, 73; her further reading, 73–75, 84; does lithographic work, 75–80; lines written by, 80; does portraiture on china, 84, 85; love episodes of, 86; enters art class, 87; takes studio, 90; enters Exhibition, 90; paints sister and child, 90–95, 98, 99; her first voyage to Europe, 100–09; in Belgium and Holland, 110–15; her quarters in Paris, 115–17; at the Académie Julien, 117–25, 172–76; visits Exhibitions and Galleries of Paris, 125–30; her first winter in Paris, 130–34; in Brittany, 135–58; on trip to Italy and Southern France, 158–69; back in Paris, 169–78; her studio at 15 rue Notre Dame des Champs, 177; visits Cambridge, England, 179–88; returns to Paris, 188, 189; painting at Cambridge, 189–92; returns to America, 193; studio work and family life, 194–97, 203–07; sends pictures to the Champs de Mars, 197, 198; her second trip to Europe, 197–202; takes studio in Washington Square, New York, 219; further work of, 219–23, 226; again abroad, 223–25; at the White House, 227–32; commissioned to paint War portraits, 235–38; paints Cardinal Mercier's picture, 239–74; paints Clemenceau's picture, 278, 280–85, 292–306; her studio at 15 rue de Cherche Midi, 298, 307–14; invited to present her 'Autoritratto' to the Medici Gallery, 316; paints Admiral Beatty's picture, 322–37; her home 'Green Alley,' 338–48
Beaux, Jean Adolphe, marriage to Cecilia Leavitt, 8; makes wife's family his own, 9; death, 205
Beaux, Mrs. Jean Adolphe (Cecilia Leavitt), death, 11, 12
Belgium, 109–15, 239–77
Benedite, Léonce, 314, 315
Berkeley-Johnson, Miss, 326, 330, 331
Bernhardt, Sarah, 126
Besnard, M., 315
Besnard, Madame, 315
Biddle, Edward, 85
Biddle, Harry, 60, 61

INDEX

Bierstadt, Albert, his 'Rocky Mountains,' 39
Bion, Paul, 198, 199; letter of, 347–49
Blake, William, 114
Blanchisseuse, a Parisian, 116
Blunt, Wilfrid, 183
Boldini, painter, 38, 137
Boulanger, artist, 120, 121
Boy Scouts, Belgian, 257
'Braddy,' Miss, 175, 176
Bradley, Mrs. Leverett, 216
Breton girls, 145–47
Brittany, 144, 145, 150
Brown, Ford Maddox, 224
Brownlow, Mr., 219
Brussels, 111, 239, 240, 255

Cabanel, Alexandre, his 'Birth of Venus,' 38
Cabot, Richard, 216
Caetani, Prince, 316
Caillaux affair, 287
Caldwell, Mr., 211, 212
Cambon, M., 229
Cambridge, England, a visit to, 179–88; life in, 182, 190; Great Saint Mary's, 183; King's Chapel, 184; a dinner at the Vice-Chancellor's Lodge (Pembroke College), 185, 186; garden-party at, 186, 187; 'the Mill' studio at, 189, 191
Champs de Mars, 197
'Chanson de Roland,' 232
Chapin, Mrs. Robert, 223
Chase, Mr., teacher in the Lyman school, 45, 49, 50, 52
Chemin des Dames, 238
Childhood recollections, 56
China painting, 84
'Christina,' painting by Miss Beaux, 223
Churchill, Winston, his 'The World Crisis,' 319–21
'Clarissa Harlowe,' 61
Clemenceau, Georges, 235, 236; compared with Cardinal Mercier, 278; his versatility, 279, 280; his physiognomy, 281, 285; reads the Treaty of Peace in the Chamber of Deputies, 282–85; speeches of, 286–90; his trips to the front, 290, 291; his stand in the War, 291; the painting of his portrait, 292–306; and Beatty, 322; visits London, 335
Clemens, Samuel L., 209
Cleveland, Mr. and Mrs. Grover, 210
Color, 108, 109, 149, 161
Concarneau, 135, 139–58
Cope, Edward D., 79, 80
Cottier, 315
Courbet, Gustave, a tree by, 38

Couture, Thomas, a head by, 37, 89
Cowles, Mrs., 229
'Cuirassiers de l'Opéra,' 172
Cusani, Marquis, Italian Ambassador to the United States, 343

D.-R., Lt. C., 151–54
Dagnan, P. A. J., 125
Darwin, Charles, 179
Darwin, Mrs. Charles, 187, 188
Darwin, George, 179, 182–84, 191, 192
Darwin, Mrs. George, 179, 181, 183–85, 188
Davis, J. C. B., American Ambassador to Great Britain, 317, 322
Death, a first impression of, 18
Delacroix, Ferdinand V. E., 316
Delorme, Capt., 304
Dey Street, New York City, 5
Dezarrois, André, 305, 315
Dickens, Charles, 189, 190
Dickinson, Emily, quoted, 33; reference to, 343
Dolls, 23–25
Dresel, Otto, musician, 6
Drinker, Elizabeth Sandwith, her diary, 60
Drinker, Ernesta, 342, 343
Drinker, Henry, 233
Drinker, Henry S., marries Aimée Ernesta Beaux, 86
Drinker, Mrs. Henry S. (Aimée Beaux), painted by Cecilia Beaux, 90–95, 98, 99
Drinker, Katharine, her studio, 57–60; her home, 60, 61. *See also* Janvier, Mrs. Thomas A.
Dublin, N.H., 216
Duchanel, French Deputy, 283
Duckworth, George, 188
Du Maurier, George, 182, 190
Duran, Carolus, 125
Duse, Eleonora, 210
Duveneck, Frank, 89
Dyer, Charles, 234

Eakins, Thomas, artist, 95–98, 214, 226
Emmet, Ellen, 220
England, 179–92
English, the, a conversational device of, 182
English character, 151–54, 323
English landscape, 180, 181
Este, Florence, 314
Evans, Ellen, 44, 45
Evans, Rosalie, 44, 45
Exhibitions, Paris, 125, 197, 213

Fargue, M., pastor, 10

Fleury, Tony Robert, 118
Florence, 164
Flushing, 109
Foch, Ferdinand, 255, 256, 289
Form, 128
Fortuny, Mariano, painter, 38
Fossils, 76–82
'Four Brooks,' the Gilders' Farm, 217
France, Anatole, 336
Francken, Chanoine, 244, 247
French Collegiate Church, 10, 11
Frère Florent, 271
Fromentin, Eugène, his 'Ancient Masters of Belgium and Holland,' 100, 110
Furniture polishing, 42

Gambetta, Léon, 290
Gardel, M., teacher in the Lyman school, 45, 52, 54
Garden-party, English, 186, 187
Gardner, Mrs. Isabella Stewart, 225, 233
Gavagnin, Natale, 341, 342
'Gayworthys, The,' 41
'Gem,' 149
Gérôme, Jean Léon, painter, 39, 120, 121
Gibson, William C., his picture gallery, 36
Gilder, Dorothea, 210, 218–20
Gilder, Francesca, 218
Gilder, Richard Watson, 208–10, 220, 297; his farm 'Four Brooks,' 217–19, 223; a line of, 293, 294
Gilder, Mrs. Richard Watson, 208–11, 217, 223, 233
Gilder, Rodman, 210
Gilder, Rosamond, 294, 295, 297, 312
Giotto, 115
Glass factory, 162
Gloubenskly, Prof., tutor in mathematics, 6
Gloucester, Mass., 338, 339
Goodheart, Mrs., 189–91
Goya, Francisco, 114
Graves, Prof., 220
Greek sculpture, 59, 70
Green, Harry, 217; his 'Theophile,' 216
Green, Miss, her school, 6
Green, Mrs., 132–34
Green Alley, 338–44
Greenock Harbor, Scotland, 193
'Guenn,' novel, 140
Guynemer, Lt., 304

Haig, Field Marshal Sir Douglas, 317
Hale, Mrs. Richard, 226
Harding, James Duffield, artist, 43, 181
Hardy, Thomas, 190
Harrison, Alexander, 148–51, 157; his

'Arcady' and 'The Wave,' 148, 150; his 'Crépuscule,' 150
Havens, Raymond Dexter, his 'The Influence of Milton on English Poetry,' 74
Heine, Heinrich, his 'Pictures of Travel,' 30
Herbert, George, 75, 203, 339
Herford, Oliver, 222
Hervey, Major, 319, 320
Hobson, Lt. Richmond P., 220
Hoeber, Arthur, 150, 151, 157, 158
'Home,' the word, 323
Homer, Winslow, 212–14
Hood, Thomas, quoted, 56
Howells, William Dean, 210
Humphrey, Charlotte, 45
Hyndman, H. M., his biography of Clemenceau, 288–91

'Imaginative interpretation,' 128
'Innocence,' 336
Ireland, Archbishop John, 229
Irwin, Agnes, Dean of Radcliffe College, 232
Italy, 158–67

James, Henry, 233; his 'The Lesson of Balzac,' 264
Janvier, Thomas A., 58, 208
Janvier, Mrs. Thomas A. (Katharine Drinker), 208; takes directorship of the Van der Whelen School, 71; resigns directorship, 75; her drawing of 'Geoffrey Rudel Dying in his Lady's Arms,' 77
Jellicoe, Sir John, 319, 320
Julia, Madame, 139
Julien, M., 59, 119, 120, 123
Jutland, battle of, 317, 319, 320

Keats, John, 75, 294
Kellogg, Mrs., 271
Kennan, Mr. and Mrs. George, 229, 230
Kent, Aratus, 41
Kent, Cecilia, 4. See also Leavitt, Mrs. John Wheeler
Kent, Sarah Evelina, 4, 6
Keyes, at Zeebrugge, 320
Kinsella, Louise, 177, 178
Kubelik, Jan, 221, 222

L., Baron and Baronne, 266
La Farge, John, 211
Lambert, John, 197; his house, 226
Laurens, Jean Paul, 99
Lazar, Charles, 127, 148, 150
Lear, Edward, his 'Nonsense Verses,' 61
Leavitt, Cecilia, daughter of John Wheeler and Cecilia Kent Leavitt, and mother of Cecilia Beaux, 4–7; takes position as

INDEX

governess, 7; goes to Philadelphia, 8; marries Jean Adolphe Beaux, 8. *See also* Beaux, Mrs. Jean Adolphe

Leavitt, Eliza, 4–6, 13

Leavitt, Emily, 13, 29

Leavitt, John Wheeler, grandfather of Cecilia Beaux, 4–6; business failure of, 7; death, 9

Leavitt, Mrs. John Wheeler (Cecilia Kent), grandmother of Cecilia Beaux, 3, 4; takes Cecilia Beaux on death of Mrs. Beaux, 13; her part in education of Cecilia Beaux, 14, 25, 40, 41; her last days and death, 205–07; reminiscences of, 207

Leavitt, Samuel, 7

Leech, John, 182, 190, 228

Lemordant, J. J., 315

Le Page, Bastien, 125, 185

Lesley, Margaret, 98

'Lesser arts,' 163

Lewis, Mrs. John F., 226

Lewis, Rebecca, 45

L'Hermitte, 125

Light and Shade, 128

Lithography, 43, 44, 59, 60, 75–80

Littauer, Lucius N., 230

Lodge, Mrs. Henry Cabot, 231

London, 181; the solitudes of, 327; weather, 332, 333

Louise, Mdlle., 266

Lucerne, 159

Lyman school (Miss Lyman and Miss Charlotte Lyman), 44–56

Mabuse, Jan de, 112

McCarter, Henry, 197, 219

McKnight, Dodge, 213

MacMonnies, Frederick W., 220

MacVeagh, Mr. and Mrs. Wayne, 231

Madrazzo, painter, 39

Malines, 240, 241; the Archevêché, 241–44, 269, 270; the Tower, 240, 262, 263; Carillon, 241, 247, 254, 262, 263, 269; convents, 244–47, 258, 259; fête in, 257; the city and the people, 259–67; châteaux, 266, 267; pictures of Rubens, 274–77

Mallory Brook, 15, 16

Mangin, Gen. Charles, 207

Manship, bronzes by, 213

Mechlin, Leila, 209

Memling, Hans, 112

Mercier, Cardinal, 235; consents to the painting of his portrait, 239; his reception of Miss Beaux, 242–44; the painting of his portrait, 247–54, 256, 265, 270–73; presentation of *Croix de Guerre* to,

255; officiates in Cathedral, 257; reviews boy scouts, 257; and his flock, 267, 268; his appreciation of American traits, 272; in the United States, 272–74; compared with Clemenceau, 278

Michael Angelo, 114

Middleton, Mr., Professor and Lecturer on the Fine Arts, 183, 184

Milton, John, 73–75

Mitchell, Mr. and Mrs. Langdon, 229

Mitchell, Dr. Weir, 220

'Modernism,' 82

'Mona Lisa,' 129, 130

Monet, Claude, 127, 201, 202

Mont Blanc, 159

Moody, William H., 230

Moody, William Vaughn, 209

Moore, Lily, 45

Morocco affair, 287

Murano, 162

Music, 30–35

Nature, the Trinity of, 128; and Art, 151

New Haven, England, 180

Newnham Grange, Cambridge, England, a visit to, 179–88

Nîmes, 168

Noyons, 238

Oakland, country estate, 5, 7

Oil-painting, 194–96

Okakura, 233

Paderewski, Ignace Jan, 210; at the White House, 230, 231

Paderewski, Madame, 230

Panama affair, 286

Paris, arrival in, 115; a pension (quarter *Pont de l'Ama*), 115–17; the *blanchisseuse*, 116; in winter, 117; Académie Julien, 117–23, 127, 172–76; Exhibitions, 125–30; Spring in, 131, 132; the 'American Colony,' 132–34; 30 rue Vaugirard, 169–72; Passage des Panorames, 172; the value of, to the student of Art, 174; after the War, 236–38; 15 rue de Cherche Midi (Hôtel Montmorency), 298, 307–14

Parrish, Maxfield, 94, 267

Parrish, Stephen, 94

Parsons, John, 220

Pastel, 191, 194–96

Pennsylvania Academy of Fine Arts, 35, 90, 98, 226

Pension, a, 116

Perry, Lilla Cabot, 201

Phillips, John, 62

Pichon, Paul, 255, 315

INDEX

Pictures, 35–40
Pinchot, Gifford, 232
Poincaré, Pres. Raymond, 255
Pont Aven, 139
Portraiture, ideal of, 165
Powell, Mr., 162, 163
Powell, Mrs., 162, 163
Pratt, Mr., 337
Pre-Raphaelites, 224
Procters, the, 231
Propriété, description of a, 140–43
Pumpelly, Elise, 215
'Punch,' 190, 228
Putnam, Herbert, Librarian, 229

'Queen's House,' Chelsea, London, 223, 224

Raphael, 114
Rembrandt van Rijn, 112; his 'Supper at Emmaus,' 113, 114, 122, 129
Renaudel, French Deputy, 283
Reverende Mère, 245, 272
Rheims, 238
Rhone, the, 168
Richardson, Henry Hobson, architect, 212
Ritchie, Susie, 45
Rivers, French, 135
Riviera, the, 167
Rockhill, Mr. and Mrs., 229
Roman remains in France, 167, 168
Roosevelt, Ethel, 227
Roosevelt, Theodore, 227–32
Roosevelt, Mrs. Theodore, 227–31
Roosevelt, Mrs. West, 231
Rossetti, Dante Gabriel, 223, 224
Rubens, Peter Paul, 110–12, 114, 163; the château where he worked, 267; his 'Adoration,' 274–76; his 'The Miraculous Draught of Fishes,' 274, 276, 277; his 'The Elevation of the Serpents,' 274
Rudel, Geoffrey, 77, 78
Ruskin, John, his 'Modern Painters,' 84
Ryder, artist, 114

St. Gaudens, Augustus, 198–200, 209, 231; letter of Paul Bion to, 347–49
St. Gothard, 160
Salon, the, 125, 126
Sampson, Admiral William T., 220
Sanford, Miss, her art school, 71, 72
Sargent, John Singer, 213, 224–26, 298
Sartain, William, 87–90, 196
Sears, Mrs., 226
Sedgwick, Mrs. Alexander, 220, 223
Sedgwick, Anne Douglas, 220
'Self-expression,' 167
Seymour, George, 193, 220

Shade, Light and, 128
Shelley, P. B., 75
Shober, Mrs., 60
Siena, 167
Silsbee, Mr., 220
Simon, Lucien, 315
Sismondi, J. C. L. de, his 'History of the Literature of Southern Europe,' 78
Size, the element of, in painting, 114
Skull, human, 69, 70
Sleeper, Henry Davis, 237
Small Country Theatre, 216
Smith, Joseph Lindon, 216, 217, 233; his Outdoor Theatre, 216
Smith, Mrs. Joseph Lindon, 216, 217
Smith, Robertson, Librarian, Cambridge, England, 183, 184
Sœur Denyse, 245, 246, 258–60
Soissons, 238
Spring in France, 131, 132
Steel engravings, 62
Strong, Julia, 45
Sullivan, Russell, 216
Supper-party, the tale of a, 155–58
Swinburne, Algernon C., 224

Taggart, Lucy, 253, 255, 257
Taste, 21
Tennyson, Alfred, 182
Testament, the Old and the New, 26
Thackeray, W. M., 182
Thayer, Abbott, 214–16
Thayer, Mrs. Abbott, 214
Thayer, Gladys, 214
Thouron, Henry, 100
Tintoretto, 114
Titian, 'Entombment,' 100, 129; 'Man with a Glove,' 129; 'Young Florentine Gentleman, Unknown,' 164, 165
Tremouille, Ducs de, 136
Tunis affair, 286
Turner, J. M. W., 83, 84
Tychefield Abbey, 152
Tyringham Valley, 217
Tyrwhitt, 321

U., Comtesse d', her hospitality, 266

Valdinaire, M., 140, 142, 158
Valdinaire, Madame, 140, 141, 146, 147, 155–58
Valor, the quality of, 318
Van der Whelen, his Art School, 64–71, 75; marriage, 70
Van Eyck, brothers, 112
Van Rensselaer, Mrs. Schuyler, 209
Vaughn, Miss, 232
Venice, 160–64

Vernissage, 125
Vibert, Jehan Georges, painter, 39
Vichy, 305
Victoria Cross, 318
Villeneuve, Mdlle. de, 115
Vitré, 135–39

Wainwright, Mr. and Mrs., 229
Wainwright, Commander, 220
War portraits, 235–38
Warren, Mrs. Fiske, 225
Weeks, Prof., 226

West, Benjamin, his 'Death on the Pale Horse,' 35
White, Henry, 237, 239, 282, 292
White House, the, 227–32
Whitlock, Brand, American Minister to Belgium, 239, 240, 273
Whitlock, Mrs. Brand, 240
Whitney, Mary, 45
Wistman's Wood, 339
Wolff, Henry, wood-cut of, 198
Wordsworth, William, 75
Wren, Sir Christopher, 223